REVIEWS

"The challenges facing us in our digital, fast-paced, multi-tasking, and stressful modern world are many. But none is more critical than the challenges of work overload that we all must face every day. This book offers commonsense, practical, and effective tools for dealing with your overload. **I can honestly say that attention to the suggestions offered could save your life.** It can certainly help you achieve a greater sense of fulfillment and accomplishment in every aspect of your life."

Archibald D. Hart, Ph.D., FPPR
Senior Professor of Psychology and Dean Emeritus, Fuller Graduate School,
Author, *Adrenalin and Stress*

"The Habashys provide an outstanding insight on the epidemic of information and work overload. This book absolutely motivates! It gives you hope that you can tackle this overwhelming issue we all are wrestling with. How? By providing content in a straight forward, easy-to-understand manner, demonstrating reader-friendly tools and techniques that tackle the issue, and sharing others' experiences and approaches through inspirational testimonials.

I found I couldn't stop reading as each page provided more clarity on triggers/drivers of information and work overload, but also direction and hope to do something about this hole we have gotten ourselves into. The outcome being our own salvation with much better health and sanity, well balanced relationships with all those we hold near and dear, and a more enjoyable and productive life!"

Pauline Maddeaux
Manager, IBM Canada, Business Controls

"This book could not have come at a better time than this, to our 'rat race' work culture. I have no doubt that this book will be a "soothing balm" to many stressed individuals. **It inspired us to enjoy a happy life by not allowing phones or e-mails or meetings to dictate the "set priorities"** of our life. In so doing, the productivity in each of the readers is sure to rise sky high!"

Ravi Chandran
Manager – Promotions, Living Truth Television

"Baha Habashy and Margaret Habashy have provided a service to busy managers everywhere by pulling together wisdom from over forty thought leaders on workplace and personal effectiveness to advance their concept of Maximum Impact for Good. They've done **an outstanding job of mixing practical, pragmatic, and theoretical solutions to common struggles and issues faced by all of us**. This book provides gripping, first-person examples, tried and tested solutions, and actionable, personal worksheets all in one place. As advances in technology accelerate information flow and the pace of our work, this book will only increase in value to any responsible executive."

Kenneth J. Bates, SPHR
Chair, Department of Business & Economics, Houghton College

"*Challenges, Changes & Cures* offers **a blend of food for thought, practical, easy-to-implement tips for putting time savers into practice**, and provocation to better define and manage roles and resources. One risk of battling upstream against overload for a protracted period is that it comes to feel like the norm. This book illuminates alternatives that otherwise may remain ignored and it is definitely worth the read."

Rudy Carson
President, IDM Research Inc.

"**I like how this book flows.** The combination of thoughts, references, exercises, and comments are very helpful in guiding the reader to recognize his or her strengths and weaknesses. The section on setting SMART goals was particularly interesting. The personal action plan is a perfect finish. This allows me to focus on certain areas where I need to improve and actually make changes."

Bill Simpson
President, Supply Chain Systems

"**This book is about dual ownership and empowerment**. Employees must be empowered to take ownership on controlling one's environment. Employers must take ownership and prioritize their leadership roles. The balance and responsibility must be collaboratively shared."

Ron Kaczorowski
Former Chairman – Kensington Health Centres

"As a pastor and coach who works with a lot of people, I see the challenges so many people deal with in effectively managing the numerous demands they face in a hectic and fast-paced society. Not only is it the individual who suffers the physical and emotional consequences; there are significant costs in the damage to family members, friends, and others as well. **Baha and Margaret have walked through that journey** and offer insightful and practical tips that can guide you to establish healthy and effective attitudes and habits to help make the long-lasting changes you need most."

Jeremy Tao
Pastor, Cornerstone Community Church

"I needed help with information overload and I got just the help I needed through this book. As I worked through this book, it has been invaluable to be able to name what I do for a living, recognizing it as part of the Information Age we now live in. One extremely novel approach the Habashys suggest is to define your job not on what you do but by what we are expected to *be*, since we are *human beings*, not *human doings*. ... This is very confrontational for a knowledge worker like me who may well pride myself on what I know.

I highly recommend reading this book, with paper and pencil in hand, to put into practice the wisdom found on its pages."

Lisa Anderson-Umaña
Director of Leadership Development, Christian Camping International

"An outstanding book to read, especially in our overloaded world! As demonstrated by the authors' personal experience, it recognizes and reconfirms our need for action plans to change our behaviour, not only for our own betterment, but to benefit our loved ones as well. It also provides easy-to-follow cures and tools by utilizing personal strategy exercises. This is a great reference book and definitely motivates you to reflect on changing one's workaholic lifestyle."

Dorota Liszewski
Director Business Information Solutions and Program Management Office,
Gamma Dynacare Medical Laboratories

"There are many books written to help us manage our time and priorities but not all of them fit the lock. This one does. While I found the opening remarks on the Challenges to be insightful, I particularly appreciated the part on the Cures—sound advice with enough step-by-step detail to help me arrange my life to make it better. It is my privilege to train Life Coaches and I will be including this book as **a vital part of the curriculum for anyone who is serious about taking charge of their life and impacting others."**

Warwick Cooper, DMin
President, Compass Coaching International

"As 'knowledge workers' travelling on our global information highway fraught with real and potential pitfalls and potholes, this book contains gems of wisdom on every page— it's a treasure trove filled with insightful analyses, voices of experience, lifestyle challenges, and practical and sound applications. The authors write with clarity and precision, providing an invaluable resource and toolbox to empower 'knowledge workers' who want to make maximum impact in one's career while maintaining work-life balance."

Andrew Lau, PHD
Lead Pastor, Cornerstone Community Church

"It is so important to feel in control rather than feeling controlled, or worse out of control! Trying to find and strike a balance between personal and professional demands is a never ending quest. I have come to learn that life is just a series of adjustments—just when you think you have it figured out, the rules change and you need another adjustment.

To help with these everyday adjustments especially in our workaday world, I would highly recommend this book. Being a very practical 'let's get it done' person, many of the topics with anecdotal nuggets hit very close to home. **The collective wisdom and commonsense solutions make this book an easy read. Brilliant!"**

Robert J. Wells
Manager of Programming and Operations Living Truth Television & Radio

Leaders collaborate

"In business like ours, time is money. Maximizing the effectiveness of time spent is key to our success and profitability. **For this reason I approached this book with interest and was not disappointed.** The book is easy to read. I really liked the exercises which helped me diagnose some areas for improvement. I found the section on filters to be of particular relevance as it provides concrete strategies for assigning priorities and, most important, choosing options where I can be most effective."
Tracey Whitehouse
Chief Operations Officer, TGO Consulting Inc.

"This book is a must read for every one in our organization especially our frontline consultants. Our people are highly skilled and much sought after; there is a fine line between working hard and working smart. Following some of the simple lessons highlighted in this book will ensure our employees are happier, more productive and can better service our clients. I highly recommend this book to any knowledge workers looking for ways to achieve a healthy work-life balance."
Orgad Gratch
Chief Executive Officer, TGO Consulting Inc.

"Life continues to ask us to do more with less time. The approach in this book minimizes the barriers that stand in our way to success. **Reading this book is helping me see how I can realize my potential.**"
Steve Ewing
Vice President of Sales & Marketing, TGO Consulting Inc.

Note: The leadership team at TGO Consulting Inc has taken our workshop and seeks to practice what we teach.

CHALLENGES, CHANGES & CURES

Improving effectiveness by overcoming work and information overload

Baha Habashy and Margaret Habashy

Using the wisdom and experience of many respected authors, clients, and friends, this book will:

- **Engage** you in honest discussion of key challenges and changes that impact personal and corporate effectiveness and productivity
- **Provide cures** in easy to personalize principles, tips, and templates to help you:
    - **Filter to prioritize** more effectively
    - **Control to improve** your communication and collaboration
    - **De-clutter to simplify** and reduce the causes of information overload.

CHALLENGES, CHANGES AND CURES
Improving effectiveness by overcoming work and information overload

Published by Integrity+ Consulting

24 Dewitt Court, Markham, Ontario, Canada L3P 3Y3

Phone: (905) 294-0380

E-mail: info@integrity-plus.com

Library and Archives Canada Cataloguing in Publication

Habashy, Baha, 1942-
    Challenges, changes & cures: improving effectiveness by overcoming work & information overload / Baha & Margaret Habashy.

Includes bibliographical references and index.
Also available in electronic format.
ISBN 978-0-9736493-4-5

    1. Personal information management. 2. Information resources management. 3. Quality of work life. 4. Work-life balance. 5. Success in business. I. Habashy, Margaret, 1948- II. Integrity+ Consulting III. Title. IV. Title: Challenges, changes and cures.

HD30.2.H28 2010   658.4'038   C2010-901721-8

ACKNOWLEDGEMENTS

This book is a true reflection of the proverb that says, "As iron sharpens iron so one person sharpens another." In this book we borrow the wisdom of many respected authors and thought leaders. Here we acknowledge with sincere thanks the following contributors:

Mr. George Abate, Vice President and Chief Accountant

Ms. Kate Agnew, Operations Manager

Mr. Matthew Anderson, Chief Executive Officer

Mr. Gerry Baranecki, People Manager

Mr. Dave Carson, Marketing Manager, Telecommunication Industry

Dr. Arnold Cook, Missionary Statesman

Ms. Marie Darling, Executive Assistant

Mr. Michael Decter, Chair of the Board

Ms. Margie Eastwood, Coordinator Provincial Information Systems

Dr. Rick Fenton, Strategist and Futurist

Ms. Shelley Fletcher, Communication Director

Mr. Ross Graham, Manager Corporate Taxation

Mr. Noel Habashy, University Student Affairs Administrator

Ms. Rebecca Habashy-Carson, Software Sales Professional

Ms. Donna Johnston, People Manager

Mr. Paul A. Kent, President and Chief Executive Officer

Mr. Paul Kim, Manager Finance

Rev. Ernest LaFont, Pastor, Police Chaplin

Ms. Violette Lareau, Director, Employee Engagement & Wellness

Ms. Karen MacDonald, Regional Director Quality and Education

Ms. Susan Malenica, Regional Director Business Development

Mr. Bruce McAlpine, President

Mr. Dave McComiskey, Executive Director

Ms. Dale McErlean, Vice President

Mr. John McGarry, President and Chief Executive Officer

Dr. Lynn Nagle, Principal and University Professor

Mr. Peter Neufeld, Partner, Management Consultants

Ms. Joelle Perez, Finance Projects Leading Manager

Ms. Andrea Seymour, Vice President, and Chief Information Officer

Mr. Doug Stirling, Director of Corporate Accounting

Ms. Cathy Ward, Manager Human Resources

Mr. Jim Wright, Operation Executive

Note: Contributors' comments are not a reflection of the opinions of the organization with which they are affiliated. For this reason their corporate affiliations are not listed.

SPECIAL ACKNOWLEDGMENTS

This book would have had many shortcomings if it were not for the invaluable editing skill and help of our friends, Kelsie McKay, Susan Malenica, and Noel Habashy. For their help we are most grateful.

Michelle Hutchison, our book design coach, you gave us your time and talent to present this book in a manner that is easy to read and simple to apply. Thank you for your prodding and encouragement.

You don't judge a book by its cover, but a good picture is worth a thousand words. Ben Allison, your creative book cover speaks louder than we could say in many words. Thank you.

For our family members, your compliments, though often biased, are most appreciated.

Above all, to our Lord and God:

- For the lessons of life You allowed us to experience, though sometimes painful, we give You our thanks.
- For the talents and abilities You give us the privilege to hold as stewards, we give You all our praise and honor.

To all who have touched our lives making us what we are today

Table of contents

CURES

Three sets of practical thoughts and tips to guide your journey as you filter and prioritize the roles you play, control to improve communication and collaboration, and de-clutter to simplify your overloaded world.

Cures, filters to prioritize

Commonsense principles that help you prioritize more effectively.

Cures, controls to improve

Practical tips to help you improve communication and collaborating and taking control of unrealistic demands and expectations.

Cures, de-clutter to simplify

A filing methodology that can help you reduce clutter and file what you need so you can easily find it when you need it.

ACTION PLAN

A practical action plan to empower you to change and to have maximum impact on your teachable people making your world a better place.

INTRODUCTION

- Confessions of a recovering workaholic
- How to use this book

1: CONFESSIONS OF A RECOVERING WORKAHOLIC

The pain of a workaholic

The attached image is from the Harvard Business Review article, *"Overloaded Circuits: Why Smart People Underperform"[1]*. In this highly recommended study, Dr. Ed Hallowell describes to a great extent my overloaded world and the negative impact it had on my quality of work and life.

People say that I am "Type A" personality. I confess that I enjoyed the hurried life. Drinking eleven to fourteen cups of coffee a day, caffeine addiction seemed to be the source of the high energy I was famous for. The hyperactive, fast moving, always changing, corporate world in which I lived seem to feed and reward such behavior. By most standards I was very successful. But now I know I was not the best I could have been. To borrow from Jim Collins' book, *Good to Great[2]*, I may have been good but I was not great.

My wake-up call came on August 12, 1999 when my doctor told me that unless I changed my lifestyle and work habits he did not want to see me any more. Ten years before that I was diagnosed with a painful condition called Fibromyalgia—a chronic, widespread severe pain syndrome that is highly aggravated by stress.

With little sleep, lots of pain and stress, you can picture the bulging eyes and grinding teeth. You can imagine what I was like when I got home from work in the late evenings! Yes, this is my story. To a great extent this book is a reflection of my life journey and the life journey of a faithful wife who has stood by me for over thirty-five years.

While I wish I had learned some of its lessons in my younger years, I must confess that I have not fully applied all the good advice given in this book. You can say that I am still a **"work in progress."** My sincere hope is that you would join me on the journey to improved effectiveness as we seek to overcome the overloaded world. My hope is that my honest confession will cause you to examine your own life and save you the risk and the painful consequences that I still carry. **BAHA HABASHY**

Challenges

In this book we will draw your attention and engage in discussion on the following key challenges:

- **The need to do more with less**. If we are to maintain our quality of life, as individuals and corporations, we must find ways to improve our productivity and/or effectiveness without sacrificing our wellbeing.

- **Winning your war for talent**. Talent is the only sustainable strategic advantage. This is a corporate and personal war we cannot lose.

- **The priority of wisdom**. In an information age, we cannot overlook our need for wisdom.

- **The risk of speed**. The misuse of technology has created risks we cannot overlook.

- **Overloaded circuits**. Negative impact greater than what meets the eye.

The marketplace is challenging at best. Corporate leaders are driven by the need for growth. Shareholders demand it and market analysts expect it. Added to this is the fact that corporate management has become very complex. In a diversified, global company like mine, we manage the business based on a variety of views. In matrix management we each have several masters who may have conflicting demands. All of this often creates demands that outstrip available resources. This is a key cause for challange and overload. **JIM WRIGHT**

Changes

In light of the challenges we face, change we must. This is especially important as we consider global economics, the movement of work, and the critical shortage of skilled talent. The accelerated culture of change offers immense opportunities for those who are flexible, teachable, and able to focus on higher value roles, objectives, relationships, and activities. There are positive changes can help us face our challenges. Some of the changes we will examine include:

- The interplay of employee wellness and engagement
- The finding of your sweet spot and capitalizing on personal fit
- The move to effective collaboration
- The effectiveness of empowering delegation

Cures

We firmly believe that each of us has an immense potential to face our challenges and impact our world for good. We each have the opportunity to be not only good but also to become great. While there is room for corporate change, this book focuses on personal cures in areas where we each exercise the greatest responsibility and sphere of influence. The cures we present are a toolbox of commonsense principles and practical tips that we hope you will apply and modify.

Foundational principles

There are three foundational principles that form the premises of the cures presented in this book:

- **Maximum impact for good:** We believe that given proper motivation, most of us would like to contribute the highest possible value or maximum impact for good to those who are important to us and to the community at large. Our goal is to provide you with facts that we believe should motivate you to seek ways to improve your maximum impact for good.

- **Best rewards:** We believe that we all deserve the best rewards possible for the value we contribute. This book provides thoughts and tips to help you significantly improve the rewards you receive for the value you deliver.

- **Tools for change:** We believe that most leaders and knowledge workers feel overloaded and undervalued and that has to change. This book offers you tools that can help you change.

The Personal Effectiveness Framework™

In the knowledge-based economy there is an interdependent relationship between information overload and work overload. Control one and you will manage the other. The results you will find are improved effectiveness and greater work-life balance. The Personal Effectiveness Framework™ is a three-part topical toolbox that can lead you in the quest to improved effectiveness:

- **The Filtering System** highlights commonsense filtering principles to guide you as you focus to prioritize your roles, relationships and the issues you face.

- **The Control Systems** provide practical tips to improve your collaboration and control unrealistic demands and the distractions created by e-mail, meetings, interruptions, telephone, and paper.

- **The Frequency of Use Filing Methodology™** will help you simplify your filing and reduce information clutter, helping you find the resources you need to play your roles and fulfill your objectives.

CHALLENGES, CHANGES & CURES

This material is based on our Overcoming Overload Workshop™. Like our workshop participants, this book can help you chart personal strategies, create solutions, and achieve impressive improvements. We have tracked the average change or improvement results experienced by our workshop participants who followed some of these principles and tips.

- **Filtering System 26% improvement:** This reflects the ability to focus and prioritize on higher value roles, relationships, and goals.

- **Control Systems 29% improvement:** This points to the effective handling of unrealistic demands and distractions.

- **Filing System 31% improvement:** This highlights the ability to create a clutter-free filing system that improves effectiveness and the timely access to needed information.

- **Work Overload 8 % improvement:** The goal is reducing excessive hours worked.

- **Meeting Effectiveness Gauge 21% improvement:** The amount of time in meetings when examined along with meeting effectiveness points to individual effectiveness in collaboration and communication.

If our workshop participants can do it so can you! We invite you to take a complimentary test of your Effectiveness and Overload Gauge™ and compare your results to the benchmark data this gauge will provide you. To do so, please go to http://www.integrity-plus.com/OG/SurveyB.asp. When there enter Project code:[3] **BOOK**. At the end you will receive an e-mail with a personalized assessment report with helpful tips and comparative benchmark data.

The Overload Gauge template appears on the following pages.

People and thought leaders

We live in very fortunate times where we have access to an increasing body of knowledge. In this book we reference more than forty respected authors and thought leaders. We encourage you to refer to their writing for more insight. This book is about people—successful people living in an overloaded world without surrendering to its negative impulses. These are people like you and me, people who face the same daily stresses you face. With stories, advice, and opinions we would like you to meet people who have touched our lives and helped us, and who have allowed us to touch their lives and help them through our Overcoming Overload Workshop™.

The Overload Gauge:

To what extent do you agree with the following statements? (5=Totally Agree & 1=Totally Disagree)	I TOTALLY Agree ←←←← →→→→ Disagree				
	5	4	3	2	1
1. I have **no control** over the amount of my voice mail, e-mail, meetings, and interruptions.	5	4	3	2	1
2. People place **urgent demands** on my life.	5	4	3	2	1
3. My roles and responsibilities cover **many subjects** and are hard to classify.	5	4	3	2	1
4. At work I do not feel **equipped and empowered** to be the best I can be and do what I love to do.	5	4	3	2	1
5. I often give up my **personal life** in order to keep up with all I have to do.	5	4	3	2	1
6. I do not have written **personal goals** that relate to my personal and corporate roles.	5	4	3	2	1
7. I treat **all people equally**; it is hard for me to define who has priority.	5	4	3	2	1
Sub-Total: Filtering System Score➔					
8. Usually my e-mail in box has more than **10 items.**	5	4	3	2	1
9. At the end of most days I have **voice mail** to which I should have responded.	5	4	3	2	1

		5	4	3	2	1
10.	I feel guilty if I have not responded to my calls.	5	4	3	2	1
11.	On an average 70% of the time spent in meetings is unproductive.	5	4	3	2	1
12.	I find taking notes in meetings stressful.	5	4	3	2	1
13.	I get too many unscheduled meetings or interruptions per day.	5	4	3	2	1
14.	My in basket usually has papers that are more than 2 days old.	5	4	3	2	1
	Sub – Total: Input Systems Score →					
15.	I feel I need more workspace.	5	4	3	2	1
16.	More than 70% of my desk is often covered by papers.	5	4	3	2	1
17.	It takes me more than one minute to find an important document in my paper files.	5	4	3	2	1
18.	It would take my associates more than three minutes to find an important document in my filing system.	5	4	3	2	1
19.	It would take me more than 30 seconds to find an item in my electronic or e-mail files.	5	4	3	2	1
20.	I am often behind on my reading. This bothers me.	5	4	3	2	1
	Sub – Total: Filing Systems Score →					
	TOTAL ALL SEGMENTS SCORE →					

2: HOW TO USE THIS BOOK

Overload is a personal matter. The definition of work-life balance is as distinct as our individual lives. You are uniquely equipped to handle the issues of improved effectiveness and the overload problem in your own unique way. In addition, no one knows your abilities for delivering maximum impact for good better than you. With this in view, this book is a resource—not a system, a program, or a work plan. This book is structured so its content can be tailored to your own unique needs and potential. Use its tools with creativity to create your own solutions. Practice the tips suggested for ongoing improvement. The following is a list of possible ways to use this book:

1. Read this book chronologically and apply its lessons as you go along.

2. Read it as an exercise book, reading one section or chapter at a time and giving yourself enough time to apply what you before moving on to the next section.

3. Skim through the pages and read the experiences of the many people who contributed to this book. As you read their thoughts seek personal applications that can help you improve.

4. Review the practical tips provided in most sections and highlight the ones you wish to apply. Write an action plan in your own words to make your application work.

5. Read or try to relate to the stories provided. Please note that while the names and titles are changed, the experience in these stories is based on participants in our Overcoming Overload Workshop

6. Examine the templates provided and use them as a guide or make your own templates using common office software tools. Feel free to use the templates at http://www.nomoreoverload.com/templates.html [4]

7. This book is designed to be a resource that you can share with others again and again. Use it as a discussion tool to coach others facing their overloaded world.

CHALLENGES, CHANGES & CURES

Whatever you do, make it your own. The ideas presented in this book are like a set of building blocks. Use them to develop your own model. Revisit them to enhance and reshape your model to meet your changing world. At all times remember, the goal is progress, not perfection. So have fun.

For ease of use as you move through the book you will find three icons:

Story

Indicates that the following is a story. While this is fictitious it greatly resembles the stories of participants in our Overcoming Overload Workshops.

Exercise

Indicates an exercise you can do or tips you can apply.

Summary

Indicates summary points often found at the end of a chapter.

Is this book for you?

- Do you need to improve your personal and corporate effectiveness?
- Do you feel overloaded?
- Are you ready to make some changes in your life priorities and habits?
- Are you concerned about someone who seems to be overloaded?

If you answered yes to any of the above four questions, then this book is probably for you. Go ahead and enjoy it.

Summary

✓ Most of us desire to deliver the highest value or maximum impact for good to our important people and our community. We invite you to join us in this personal and corporate challenge.

✓ You all deserve the best rewards possible for the value you deliver. This book is collection of the wisdom of many authors that can help you find opportunities for changes that can maximize your rewards.

✓ Most leaders and knowledge workers feel overloaded and undervalued. In the form of commonsense principles and practical tips this book presents cures that will help you change.

✓ If you battle the overloaded world or feel the need for improved effectiveness then this book is your toolbox.

✓ This book is a toolbox that you can use when you need it. It is a topical framework that you can personalize to your unique talents and circumstances.

CHALLENGES

- More with less

- The war for talent

- Information, knowledge, or wisdom

- Speed kills

- Overloaded circuits

3: MORE WITH LESS

When Doris Janzen Longacre started to compile the material for *The More-with-Less Cookbook*, it is doubtful that she dreamt of the success her book would have. Her book was a bestseller and became a guide for those seeking to solve one of our world's greatest challenges.

Longacre's book[5] is a collection of recipes and suggestions on how to eat better and healthier meals while consuming fewer resources. Her second book, *Living More with Less*,[6] is filled with personal stories and testimonies of people searching for ways to simplify their living and be more fulfilled and productive. In these two books this wise woman challenged us to examine why we do what we do and in so doing find ways for improved effectiveness in the use of our time and resources.

In many ways the problems we face today are similar to those Longacre tried to highlight and the solutions she proposed give us guidance as we face our personal and corporate call for more with less.

The law of diminishing returns

Simply put, the law of diminishing returns means that the more we have, the less we are satisfied and the more we want what does not satisfy. We want more of what we have and crave what we do not have.

To demonstrate this, consider our growing attraction for bigger and bigger homes. As we move to bigger homes, along comes the need for more and different stuff to fill these bigger homes. Yes, we are victims of our desire to keep up with the Joneses in our bigger and better neighbourhoods.

Or consider the love affair North Americans have had with the automobile. Instead of one family car, two cars seem to be the norm. And when our kids became teens we wanted three or four cars. We demanded more options and choices in our buying frenzy for bigger, gas guzzling automobiles. Car manufacturers responded to our desire for more choices and car dealerships became auto-malls filled with more brands, models, and options than we could imagine.

Grocery stores have become supermarkets. Markets have become shopping malls and gallerias. The growing options list goes on to include everything from movies to home theatres. Our holiday is no longer a visit to Grandma or to Aunt Betty. The options include sport camps, cruises, and an all-inclusive experience in some far away resort.

There is nothing wrong with seeking the best lifestyle we can have, as long as we agree that the price has to be paid. Our growing demand for goods and services means we have to produce more or work more to pay for what we want. Our demand generates opportunities for others to work harder so they can pay for their own growing demand. And so it goes on and on.

Living above our means

When this growing demand for products and services exceeded our normal value contribution we welcomed easy credit. The temptation of easy credit and manipulative advertising fuelled our buying desires. Credit practices encouraged us to spend more than our present buying power. As individuals, corporations, and even governments living off easy credit we spend today more than our economic value contributions with the hope of what we will earn tomorrow. As we chased this illusive mirage we worked harder to catch up with our ever ballooning debt and associated credit costs. The result is that we work harder and harder to pay more and more for what we have and what we crave.

In a recent speech Mr. Mark Carney[7], the Governor of the Bank of Canada, warns that every Canadian stands to lose about $30,000 in income this decade as a result of the country's "abysmal" productivity levels. What Mr. Carney is suggesting is that the central bank cannot continue subsidizing our present spending levels by its low interest rate policies and deficit government. Our personal and corporate productivity cannot support our present standard of living.

The answer to Mr. Carney's warning is not a call to longer work hours. As individuals we have been lulled by the mindset that if we work longer and harder we can spend more and more. If the truth be known, on average, we need to work less hours. If we want to see things changed we have to change the way we think. There is a limit to how hard and long we can work before our health and life are compromised.

What are our options?

As we write this book we are in the midst of a global economic and financial crisis grounded in the law of diminishing returns fuelled by the temptations of easy credit. There will have to be a day of reckoning. Our personal debts will have to be repaid. Our government deficits will have to be reconciled. We cannot leave this to our children and our grandchildren.

If you agree with the above realization you will see that our way out of this crisis lies in one or a mix of the following options:

1. **Reduce our spending appetite:** While the reduction of our demands and consumption is needed and admirable, I do not believe this in itself will be enough to solve our problems. This especially true as our governments and the advertising world encourage spending and easy credit.

2. **Pay more taxes:** This is a reality that we will most surely face in order to reduce our per capita local and national debt. Whether we like it or not, this will happen. Regardless of political promises, governments will have to reduce their debts to remain solvent.

3. **Improve our personal and corporate productivity**: If we are to maintain our standard of living, improving our productivity will have to be the goal. This will be mandatory, not only because of our present debt load but also because of the expected inflationary pressures that will take place as a result of the present government deficit budgets.

Some may think that we are suggesting that we have to work harder. Regretfully, working harder is not the solution. No. There is a finite limit to how much harder and how much longer we can work. As we will see in later chapters, there is strong evidence that work overload has a negative impact on productivity and effectiveness. In a way we are in a war for talent that seeks to enhance our personal and corporate productivity. Our call is to face our challenges by examining our **roles and priorities and focusing on higher value objectives** and in so doing find ways for effective delegation and collaboration that seeks maximum impact for common good.

Summary

- ✓ More with less is not an option; it is the new personal economic reality.
- ✓ The law of diminishing returns, while encouraging a constant search for more, has led us into unsustainable debts that must be repaid.
- ✓ If we are to maintain our present quality of life the challenge is to find ways to improve our personal and corporate effectiveness. This is the only reasonable option.
- ✓ Working harder and working longer are not the answers. The need is for improved effectiveness. This is our quest. Let us join together on this journey.

4 : THE WAR FOR TALENT

In 1997 the global consulting firm, McKinsey & Company, published a report called *"The War for Talent"*[8] that gained a lot of press. That report was later updated in 2001 with almost the same findings. At its core this report had two key messages:

- **Talent is the only sustainable corporate competitive advantage.** Organizations that focus on developing and optimizing their talent pool are the ones that are most likely to thrive in a tough competitive market. Whether we examine this at the corporate or even on the national level the message holds true. Organizations that care and cultivate learning and growing cultures are the ones likely to retain good talent in a competitive market. In a global economy, countries that reward learning and innovation will attract the immigration of talented people and investments.

- **Ongoing personal development is not optional.** In a globally competitive world individuals who value and develop their personal skills and talents are the ones most likely to take advantage of emerging trends and opportunities for progress.

With twenty years experience in the executive search and recruiting business I can say that good organizations are always in a war for good talent. Even in tough economic times it is critical that we do not lose sight of maintaining human capital. This is exceedingly critical as we examine the demographic shift that we are facing now and which will become more serious in the near future. **BRUCE MCALPINE**

Supply and demand economics

As we discussed earlier, the law of diminishing returns created the need for each of us to work more and more. Our collective demands created the opportunities that helped fuel economic growth. Economic growth provided more work opportunities for those who had to work to fulfill their growing personal expectations.

Basic economics tells us that there is a strong relationship between supply and demand for labor in the marketplace. With this in view, as early as July 2002 the Organization of Economic Development and Cooperation warned that the industrialized world would face a significant shortage of skilled labor.

Over the past nine years I have been the board chair of a very fast growing healthcare organization. We have had a 1600% growth in what may be considered an environment where talent is in very short supply. Our growth has been primarily due to the outstanding talent we have in the organization and the how the leaders focused on nurturing and developing the talent of the organization.

More than ever we need to look at human resources as a most vital asset to nurture to grow. Developing a culture of cultivating talent applies to all levels of the organization from the VPs to the front line nurse or caretaker. **MICHAEL DECTER**

The demographics leave no doubt that we are in a war for talent. While there may be a cyclical downturn we will be in a long period where good talent is in short supply. Organizational leaders need to focus more on employee wellness and life balance as older employees stay in the workplace longer than originally planned and younger ones are in need of flexibility to raise their family and/or want to have a life outside of work. **VIOLETTE LAREAU**

I have a personal responsibility to manage my personal war for talent. This is critical in our fast changing world. I try to spend five per cent of my time looking for my next development move. This does not mean that I am looking for a new job or organizational change but rather seeking new opportunities to grow, develop, and offer higher value. I do this by networking with colleagues in the organization, friends, and thought leaders, and taking advantage of training and learning opportunities. I track my potential contribution on a three to six month horizon. If I do not sincerely believe that I have a potential of making a significant contribution over the next three to six months I have a personal responsibility to discuss this with my boss and together look at how I can contribute. **PETER NEUFELD**

Using the year 2000 US census data as an example, the following **table and its related graph** provide us with an interesting picture of the projected supply and demand problem referred to by the Organization of Economic Development and Cooperation. It is safe to assume that the rest of the industrialized world will face a similar picture.

WORKING POPULATION SUPPLY AND DEMAND PROJECTIONS			
Year	**(A)** Population Projection (ages 16-64)	**(B)** Population Demand = Year 2000 + 3% for GDP Growth	**(C)** Population Demand Discounted by 50%
2000	178.0	178.0	178.0
2005	188.1	206.3	191.7
2010	196.6	239.2	206.5
2015	200.5	277.3	222.5
2020	202.5	321.4	239.7
2025	203.7	372.6	258.2
2030	206.9	432.0	278.2
2035	213.3	500.8	299.7

- **Line (A)** provides the US population projection for people ages 16 to 64 between the years 2000 and 2035.[9] This population is expected to grow from 178 million in the year 2000 to 213.3 million in 2035.

The War for Talent

- **Line (B)** uses the year 2000 as a base point representing the demand for work in the marketplace. It also assumes that the economy will grow because of increasing demand and population growth by a compound average of 3% per year. This is what is called the average GDP (Gross Domestic Product). GDP growth results in increased need for workers from 178 million in the year 2000 to 500.8 million in 2035.

- **Line (C)** suggests our hope for productivity improvement and economic structural change. Structural changes will provide for some work to be delegated or transferred to parts of the world where there is a greater supply of workers. This is what is often referred to as "outsourcing." Based on this assumption, we discount the demand for work by 50%.

Please note the gap between (A) the supply of workers and (C) the modified demand for work. By 2035 this gap grows to more than 86 million workers or 40%. This is the significant challenge. Basic economics tells us that when the demand exceeds the supply this presents increased pressures on those in the supply line. Granted, those of us in the workplace at that time will be able to ask for more money and get it. However, if you intend to be in the workplace at that time you will be facing an ever-increasing pressure to produce much more in response to the growing demand that will exist in the marketplace.

CHALLENGES, CHANGES & CURES

It is important to realize that the focus of senior corporate leaders is and will remain on the demand columns and line (B) and (C). The leader's priority is to maintain market share or grow it. If the president of any organization announces a planned decline in market share this would be a career terminating move. The problem is the same in the not for profit or public services field. For example, in Canada the focus of healthcare executives and regulators is on surgical wait lists and the inability to meet the growing needs of our aging population. With this in view we must ask in light of growing demand who is responsible for growing the talent supply line? As we examined the supply column and line (A) we see that it is finite. Even when we allow for immigration, improved effectiveness, and global outsourcing the demand will exceed the supply.

- **Line (D)** illustrates what we believe is the only solution to this dilemma. If we are to have a positive impact on this crisis, if we are to maintain our quality of life, we each must seek to raise our personal value contribution and seek ways to make maximum impact for good by:
  - **Focusing** on higher value roles, goals, and activities
  - **Delegating** lower value roles and goals to others who grow through effective delegation, coaching, and training.
  - **Collaborating** to create leveraging opportunities that serve the common good on the personal, local, national, and even global level.
  - By effective delegating and collaborating we can all aspire to deliver maximum impact for good (MIFG).

Summary

✓ Talent is the only sustainable strategic advantage.

✓ Supply and demand indicate that there a great gap between the needed work and the growing need for skilled labour.

✓ While there may be some cyclical changes in certain professions or geographies the problem is more likely to grow.

✓ The only solution is that each of us as individuals find ways to enhance our talents, improve our effectiveness and seek to deliver maximum impact for good.

5: INFORMATION, KNOWLEDGE OR WISDOM

In our changing environment the industrialized world has raced to a knowledge-based economy like a train out of control. This race was fuelled by technological achievements that made it easier to create, exchange, and accumulate more information than we ever dreamed possible. This in turn has created "information overload" or should we call it "work overload?"

You and I are called **"knowledge workers"** because our economic value is tied to our ability to process information, make wise choices, and take actions based on the knowledge we create as we process the information we accumulate. In so doing we are expected to share our knowledge with our information exchange partners through a variety of media and most of us are suffering from work and information overload.

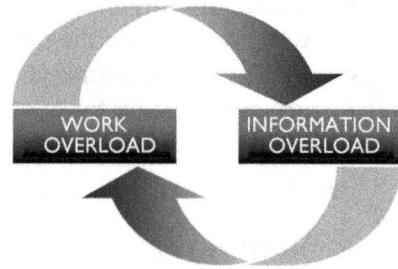

Work and Information Overload

From my years as Chief Information Officer, I believe that good information begets knowledge and good knowledge along with experience begets wisdom. Yet I also see that wisdom is often lacking. Often people are not willing to learn from their own experience or that of others around them. The results—we act unwisely and make the same mistakes over and over again.

In many ways I attribute my success to the wise mentors and coaches I have had in my career. In today's work environment what is lacking is the coaching and wisdom of people who can help a new or younger employee to grow. **Lynn Nagle**

What comes first? Does information create work or does work create information? Does work overload create information overload or is it the other way around? The answer may vary from one person to the other. One common fact is that in our knowledge-based economy work overload and information overload are highly interlinked and interrelated. We cannot solve one problem unless we manage the other. Whether it is in our offices or at home performing simple domestic tasks, the amount of information that we have to deal with is often overwhelming.

> In our world today we have far too much information; our need is to learn how to quickly filter through the clutter to find the needed knowledge and gain the wisdom that is critical to our business. In the present work environment, this does not come naturally. I recently decided that this requires investment in training my directors and managers on how to de-clutter our world and become more focused and effective. **GEORGE ABATE**

May we suggest that we have two similar health problems in our society? The first problem is the problem of overeating. Food is advertised and glamorized to us; we overeat and carry the consequences. In a similar way, we have become addicted to having too much information.

You see, our minds were created to handle information in a similar way as we handle food. We are expected to take food into our bodies in reasonable quantities. As we digest the food we turn it into energy that is used as we perform our duties and bring value to our society.

Some time ago we used to say, *"Information is power."* The truth is that **information** has no power at all. Information in itself has no value until it is digested through the thinking and learning process and changed into **knowledge**. Knowledge in itself has little value until it is related to the outside world in a timely and proper manner in what is called **wisdom**. This diagram illustrates what we call the balanced

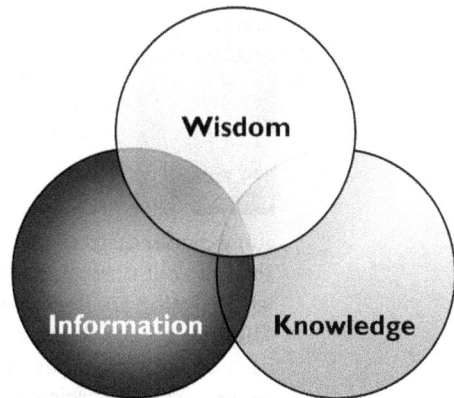

Balanced Information Processing Model

information-processing model. Information digested through the learning process gains its true value when it is related to the outside world in a proper and timely manner as wisdom. This is very much like eating balanced meals and using the energy produced by the digestive process to help us do valuable work.

In our hurried world, information is thrown at us in such large quantities that we do not have time to digest it properly. While we may have lots of information, knowledge is compromised. We tend to act in haste and wisdom falls by the wayside. This is what is called overload. The Information Overload diagram illustrates this reality.

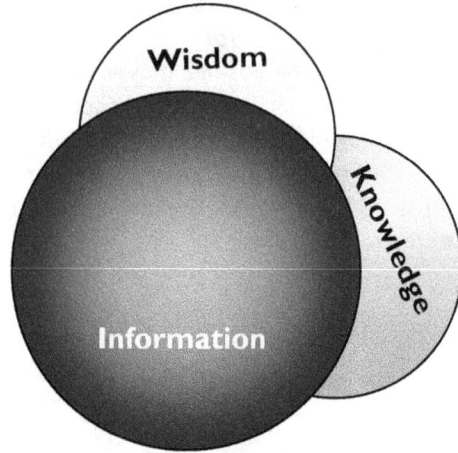

In his book, *The Overload Syndrome: Learning to Live within Your Limits*,[10] Dr. Richard Swenson illustrates this overload crisis in an interesting way.

Information Overload

We all like our doctors to be well informed and keep up with medical research. Right? Well, the author quotes Dr. Octo Barnett who writes *"If the most conscientious physician were to attempt to keep up with the literature by reading two articles per day, in one year this individual would be more than eight hundred years behind."*[11] The reason is that we publish almost half a million medical papers annually.[12]

Wisdom suggests that doctors should spend more time with patients helping them to take control of their own care plan. Regretfully, under time pressures, it is much easier for the doctor to prescribe the latest drug based on the information he or his patient received through the TV or Internet or the last sales visit from the pharmaceutical rep. The result is that in North America we have the most overmedicated and drugged population in the world.

Today we are bombarded with information, data, and stats and we have a hard time distilling it into insight and intelligence. The result is a numbness that leads to some sort of mental paralysis that holds us back from acting in a timely manner.

Wisdom is the ability to bring to bear the insight and experience to the current circumstances. Wisdom is the ability to cut through the mountain of data and be able to see what is going on. Regretfully, wisdom has become in short supply. This may be due to the complexity of our present world or because we sometimes assume, wrongly or not, that the experience is not relevant. **MICHAEL DECTER**

This problem of information glut or information indigestion is not limited to our physician's office. It is evident in our workplace and our homes. Our minds have become the proverbial inbox for often meaningless data.

Eating disorders are not caused only by the amount of food we take in but also by the speed at which we eat or sometimes inhale our food. In a similar way the speed offered by today's technology feeds a very destructive culture of urgency and impulsive behavior. In so doing, we greatly compromise the thinking process that is critical to the success of the knowledge worker. The results we often see are frequent miscommunication and dangerous business and life choices.

Wisdom is one outcome from the processing of knowledge. Wisdom can be enhanced over time by being tested. Education and degrees while a noteworthy significant accomplishment, without experience is not a certain path to wisdom. Time and experience, often in difficult and challenging circumstances, provides the knowledge which can evolve into wisdom which is recognized and valued by others.

I serve on several corporate as well as not for profit boards. While I enjoy them all, I find the not for profit boards to be more challenging and requiring more wisdom. On such boards you have unique diversity of membership that is refreshing. Here you may have a plumber, a housewife, a medical professional, and a business executive put together on the same board. Their link is a common interest in a good cause, their effectiveness as a Board starts with this common interest but the organization can be propelled forward if they share a common value system for the work they oversee and the outcomes they desire for the organization. **PAUL KENT**

Summary

✓ Today most of us struggle with information indigestion.
✓ Information has no value until it is digested into knowledge.
✓ While knowledge is good, wisdom which is the proper application of knowledge is what we each must seek.

6: SPEED KILLS

Have you seen this man walking?

You may know this man or you know someone like him. He walked ahead of me on a busy street in the financial district. Dressed in his dark gray pinstriped suit he looked like my financial advisor. I do not know his name but he was so typical of the many I saw every day where I worked downtown.

He had a hot dog in one hand and his smart phone in the other. The smart phone seemed to take priority. I sped up to watch the speed of his fingers moving on that little keypad. While I had to stretch my stride to keep up with his intense pace, I suspect his fingers must have been moving at twice that speed. Finally he was stopped by a red traffic light. That is the moment when he glanced at the hot dog and took a big bite. Then back to his smart phone.

Between his impatient glances at the traffic lights he continued to work his smart phone. He was totally oblivious to my presence beside him. I was so close I could see he was not playing a game but doing his e-mail. Right then my thoughts went to a selfish mode. If he were my financial advisor, would I trust what he was telling me in this e-mail? In his urgency driven world, what attention was he giving to my issue, concerns, and the complexity of my financial affairs?

You see, if he were my financial advisor then his value to me is in his ability to:

- Carefully examine my questions
- Research all financial factors that relate to my status and might have an impact on my retirement plans
- Outline the possible alternatives
- Respond to me describing my options as well as his advice of what actions I should take.

Now if this is my financial advisor, can I really trust his hurried judgment? Can I rely on the wisdom that is compromised by the culture of urgency created by the misuse of this technology? You see, if he is my financial advisor the quality of his advice is *related to his ability to process and convert all relevant information into knowledge and ultimately wise advice. This he must do through a thinking process that requires focus and time. The quality of output, which is wise advice, is directly related to the amount of focus and time invested. Is it any wonder why many of us are in such a bad financial state?*

As the traffic light changed, he darted into the busy road dodging delivery men on speeding bikes and equally rushing men and women. As he raced ahead of me, I wondered, if he were my financial advisor would he be taking as much risk with my retirement portfolio as he is taking with his own health and eating habits. Is he as concerned about the safety of my nest egg as he is with his personal safety on a busy road filled with cars, buses, and bikes?

Well, maybe I am to blame. I am a product of that urgency-driven world as well. If this were my financial advisor, what was the tone of the questions I sent him? Did I communicate unrealistic expectations of responsiveness? Did I place undue stress on him by overreacting to market rumours, misinformation, and the latest analysts' briefings? Has my contagious adrenalin addiction contributed to his bad work habits?

As I recall his face and that of many other men and women who rushed every day on that busy downtown street, I wondered how many have compromised their health and safety because of the urgency-driven culture in which we live. I remember associates who faced premature ill health because of their adrenalin addicted urgency-driven life. OOPS, yes I do recall August 1999 when my doctor told me unless I changed my work habits not to bother coming back.

We seem to have substituted fast for good. We falsely assume that if I get an answer quickly that is good. While the reverse is often the case. A well thought deliberate reply to a question is more helpful. This is very critical in professional fields where we deal with complex issues.

There are people in my organization that I know I can send them an e-mail any time and I can reach them almost 24-7. I know that I will get a response within a very short time. As an employer I may think this is great. But I also must realize too, there is a problem out there that I need to deal with. As a leader I have to be aware of the long term risks associated with such behavior. Leaders who encourage and reward such behavior run the risk of creating a destructive, short- sighted work culture.
MATTHEW ANDERSON

In his booklet, *Tyranny of the Urgent,*[13] Charles E. Hummel writes, **"Jumbled Priorities?** *When we stop long enough to think about it, we realize that our dilemma goes deeper than shortage of time; it is basically a problem of priorities. Hard work doesn't hurt us. We all know what it is to go full speed for long hours, totally involved in an important task. The resulting weariness is matched by a sense of achievement and joy. Not hard work, but doubt and misgiving produce anxiety as we review a* *month or a year and become oppressed by the pile of unfinished tasks. We sense uneasily our failure to do what was really important. The winds of other people's demands, and our own inner compulsions, have driven us onto a reef of frustrations. We confess, quite apart from our own sins, 'We have done those things which we ought not to have done and we have left undone those things which we ought to have done.'"*

As a futurist, I see two emerging developments that will exasperate the overload problem. The first one is what I call "PDAitis." The growing use of PDA or Personal Digital Assistants will reduce the latency of our demand expectation to zero. The expectations of time to respond will be reduced significantly, placing more urgency and higher demand on all of us.

The second factor is the notion of constantly identifiable presence. Emerging technologies will make it possible for people to identify your point of presence at any given time and thus maintain a persistent and contextual demand. In a way, you can run but you cannot hide.

Unless we culturally adjust to these factors, I will remain concerned about what the future holds for the overload problem
RICK FENTON

The workplace has become a frantic environment. The use of smart phones and such technologies has created an environment that needs to be addressed by leaders and individuals. I coach leaders on the need for time blocking.

Leaders realize that if we do not block time for the important matters the day will be filled up putting out fires. It is important to avoid the culture of urgency. This is often counterculture and brings higher risks. For this reason, it is critical that your boss understands and supports your changed behavior; otherwise this will not work. To succeed in this, it is critical that you deliver, document, and communicate the positive results that come from your changed behaviors. **PETER NEUFELD**

Summary

✓ Speed has a price called risk.
✓ Technological changes that are designed to help improve our effectiveness may lead to compromised quality and increased risks.

7: OVERLOADED CIRCUITS

Dr. Edward M. Hallowell starts his Harvard Business Review article, "*Overloaded Circuits: Why Smart People Underperform*"[14] by describing someone you might know. "*David drums his fingers on his desk as he scans the e-mail on his computer screen. At the same time, he's talking on the phone to an executive halfway around the world. His knee bounces up and down like a jackhammer. He intermittently bites his lip and reaches for his constant companion, the coffee cup. He's so deeply involved in multitasking that he has forgotten the appointment his Outlook calendar reminded him of 15 minutes ago.*

Jane, a senior vice president, and Mike, her CEO, have adjoining offices so they can communicate quickly, yet communication never seems to happen. "Whenever I go into Mike's office, his phone lights up, my cell phone goes off, someone knocks on the door, he suddenly turns to his screen and writes an e-mail, or he tells me about a new issue he wants me to address," Jane complains. "We're working flat out just to stay afloat, and we're not getting anything important accomplished. It's driving me crazy."

David, Jane, and Mike aren't crazy, but they're certainly crazed. Their experience is becoming the norm for overworked managers who suffer—like many of your colleagues, and possibly like you—from a very real but unrecognized neurological phenomenon that I call attention deficit trait or ADT. Caused by brain overload, ADT is now epidemic in organizations. The core symptoms are distractibility, inner frenzy, and impatience. People with ADT have difficulty staying organized, setting priorities, and managing time. These symptoms can undermine the work of another wise gifted executive."

In this article Dr. Hallowell explains ADT is a cousin of ADD, Attention Deficit Disorder. He explains how they both share the same brain chemistry. Under the influence of overload and stress chemical reactions affect our brain in a manner very similar to the plight of children with ADD or Attention Deficit Disorder.

In *Crazy Busy* Hallowell *writes "Without intending for it to happen or knowing how it got started, many people now find that they live in a rush they don't want and didn't create, or at least didn't mean to create. If you feel busier now than you've ever been before, and if you wonder if you can keep up this pace much longer, don't feel alone. Most of us feel slightly bewildered, realizing we have more to do than ever—with less time to do it."*[15]

The industrial revolution transformed the manufacturing world and the work processes of those who earned their living making parts and products based on physical labor. The information revolution multiplied the sources of raw material available to the brains of knowledge workers without significantly enhancing the thinking process and work habits of those who make their living based on intelligent decision-making choices. We believe this is the key cause of attention deficit trait.

I am very concerned about the culture of pushing people to the limits. We often think that by subjecting new recruits to unrealistic expectations sort of puts them to the test to see if they can survive. This has very negative, long-term consequences. In the healthcare system, where I have very special interest, I see this in the demands we put on new doctors or new nurses. Sometimes this work environment borders on being abusive. This often scars them for life. This does not create the best work environment.
MICHAEL DECTER

"I work better under stress"

Many of us believe that we perform better under stress. There is a great deal of truth in this. We all can perform great physical achievements thanks to the surge of adrenalin that comes as we face personal challenges. We can easily see this if you ever watched a sprinter run the 100 meter dash, or a mother run to the rescue of a child in danger, or a farmer race against the elements of nature to harvest his crops in time. From these examples we can see that stress is good when it is exercised for short time spans.

Psychologists have what they call The Yerkes-Dodson law[16]. This is an empirical relationship between arousal, stress, and performance. This law dictates that performance increases with physiological or mental arousal, but only up to a point. When levels of arousal become too high, performance decreases. The

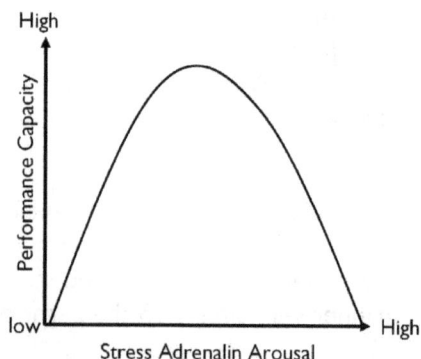

process is often illustrated graphically as a curvilinear, inverted U-shaped curve which increases and then decreases with higher levels of arousal or stress.

Research has found that different tasks require different levels of arousal for optimal performance. Tasks that demand stamina or persistence may be performed better with higher levels of arousal (to increase motivation), whereas difficult or intellectually demanding tasks may require a lower level of arousal (to facilitate concentration). Dr. Archibald Hart supports this view in his book, *The Hidden Link between Adrenalin and Stress*[17], where he highlights the negative impact of stress on our creative and cognitive skills by saying **"more stress less creativity."**

As a leader I see that this has a business and a personal dimension. The personal side became clear to me in April 2004 at age forty-two. Our international company had just survived a most brutal business experience. I had personally buried myself in the commitment of corporate survival. I will never forget that day. As I got out of bed that morning my room was spinning before me; my legs seem to give way and I was totally unable to hold my balance. Fortunately, a diagnostic test revealed it was a stress-induced condition that responded well to rest and medical treatment.

As VP and Chief Accountant responsible for financial integrity, I realize that overload may result in material risks to business and corporate integrity. Following my personal wake-up call I have a personal responsibility to guard against the work overload risks for my managers and key staff. I see this as part of my leadership responsibility.
GEORGE ABATE

The sad reality is that, in our fast-paced culture, most of us have become accustomed to a higher than normal arousal levels. As Dr. Hart puts it we have become addicted to higher doses of adrenalin in our blood. Whether in our work or entertainment we seek out more demanding, stimulating, and even more stressful endeavors because we crave the high that comes with the increased adrenalin in our blood. Adrenalin is a chemical drug and those accustomed to its higher levels face physical and productivity challenges similar to those facing other drug addicts.

So for those of us that believe we work better under stress, this is true as long as we are involved in physical tasks that do not require much of our creative thinking. Regretfully, this is not the case with most leaders and knowledge workers where our value contribution is directly related to how we think and create value by the creative and wise choices we make. As a matter of fact, it is safe to say that excessive arousal of stress may result in negative contribution due to mistakes, misjudgment, and miscommunication.

The power of sleep

During sleep our bodies and minds are actively at work performing functions that are very critical to our lives and our productivity. During sleep our cells perform at a higher degree of rejuvenation to repair parts that have been damaged in the process of life. During deep sleep our brains are hard at work organizing the masses of information and experiences we encountered during the day in our communication and interactions.

Two friends discussing their busy life brag about how little sleep they get. It sounded as if there is an element of resiliency or strength that keeps them from overcoming the need to sleep. We have developed a culture where those who sleep are perceived as slackers and do not perform as well as others. This is totally contrary to the truth especially when it comes to leaders and knowledge workers who deal with complex issues. Research in several universities has shown that students who had adequate sleep constantly achieved higher grades than those who were sleep deprived.

It is true that many will find that they have trouble falling asleep quickly. Others will wake up and cannot go back to sleep. In *The Hidden Link between Adrenalin and Stress* Dr. Hart highlights that this is primarily due to our adrenalin addiction. It is very similar to the alcoholic or nicotine addict who would wake up at night to get his fix. To overcome our adrenalin addiction we need to train our bodies in better sleep habits. This can be done by reducing mental and physical stimuli before going to bed and by adjusting our schedules we need to give ourselves permission to sleep longer.

How much sleep do you need? While less than 5% of us can survive with little sleep it is well established that most of us are sleep deprived. Our need for sleep depends on many factors that include our physical metabolism and the pace and complexity of life we lead. Here is one of the tests Dr. Hart suggests to help you define how much sleep you need. Recall your last extended and relaxing vacation of at least two weeks. **Think of how much sleep you got after your first relaxing week**. The amount of sleep you got after the first week is how much sleep you should get every night. If you cannot recall such an extended relaxing vacation, the suggested norm calls for eight to eight and a half hours of uninterrupted sleep for an average adult.

How do you feel today?

Work and information overload display themselves in many ways. In our research we came across several terms that are repeatedly referenced to describe our overloaded circuits. These we listed in the following table. Take few moments and examine them to see if you identify with any of them.

Do you relate to these symptoms or feelings? If you do, indicate how often → → → →	Quite Often	Some-times	Seldom
1. Feeling overwhelmed, flooded, or claustrophobic			
2. Forgetfulness, hard to recall details			
3. Difficulty finding information, workspace disorganized			
4. Inability to make decisions, procrastinating far more than usual or ever before			
5. Irritability and feeling "edgy" especially with family members and those closest to me			
6. Resentment of voice mail, e-mail, and meetings, especially when the sources are friends or family			
7. Chronically talking about not keeping up or always saying, "I am very busy"			
8. Feeling guilty over being behind			
9. Giving time and attention to low priority matters at the expense of more important things to do			
10. Thinking others understand all that you do not comprehend			
11. Fear of saying "No" and "I do not know"			
12. Compromised social and family life			

As I researched the area of employee wellness and engagement, I learned that about twenty per cent of workers struggle with some issue of compromised mental or emotional health, ranging from mild depression cases to total burnout. As a result productivity is significantly affected. Regretfully, managers and leaders often fail to recognize the signs and often engage in management behaviors that can have disastrous consequences for both the individual and the organization.

We all know that personal and work life overlap and impact each other greatly. Employees, both men and women are more vocal in their demand for balance, flexibility, and reasonable work hours and workload. Managers who are attuned to their employee needs will attract and keep good people. Having a peak in workload and having to work long hours does happen from time to time. It is when it is considered standard practice that it becomes destructive. **VIOLETTE LAREAU**

Examine the items you marked as **"Quite often"** and mark the top two. Prioritize them as A and B based on the ones which concern you the most or give you the most stress. Later, as we discuss some solutions, thoughts, and tips try to relate them to the critical symptoms you identified.

Note: These thoughts are not intended as a clinical diagnostic tool. If you have a feeling of stress or anxiety that persists seek appropriate professional help.

Good or bad, I inherited many of my personal traits from my parents. I am a perfectionist; I got this from my mom. I am also a workaholic. This I get from my dad. I started my first career in a large, international technology corporation. I found the business world a fertile soil for my perfectionist, workaholic nature and I thrived in it. Working sixty or seventy hour weeks became a normal lifestyle for me. I admit I enjoyed the adrenalin rush provided by this fast paced project oriented world.

One day a senior executive in our corporation had a candid talk with me. He explained that I would be of greater value to the corporation and myself if I had more balance in my life. He gave me some good thoughts regarding my career and work-life balance. His advice gave me courage to examine my priorities and work habits. Since then I have made several career changes that have enabled me to have more balance, for which I am very glad.

REBECCA HABASHY-CARSON

Summary

✓ We each respond to stress and overload in our own unique way. Overload is a personal problem and must be owned by each of us personally.

✓ Today, as we need to enhance our personal effectiveness and improved corporate productivity we cannot ignore the risks associated with the overload syndrome. As individuals we have a personal responsibility to seek personal solutions.

✓ Business leaders own a significant share of the solution. Paying good attention to employee personal health is not an optional leadership responsibility; it is a mandatory performance objective.

CHANGE

- Desire, willingness, and ability to change

- Wellness and engagement

- Finding your sweet spot

- Effective collaboration

- Effective delegation and coaching

8: DESIRE, WILLINGNESS, AND ABILITY TO *CHANGE*

Do you know a Jim or Janet?

It was 6:35 P.M. Jim had just walked out of a meeting with a pile of papers and a long "To Do" list. Now he knew why his boss asked him to come to this Senior Management meeting. Jim's name was not on the agenda. He always seemed to get dragged into these meetings on short notice. "It is going to be a short meeting and there's nothing to worry about," his boss had said. Lately Jim had been on the short end of some harsh comments due to some minor mistakes by his junior staff. Over cautious, he had been working fifty to eighty hour weeks for the past year or two. His boss had been asking him to take time off while at the same time piling new responsibilities on him!

On his way out of the conference room his boss looked at him, almost sympathetically, and said, "Hey, Jim, thanks a lot. Take care of yourself. OK?" Jim did not even reply.

Now he was very tired and had a splitting headache along with neck pain. His mind raced back to the events of the last few months. Business travel had taken him away from his family far more than he liked. He had promised his kids Justin, 11, Jill, 7, and Joe, 6, that he would be more consistent in attending school and sports events this year but here he was at the office thinking of the number of soccer games he had missed.

Jim felt like a sucker as he picked up the phone to call Janet, his wife. He had to tell her that he would not be home for supper. Janet was gracious in her response but the manner in which she hung up the phone spoke louder than words.

Struggling with his a feeling of guilt Jim knew this could not go on. As he glanced at the flashing phone message light he had an idea. "I know what I should do," he said to himself…

At 6:45 P.M. disappointed by Jim's phone call, Janet collapsed on the chesterfield wondering what to make for dinner … feeling guilty about not having a good dinner for the kids. Yet, she was utterly exhausted. Lately she felt more like a single mom. For her part, she had been very patient with Jim's work habits. She was aware of her own pitfalls. Her sales forecast was dismal and she had been more irritable with the kids over every little thing. When Jim went away she played both mom and dad filling in the gap. Some days she felt that this was more than she could handle…

Driving kids to school, keeping house, and having a demanding marketing job required eighteen working hour days. Her mother used to help a great deal until she fell down and needed hip surgery. Now she understood what it meant to be part of the sandwich generation. An overwhelming sense of responsibility for her own children and a need to offer care for her aging parents were more challenging than she had ever experienced.

Janet knew it was late for the children's supper but she was totally unmotivated to move from the chesterfield. Then she thought, "Why don't we surprise Jim?" Just then the phone rang. She did not feel like speaking to anyone. She would rather think of something creative to do with Jim and the kids. The persistent phone ring called her to finally answer.

"Honey", the voice said. "Why don't you get the kids ready? I'll come by and we can go to the Pizza Palace for dinner and then I'll come back and finish my work."

While the kids ate their pizza Jim and Janet talked about the need for change. They agreed to take a weekend away to talk about the changes they needed to make. When they were away they agreed on the following changes:

They committed to a go to the gym together every Thursday, 8:00 – 10:00 P.M. Janet would seek a new marketing role where she could collaborate with partners instead of her present sales responsibility. Her VP had told her that she would be a good fit, while she may not make as much money it would be a good career move and she could work from home 3 days a week. Jim, in order to reduce his travel by 30%, would delegate more oversight to his regional managers.

Desire, willingness, and ability to change

It has been said that the only one who likes change is a baby in a wet diaper. While this may be true for most of us we all agree and accept that change is an unavoidable part of living. In addition, while most of us do not like change we all love progress. Progress is the reward that compensates for the pain or challenge of change.

Most of us desire change in return for the promise of something better or less pain. We accept change when the promise of progress or reward is attractive and appealing or if the pain we carry is more than can cope with in our daily life. For example, we all would be prepared to trade in a problematic 1995 Ford for the latest model BMW. As we get older we all would jump to the dream of less aches and pains if we are given the chance.

The willingness to change is different. There is no change without cost. The willingness to change comes when we are prepared to pay the price for change. While we all would be willing to trade our older car for a new one most of us would not do this unless we are prepared to carry the new car payments or unless we were stranded on the side of the road with a broken transmission. While all of us would dream of a younger, healthier body very few of us are prepared to pay the disciplines of regular healthy exercise and better eating habits, that is, until we get a medical warning of an impending health crisis. You see, while most of us would welcome change with the promise of progress, change does not happen unless the rewards exceed the possible price or the consequences are too great to bear.

The ability to change often involves elements that are outside our immediate or present control. For example, while we may desire to trade a 1995 Ford for a new BMW and are willing to carry the extra car payments, change may not happen if the bank would not allow the credit needed for the transaction. If, for the promise of improved health, I am willing to give up my bad eating habits, this will not happen if the family culture is based on high fatty foods and bad drinking habits. You see, in some cases, the ability to change may involve environmental, cultural, or economic factors that may be outside our control.

Complaining is not something I enjoy. I tried to keep my concerns to myself as I observed my husband's deteriorating health and his irritability with me and with the children. I could understand the pressures he was facing and did not want to add to his concerns.

Caring for the children, professional, and community activities kept me busy so I had no time for complaining. There was always the hope of a better tomorrow. With every promotion or job change, we hoped that things would improve as routine would be established and work demands would slow down. I was told that in the beginning there would be more work but things would surely get better as time goes by. That was a faint promise, if I ever heard one.

I thought life would get easier when the children got older. That was a dream. Only those who have had teenagers would truly understand why things became harder. With teenage mood swings and a tired, irritable husband, life was going from tough to tougher.

One thing I learned was that life is like a garden patch. Left to its natural state it will always deteriorate. Unless specific actions are taken to make things better, circumstances will always get worse. Based on our experience, the future can get better for those who are committed to choices that bring about balance in life.

During those days I tried to keep my sense of humor and I certainly related to the old woman who after many years of marriage was asked if she ever considered divorce. "Divorce? No," she replied. "Murder? Yes!"
MARGARET HABASHY

Change we must

Because change always has a price, most of us are reluctant to change unless there is a significant reward or negative consequences. In the confession of a workaholic we shared the personal price paid that compelled us to change. In other stories the promise of improved family life was the driver for Jim and Janet to change. Whatever your personal currency you need to be clear on what will drive you to change because in our changing world, change you must.

In the first part of this book we discussed the challenges that call us to change. In the coming section we will discuss key points that we hope will encourage and support your willingness to change. We will review the trends and cultural elements that may strengthen your ability to change. Today more than ever before, there is a strong awareness of the need to change and focus on long term values.

9: WELLNESS AND ENGAGEMENT

Sarah Cook in her book, *The Essential Guide to Employee Engagement*, writes, *"As more and more businesses recognize that enthusiastic and committed employees add value to their organization not just in terms of productivity but also customer satisfaction, retention, profitability, and long term stake holder value, 'employee engagement' is a much talked about issue at the highest level in organizations today"*[18]. While employee engagement is the goal of corporate leaders, wellness is a personal responsibility.

Carr Cooper, professor of organizational psychology and health at Manchester University in the United Kingdom, is credited with coining the term "presenteeism" to describe the feeling of overwork and job insecurity. Since then, many respected organizations have trumpeted concerns over the problem of presenteeism and its economical and personal costs. In recent years growing healthcare costs have placed the United States in a less favourable global competitive position. Today more business leaders are seeking changes to reduce the negative impact of presenteeism.

In October 2004 Harvard Business Review published a study titled *"Presenteeism: At Work—But Out of It"*[19]. In this article Paul Hemp highlights the cost of ill health among employees who are not sick enough to be out of work. This is the cost of employees who come to work while feeling the effects of compromised health. The article refers to a year long survey dubbed the American Productivity Audit which calculates *"the cost of presenteeism in the United States to be more than $150 Billion a year."* The article highlights this problem by providing the results of Bank One estimates of its healthcare costs breakdown to be as follows:

- Absenteeism, 6%
- Presenteeism, 63% (Ten times the cost of absenteeism)
- Medical and Pharmaceutical, 24%
- Short term Disability, 6%
- Long term Disability, 1%

In Chapter 7: Overloaded circuits we referenced the work of Dr. Hallowell on the reasons why smart people underperform. Common sense leads us to quickly appreciate that employees who are not well or who are overloaded cannot be fully engaged in the business. If we are to seek maximum business engagement, effectiveness, productivity, and profitability then we need to seek employees whose business engagement is supported by optimum physical and mental health.

Employers need to realize that there is significant gain in helping their employees have interests outside the workplace. By encouraging an environment where employees work to live, not live to work, you will create an atmosphere of trust that leads to higher value from the time spent at work. I believe that having "avocation" leads to energy and success in your vocation. The more you are able to refresh yourself outside the workplace, the more successful you will be in the workplace. **JOHN MCGARRY**

Personal wellness should be the highest priority of every leader and knowledge worker. The changes that lead to wellness cannot happen without personal ownership and accountability. Today leading organisations are making significant efforts to leverage the interplay between employee wellness and engagement. Business leaders are acutely aware that corporate survival depends on the changes they make to ensure employee wellness and engagement. On the personal level, knowledge workers need to do likewise.

According to a national survey on health conducted in 2006 by Desjardins Financial Security[20], *"more than two-thirds of Canadian workers drag themselves into work feeling unwell, in pain, stressed and depressed. ... Then there's technology, where wireless phone and e-mail devices have blurred the boundaries of the traditional work day. More than 80 per cent of Desjardins respondents say wireless technology maintains or increases stress levels. It's a cycle. Family financial pressures, corporate cultures that emphasize "do more with less," longer commutes, and other factors, all contribute to skewing work-life balance, leading to less time for family and relationships, more stress and depression, and a greater risk of illness and injury. 'The costs and effects on people and companies are tremendous,' said Alain Thauvette, Senior Vice President of group and business insurance for Desjardins in Montreal."*

Robert Cunningham,[21] Vice President of Human Resources and Corporate Services at the National Association of Manufacturers, encourages employees to adopt healthy lifestyles by keeping their professional and personal lives in balance. *"We don't give medals to people who are working 15-hour days and Saturdays and Sundays,"* he explains. *"We expect people to work hard during the day, and we have pretty high standards, but we also expect people to have personal lives. We want employees to be energized and refreshed, to take their vacations, and to spend time with their families or loved ones. We don't pressure them to work 70 to 80 hours a week. People who do that run down, which impacts their productivity."*

Presenteeism also has been identified in studies of work-life balance. In a 2001 study of work-life balance in Canada, Linda Duxbury from the University of Ottawa and the University of Western Ontario's Chris Higgins, found high work-life conflict often caused people to go to work when unwell. More than four out of five employees with high work-family conflict reported doing so, significantly higher than other employees. The Duxbury-Higgins research also underscores how work-life conflict is highly correlated with stress, burnout, and depressed mood and therefore, presenteeism. Depression in the workplace may result from unsupportive supervision, job pressures, lack of flexibility, and generally unhealthy conditions.[22]

More than ever before business leaders are aware of the need for change. More and more organizations are offering incentives to employees who are willing to change and improve their wellness. Employee assistance programs often provide support for maintaining optimum health, weight loss, psychological counseling, parenting and marriage counseling, and fitness programs. In addition, many employers offer valuable employees preplanned sabbatical leaves to allow them to refresh and rejuvenate their mental and emotional health.

They say that "If you want something done, give it to a busy person" and I became that busy person. In a consensus oriented culture I found myself on twenty-seven different committees, most of them meeting at least once a month. The volume of work that these meetings generated became overwhelming and next to impossible to complete to my satisfaction. One day I was faced with the reality that I lived, ate, and drank work. The price for my work overload became a reality. My immune system became compromised and I developed an environmental allergic reaction to almost everything including my own body. The result was excessive fatigue and I felt as if I was just dragging my body from place to place.

Faced with that reality, I had to re-evaluate my roles and what I wanted to do with the rest of my life. Now, months later, I am glad I took control. **MARGIE EASTWOOD**

Regretfully, employee participation in such employer offerings is often well below what would be expected. While leaders are often ready to help, most employees go on complaining as they suffer with ill health. We must realize that the wellness problems we face are personal problems. Knowledge workers who are concerned about their own effectiveness, productivity, and even their competitive positioning must apply to their caring leaders and seek to take

　　CHALLENGES, CHANGES & CURES

advantage of the growing corporate trend that places a high priority on employee wellness and engagement.

Adrenalin addiction

The adrenal glands serve very wonderful and complex roles in our body. They respond to the demands and the stimuli we have in our lives by producing many chemicals that help us respond and cope. The various stimulators we encounter, good or bad, arouse our adrenal glands and they respond by producing chemicals we call adrenalin.

Today we live in highly stimulating environments. Our work is stimulating; our social life is highly engaging and even our entertainment is fast and high energy. The result is that we live in what Dr. Archibald Hart[23] calls a constant "**state of distress**" where our bodies become used to a higher than average adrenalin flow. Like any other drug this chemical has negative side effects. Taken in quantities beyond normal needs it weakens the most vulnerable parts of our body. The result is seen in many symptoms including headaches, ulcers, digestive problems, muscle spasms, repetitive low grade infections, as well as immune system deficiency.

To help you identify the level of distress in your life Dr. Hart provides the following simple test[24].

Answer the questions listed below according to the following rating scale:

0 = I do not experience this symptom at all.

1 = I sometimes (perhaps once a month) experience this symptom.

2 = I experience this symptom more than once a month, but not more than once a week.

3 = I experience this symptom often (more than once a week).

Symptom Of Distress	Rating
1. Do you experience headaches of any sort?	
2. Do you experience tension or stiffness in your neck, shoulders, jaw, arms, hands, legs, or stomach?	
3. Do you have nervous tics, or do you tremble?	
4. Do you feel your heart thumping or racing?	
5. Do you get irregular heartbeats, or does your heart skip beats?	
6. Do you have difficulty breathing at times?	
7. Do you ever get dizzy or lightheaded?	
8. Do you feel like you have a lump in your throat or you have to clear?	
9. Do you get colds, the flu, or hoarseness?	
10. Are you bothered by indigestion, nausea, or stomach discomfort?	
11. Do you have diarrhea or constipation?	
12. Do you bite your nails?	
13. Do you have difficulty falling or staying asleep?	
14. Do you wake up feeling tired?	
15. Are your hands or feet cold?	
16. Do you grind or grit your teeth or do your jaws ache?	
17. Are you prone to excessive sweating?	
18. Are you angry or irritable?	
19. Do you have general pain (back pain, stomach pain, head pain, muscle etc.)?	
20. Are you aware of increased anxiety, worry, fidgeting, or restlessness?	
TOTAL SCORE	

Turn the page over and compare your total score to Dr. Hart's assessment

Answers to Dr. Archibald Hart's distress symptoms survey[24], Where you total score is:

0 – 10: **No stress.** Are you sure you are alive?

11 – 20: **Mild stress.** You are basically healthy, but occasionally bothered by stressful life events.

21 – 30: **Moderate stress.** You should be concerned abut your life pressures and how you handle them.

31 – 40: **Severe stress.** Your life is out of control and you probably need professional help.

41 – 60: **Dangerous stress levels.** You need immediate help.

When I was in charge of employee health and safety in a large national organization, I noted the very high and growing cost of compromised health, especially in areas related to mental health. The growth of these costs was unsustainable and or could have a very negative impact on our viability and profitability. As we surveyed our organization we noted that while short term absences for mental heath reason were increasing, the recovery period was six to eight weeks shorter in the presence of a healthy and supportive manager/employee relationship. This became a priority to me. We trained managers on how to recognize the signs, help them identify the issues, and gave them tools and support to deal with the issues. **VIOLETTE LAREAU**

Summary

✓ Personal effectiveness, productivity and even competitive positioning are highly related to our physical and emotional wellness.

✓ Corporate leaders are more than ever before aware of the interplay between wellness and engagement and are prepared to encourage, invest, and support employee wellness programs.

✓ If we are to face today's challenges, individuals need to take ownership of personal wellness and seek ways for optimum health that will lead to improved productivity.

10: FINDING YOUR SWEET SPOT

"Golfers understand the term. So do tennis players. Ever swung a baseball bat or paddled a Ping-Pong ball? If so, you know the oh-so-nice feel of the sweet spot. Connect with these prime inches of real estate and kapow! ... Life in the sweet spot rolls like a downhill side of a downwind bike ride."[25] Living in your sweet spot is like your engine optimized and humming nicely and on all cylinders. Living in your sweet spot is the spot where you are most effective, productive, and fulfilled. While this may be an illusive optimum state, it should be the target to which each of us must aspire.

Donald O. Clifton, Ph.D., was cited by the American Psychological Association as the Father of Strengths Psychology and the Grandfather of Positive Psychology. He was a chairman of Gallup, the well-known survey and research organization, where he invented the Clifton Strengths Finder, an assessment tool that has helped millions of people around the world discover their talents and focus on their strengths.

When we examine Dr. Clifton's work we find a simple theme. We are our best when we focus on our strong talents and abilities. We are most effective, do the best work, and enjoy our work the most when we are in our best fit. Life is most fulfilling when we live in our sweet spot.

Gallup Research asked thousands of people to what extent they agree with the following statement: *"At work, I have the opportunity to do what I do best every day."*[26] Regretfully, only one-third of those surveyed strongly agreed with that statement. In other words, two-thirds of us potentially are not living our sweet spot at work. If such an option is not present at work, where we spend most of our day, our level of enthusiastic involvement in work will always be limited.

In his book, *Strengths Based Leadership,*[27] Tom Rath says that as a leader if you help your employees focus on their strengths the possibility of their engagement increases to 73%. Compared with organizations where leaders ignore the need to focus on employee strengths the probability of engagement drops to only 9%. This is a staggering difference that calls for leadership action and priority.

There is a strong element of personal responsibility in living in our sweet spot. Opposites attract. Instead of focusing on what we are good at, we envy those who are better than we are in certain areas and try to be like them. This is engrained in us from early childhood. Parental statements like, "Why can't you be like your sister?" or "Your brother is very smart; he gets As in math" or "If you really want to be successful you have to do well in sciences." This is carried with us into adulthood. The danger comes when, driven by personal greed, financial pressures, social status, family or peer expectations, and even corporate dysfunction, we try to fit into a mould that does not match our best fit. Life becomes like fitting a square peg into a round hole.

Instead of focusing on what we are good at, we seek training that focuses on our weaknesses. Most corporate training budgets are spent on programs to make us what the company needs, regardless of whether we are a good fit or not. It is good to seek improvements but we need to be aware of our weaknesses and avoid the traps created by them. Our focus needs to be on how we can best leverage our strengths.

Based on our interviews and leaders' comments we believe that finding your sweet spot is a dual employee/employer responsibility. As individuals we own the initiating responsibility while employers have the supporting role. Individuals need to take an active role to frequently assess and calibrate their roles and responsibility to ensure living in their sweet spot.

Having the best fit is the most important factor in a fulfilling and most productive career. This is a shared employee/employer process. The employer is responsible for creating the environment that encourages the employee to find their best fit. As an employee I am the one that is most sensitive to the issues surrounding my personal fit. So I hold a big portion of the responsibility but not one hundred per cent of the responsibility. It is the employer's responsibility to create the environment that encourages the employees to seek opportunities where they fit the best because that is where they will deliver the best.
MATTHEW ANDERSON

Exercise: Finding your sweet spot

The Strengths Finder research identifies 34 key talents or themes presented in 34 chapters. We recommend this book and its related survey. Near the end of this chapter is a list of the strengths finder themes. For each theme we listed key adjectives that we believe describe each theme. Here is what you can do:

1. **Personal identification:**

    A. Thoughtfully examine the themes list and select the **top five themes** that best describe you.

    B. From each selected theme, select the **best adjective** that best describes you.

    C. **Prioritize the 5 adjectives** you selected and use them to complete the following sentence

"**I am** _____, _____, _____, _____, and_____."

2. **External validation:** Let us suppose your name is Tom.

    A. Seek input from 5 friends who know you well, give each of them a slip of that looks like the following example and you will have 25 adjectives/attributes that describe you.

Could you help me identify and focus on my best character attributes? As candidly as you can, please complete the following five sentences with the most important attribute or adjective that I demonstrate. Use one adjective per line:

- Tom is_____

- Tom is_____

- Tom is_____

- Tom is_____

- Tom is_____

    B. Compare these attributes to the ones you selected in your personal identification. Hopefully you will find some similarity between your chosen adjectives (personal identification) and your friends' external validation.

    C. Use your candid best judgment to focus on what you deem to be the most important character attribute.

    D. Update your "I am statement".

3. **Historical validation:**

    A. Reflect back on your life events, think of situations where you feel you displayed these character attributes.

    B. Write these thoughts and experiences as your story. Hopefully, these will be pleasant thoughts and joyful experiences.

4. **Application:**

Update your resume to:

A. Start with a brief three to five sentence character profile that uses your most important character attributes. This should clearly describe who you are or who you wish to be known as. We believe this is the most important part of a resume.

B. List or highlight career and personal achievements where you capitalized on your strengths and where your character attributes were leveraged in the best light.

Dreaming is good and healthy. Imagine work and social engagements where you can be the person described by the attributes you listed. Write your thoughts in a document called "What I want to be and why." Later, under the heading of "Living your Sweet Spot" we will give you more practical thoughts and tips.

Begin to seek out venues and opportunities where your imagination can become a reality. In Chapter 4: The war for talent we highlighted that the demand for talent is greater than the forecasted supply. With some flexibility and perseverance you can find your best fit.

Ensuring employee fit is one of the most challenging leadership roles. Optimum fit in the workplace is a joint responsibility between the employee and his or her leader that requires constant alignment and active monitoring.

Leaders often have the advantage of a wisdom that comes from experience and a more complete understanding of corporate opportunities and limitations. On the other hand, employees own the responsibility to realistically communicate their own talents, abilities, and career objectives.

An important component of fit is ensuring the employee, employer, and corporate leadership share common values. Unfortunately, while this is critical, regretfully, values are often the most neglected part of the employment or promotion discussion. The young professional with lots of upward potential is rarely taught by their superiors and leaders to recognize, discuss, and negotiate value. I recommend that companies, their leaders, and staff should incorporate value alignment into their professional development activity. **PAUL KENT**

Character themes

- **Ambitious:** Energetic, Goal-oriented, Hard working, Motivated, Self-disciplined
- **Action Oriented:** Impatient, Learning, Practical, Results-oriented, Tenacious
- **Adaptable:** Calm, Flexible, Productive, Reassuring, Responsive
- **Analytical:** Dispassionate, Interrogative, Logical, Objective, Rigorous
- **Coordinative:** Adaptable, Creative, Flexible, Innovative, Resourceful
- **Belief and Values Oriented:** Altruistic, Dependable, Family-oriented, Responsible, Spiritual
- **Commanding:** Clear, Confrontational, Direct, Honest, Risk-taking
- **Communicative:** Articulate, Captivating, Conversational, Descriptive, Expressive
- **Competitive:** Aggressive, Aspiring, Challenging, Driving, Striving,
- **Connected:** Accepting, Caring, Considerate, Humble, Spiritual
- **Consistent:** Balanced, Ethical, Even-handed, Fair, Unprejudiced
- **Context Oriented:** Counterintuitive, Experienced, Interrogative, Perceptive, Reflective
- **Deliberate:** Careful, Contemplative, Private, Serious, Vigilant
- **Developing:** Challenging, Coaching, Encouraging, Helpful, Nurturing
- **Disciplined:** Efficient, Exact, Orderly, Predictable, Structured
- **Empathetic:** Anticipating, Appreciative, Kind, Sensitive, Understanding
- **Focused:** Collaborative, Efficient, Goal-oriented, Independent, Impatient
- **Futuristic**: Energizing, Foresighted, Inspirational, Motivating, Visionary
- **Harmonious:** Agreeable, Deferential, Non-confrontational, Peaceable, Personable
- **Ideas Oriented:** Abstract thinking, Contemplative, Conceptual, Creative, Visionary
- **Inclusive:** Accepting, Connecting, Loyal, Non-judgmental, Social
- **Individualizing:** Encouraging, Impatient, Intuitive, Listening, Observant
- **Acquisitive:** Quick-to-learn, Inquisitive, Interested, Interrogative, Studious
- **Intellectual:** Inquisitive, Introspective, Reflective, Studious, Thoughtful
- **Studious:** Assimilative, Energetic, Inquisitive, Motivated, Studious
- **Maximum Oriented:** Demanding, Discriminating, Focusing, Productive, Refining
- **Positive:** Energetic, Energizing, Enthusiastic, Light-hearted, Optimistic
- **Relational:** Caring, Close, Genuine, Risk-taking, Sharing
- **Responsible:** Conscientious, Dependable, Ethical, Hardworking, Available
- **Restorative:** Analytical, Fixing, Identifying, Rekindling, Resuscitating
- **Self-Assured:** Certain, Confident, Independent, Risk-taking, Self-confident
- **Significance oriented:** Achieving, Credible, Focused, Goal-oriented, Independent
- **Strategic:** Intuitive, Observant, Predicting, Problem solving, Reflective
- **Woo-Charismatic:** Conversational, Friendly, Initiating, Networking, Sociable

Warning, change is not easy. This exercise is not easy and you may face:

- A balancing act between your sweet spot or best fit, corporate structures, and demands, as well as the expectations of others. In a changing world, this will require constant negotiation and realignment.
- A need to change employment or even career.
- An opportunity for lifestyle and financial compromises.
- Your ego or pride hindering you from doing what you know is best.

In our recruiting firm, when we engage with a client to find senior staff, our priority is to understand the corporate values and map this to potential candidates' values and character. I believe that employers have the ultimate responsibility of communicating clearly the behaviors and attitudes they expect the employee to exhibit.

On the other hand, I believe employees have an equal responsibility of accepting responsibilities for what they can be passionate about. The worst thing a person can do is to have a job that does not motivate them regardless of how much it pays. As Jim Collins says, "People are not your greatest asset—the RIGHT people are." **BRUCE MCALPINE**

Today we see a great shift in value. For example, to my father, a doctor from the old school, life was work; you never refuse a call and never say no. Today many of our new healthcare practitioners do not want this. They want to be assured that they can have more balance in their practice and are able to close the door and take long holidays. We see this not only in the healthcare field but I see it in most other professions. **MICHAEL DECTER**

Summary

✓ Today more leaders are aware of selecting employees based on cultural and personality fit.

✓ While selecting fit is a dual employee—employer responsibility, the lion's share of that responsibility lies in the hands of the employee.

✓ You know yourself better than anyone else.

✓ Taking advantage of this emerging change is your gateway to improved effectiveness and overcoming work and information overload.

11: EFFECTIVE COLLABORATION

In the early 1600s the English preacher poet John Donne penned a few simple words that embody the true meaning of collaboration. He wrote "No man is an Island entire of itself; every man is a piece of the Continent, a part of the main."[28] In our global village, these words ring truer today than ever before. Leaders and knowledge workers today must constantly seek changes that enhance their ability to collaborate more effectively. As we face a challenging and more demanding world we must make effective collaboration a top priority. Effective collaboration is critical to our success if not for our very corporate survival.

For a very long time organizations leveraged the power of collaboration by sharing expensive assets and resources. Co-operatives were established and credit unions thrived on a foundation of collaboration. Nations, tribes, and people groups established alliances to fight a common enemy and survive natural disasters.

Today, rapid and dynamic global integration has increased our dependence on each other. Technology that enables us to break down the boundaries that separate us has never been more accessible. At the same time effective collaboration remains a challenging goal in many of our work habits. While business leaders preach it and call for it, today most organizations struggle with its implementation. So we stop and ask, why do we struggle so much with effective delegation. If our future success strongly depends on it why do we, so easily abandon our commitment to it?

Many books and academics have tried to define, explain it, and create policies and structures to enforce it. It is an issue of corporate culture, yes, but more importantly it is an issue of personal culture. While corporate leaders preach and call for it, it often crumbles at the feet of our selfish motives and egotistical behaviors. Effective collaboration calls us to seek a much broader view of achieving maximum impact for good, for common good, for broader more lasting good.

The greatest achievements are fulfilled through effective collaboration. Effective collaboration requires that we are honest enough to know that we cannot solve problems by ourselves. The more complex the problems we face the more critical is the need to collaborate effectively. In the global relief world where I work, we have learned that unless we collaborate effectively we will most certainly fail. In my view there are three key foundations for effective collaboration:

- Common and compatible values, visions and objectives that are of high value
- Different but complementary skills and/or resources
- Equal respect and trust for all members in the collaboration partnership. This is the most critical part of the equation. This is the glue that holds it together. For example, in our business those who bring the financial resources or medical expertise should not be considered greater than the frontline workers who dispense compassionate care.

The greatest risks to effective collaboration are of self, pride, jealousy, and a competitive spirit. **DAVE McCOMISKEY**

For me the importance of collaboration cannot be overstated in today's economy. I do not define collaboration as two people talking. There is a lot of that with no results. Collaboration is going way beyond the talk to getting results. In my opinion effective collaboration requires:

1. Choice: All the people at the table must be there of their own voluntary choice and desire to be part of the collaborative process. If you are forced to come to the table, it is almost impossible to be a real team player.

2. Mutual trust: Without trust it is impossible to accomplish anything. In my experience this is often the first hurdle that you must overcome. Very often we assume that there is trust. But trust has to be earned and built before you go much further.

3. Commitment to stay focused on outcome: Having a clear common outcome that is supported by all those at the table is the critical third leg on which collaboration will stand or fall.

If people are there by choice, trust each other and stay focused on the outcome; the rest is trapping that can be as simple or as complex as we have to make it. The more complex the issues the more important are the elements of choice, trust, and focus. **MATTHEW ANDERSON**

Great life achievements require collaboration. Regretfully, in most of our life we are not trained to collaborate as much as we are encouraged to compete.

While the work environment may give lip service and say that we want collaboration, most business culture and compensation plans still reward competitive behaviors. I know that this is a cultural shift but it needs to happen.

When we examine our younger recruits coming out of university they are used to a team work culture with a high degree of collaboration. Some may find fitting in a competitive work culture unsettling. I believe leaders need to set examples and modify compensation plans to encourage a collaborative work environment. **MICHAEL DECTER**

Collaboration, at its core, is the willingness to compromise some objectives in order to embrace and advance towards some of the objectives of someone else such that both progress towards the ultimate desired end state. Through sincere respect for the other party and constructive dialogue and communication we seek a higher goal than the parties can achieve on their own. Collaboration has its roots in exchange of recognizable value. As you exchange statement of value and make it important to communicate and honor these values then trust is established and effective collaboration can find its way. Without value alignment, the effort to collaborate is on a shallow foundation and is likely to fail. In collaboration, values do not necessarily have to be identical but they must be complementary, aligned, and fully respected. **PAUL KENT**

A word about collaboration technology: In the book, *Wikinomics,* [29] Don Tapscott and his team highlight the phenomenal impact new technological tools, trends and development will have on our ability to globally collaborate. In their book they stretch our thinking and help us dream of endless possibilities. And that is great. Admittedly, they suggest that the younger tech savvy generation will be able to leverage such technologies better than the boomer generation. But we must be warned that this is could be a double-edged sword.

Collaboration is an attitude before it is a technological innovation. Collaboration tools and technologies are filling our inbox with news of new products or Web-based services. Social and business networks are popping up with tantalizing offers. Web 2.0 concepts and desktop tools promise to be the panacea of every application developer that wants people to collaborate and cooperate. Smart phones promise to give you access to all you want and all who want you any time anywhere. All of this is great, but:

- Unless we control it, it will become the monster that will destroy our effective collaboration ability.

- Unless we learn how to use correctly it will be more dangerous than fire in the hands of a small child.
- Unless we master it, it will become a demanding master.
- Unless we invest in it wisely, it could lead to our financial ruin.

While I totally agree with Don Tapscott on the value new technological tools can bring to our collaboration theaters, I believe that Don Tapscott would most likely agree that **technology provides access; control is, and must remain a leadership and personal responsibility.**

"'Effective Collaboration' touches key points surrounding collaboration in today's workplace. Items such as shared values, mutual trust, and the willingness to compromise some objectives in order to collectively reach a greater goal, are all on-point in today's work environment. In my estimation, the key requirement for effective collaboration is the importance of having a "clear common outcome that is supported by all those at the table."

Having worked in the telecommunications industry for a number of years, it has been my business to find ways for people to work together more effectively using cutting edge technology. What is often omitted, however, is the need for clear communication and ensuring that all parties are working towards the same objective. So while terms such as "fixed mobile convergence" and "telepresence" may sound like they're enhancing collaborative efforts, it is the ability to work towards a common goal that lies with each of us. This ability can never be replaced by the latest and greatest technological advancement." **DAVID CARSON**

Summary

✓ Effective collaboration is not an option. It is a foundation for our future survival.
✓ While corporate leaders call and advocate for it, collaboration will never take root until individuals wholeheartedly embrace it.
✓ As individuals we must put aside our competitive spirits and personal biases and embrace common higher value goals.
✓ Effective collaboration takes root only when we sincerely seek a higher level of thinking that seeks maximum impact for good.
✓ Personal effective collaboration hinges on our ability to put aside personal egos and self-glorification in favor of seeking maximum impact for common good.

12: EFFECTIVE DELEGATION AND COACHING

Andrew Carnegie is quoted for saying *"No man will make a great leader who wants to do it all himself, or to get all the credit for doing it."* [30] Effective delegation is a cornerstone of business leadership. As we face our present challenges we must seek changes that enhance our ability to delegate and reward effective delegation. Effective delegation is sharing the adventure.

Effective delegation shares the stage with its twin—effective coaching. They both share a common high value objective—growth. Effective delegation and effective coaching leverage each other by providing an optimum mix of opportunity, empowerment, authority, and accountability. The outcomes are multiplied benefits to the leader and his or her protégé.

Absence of effective delegation is a major contributor to the overload problem and a stumbling block to individual and organization growth. Working with clients, there are three key symptoms that we observe that often indicate the inability to delegate effectively:

- **E-mail overload:** As a manager or leader, the amount of e-mail you get from your staff, or from those who should be dealing with your staff, is a strong indicator of level of effectiveness in your delegation skills. The amount of e-mail you are copied on is a further strong indicator of ineffective delegation or lack of empowerment.

- **Meeting overload:** The amount of time you spend in meetings, with your staff or with others in the presence of your staff, often has a direct correlation to the level of empowerment, support, and authority you delegate to your staff.

- **Interruptions:** Constant interruptions by your staff or by those who should be dealing with your staff may be good indicators of your need to examine your delegation skills.

Why delegate?

The primary objective of delegation is not getting work done, or getting rid of stuff you do not feel you have the time to do. The primary objective of effective delegation is growth and progress. For delegation to be most effective it has to:

- help you grow by focusing you away from roles and responsibilities that you have outgrown

- help others grow by taking on new roles and responsibilities that can cause them to be passionate and excited

- help you and your protégé gain greater appreciation and commitment to each other and the common goals you share

Leaders who do not learn effective delegation hurt themselves by limiting their growth potential and do their organization great disservice. In my role I spend a great deal of my time overseas. I had to realize that unless I delegate effectively I will be the greatest liability to my organization.

Effective delegation has a multiplier effect. Used wisely, it enables a leader to accomplish many times what he or she can do. Effective delegation involves first giving power away. Some individuals struggle with that, especially if they are a bit insecure. It also involves coaching, equipping, supporting, and serving those you delegate to. In our busy lives very often leaders neglect this and delegation fails.

Very often delegation is viewed to be more hierarchical—a boss delegating to an employee. It does not necessarily need to be that way. For example, I have worked on teams where the leader was one of my staff and had a strong leadership role. In that capacity, she delegated to me certain roles and I was accountable to her.

Effective collaboration and effective delegation are twins bearing similar DNA. Done well, this is the place where we see delegation and collaboration intertwine to bring the greatest benefits. **MICHAEL DECTER**

Why do we fear delegation?

There are many reasons that hold us back from delegation:

- **Fear of losing control.** "If I delegate, something may go wrong and I am not sure how to deal with this."
    - There is always risk but if you have done your leadership role with proper coaching, empowerment and accountability, the risks are reduced and the rewards are worthwhile.

- **Fear of diminished value:** "If I delegate this will reduce my role or authority."
  - The best thing you can ever do for your career is to train others in such a way as to work yourself out of a job.
- **Fear of perfectionism:** "No one can do it as well as I can" or "If someone else does it better than I can, I may lose my reputation."
  - You were never that good until someone gave you the chance to try.
- **Fear of coaching:** "I have no time to teach someone else; it is easier for me to do it myself."
  - **The** investment you make in coaching not only adds to your achievements, it multiplies them.
- **Fear of overloading others:** "They are so busy already; I hate to put more on their shoulders."
  - Your protégés are big kids. Give them the choice. As they prioritize, coach them to delegate likewise. Often they will uncover options that you cannot see.

Effective delegation is never abdication. Never delegate to avoid responsibility or negative outcome. Effective delegation carefully considers the learning needs and ability of the person to whom you are delegating. Take lots of time to communicate all expectations, timelines, process, and authority. Be sure you are able to provide appropriate feedback and support as well as needed authority. Delegation often takes more work than doing something yourself but it is critical for the growth of the intellectual capital of an organization.
SUSAN MALENICA

Tips on effective delegation

1. **Delegate roles not tasks.** Most delegation happens along organizational lines. The risk that comes with this is that we end up delegating tasks to get rid of work assignments. However, in delegating roles you need to make sure the individual has the optimum mix of:

   A. **Skill and character attributes**: Ensuring character fit is the most important aspect in defining a role and therefore the most critical element in effective delegation. The most important job of an effective delegator is to define the needed character.

   B. **Competencies, knowledge, experience and/or information:** If these elements are not available you need to ask if they can be easily acquired in a timely manner.

C. **Ability or the time** and effort that can be dedicated to that new role. The time horizon and needed effort are critical to ensuring people have the bandwidth needed to carry the role. If not, can they be empowered to delegate some of their present obligations?

2. **Empowerment, authority and accountability** are the three-legged stool of effective execution in effective delegation.

   A. There is no delegation without empowerment.

   B. There is no empowerment without authority.

   C. There should be no authority without accountability.

3. **Focus or progress**: In delegating roles you encourage ownership of the process. The person you are delegating to brings unique skills, talents, and perspectives. As you delegate you hold responsibility **for a dashboard of progress** but the outcome and consequences are transferred to the person to whom you have delegated.

4. **Protect the priority of communication:** Communication is the fuel that keeps effective delegation going. As you monitor progress you provide feedback, support, encouragement, and corrective input. The communication format and frequency need to be agreed upon in the delegation agreement.

5. **Keep track:** Delegation is important business. As you delegate you assume the role of a coach or an overseer. Keeping an appropriate record of the delegation process and the delegation dashboard are critical success factors.

6. **It is not a life sentence:** When good actors contract for a role in a theatrical performance they usually have a contractual term. When delegating a role, keep the delegation within a specific time horizon. This could be bound by the project completion date or a specific review point.

7. **Allow for contingency:** The best of plans may fail so allow for contingency. The contingency may include corrective actions if the delegation agreement fails to bring acceptable outcomes. This should be agreed upon upfront and should not be a surprise to either party.

8. **Celebrate:** It is your responsibility to track and profile the success of your protégé. Sincere compliments and proper public acknowledgement are the greatest motivators so be very generous with them.

Effective delegation takes time and requires initial planning and clarity in communication by the delegator. It also requires follow-up support and encouragement. When delegating we make two common mistakes. The first is that we often quickly delegate prescribed tasks rather than carefully communicating the role that we are delegating. Delegating roles allows the protégé more latitude in using their judgment, and in the end brings greater development, a greater sense of achievement, and likely a better result. The second common mistake is that we can sometimes treat people like a "fire-and-forget missile."

We hand it to them and don't follow up, perhaps leaving them to flounder on difficult issues. It is important to be available to the protégé to provide a regular point of support and encouragement. This is the reason why effective delegation and coaching go hand in hand. **DOUG STIRLING**

Effective delegation is founded on three pillars:

The first and most important is to know the person you are delegating to. You have to know not only their competencies but, more importantly, their skills and abilities.

The second is clear communication of what it is that you are delegating. For example, if I get a request for a financial analysis from someone above me and I delegate this to one of my staff without clearly understanding the objective and expected content of the report I will most likely cause more work overload and resentment than I should.

The third is a commitment to guiding support and coaching. This ties the two first points together. Based on knowing the person and what it is you are delegating as a leader you need to define what, where, and when coaching is needed. **GEORGE ABATE**

Summary

✓ Effective delegation and its twin, effective coaching, are two of the most important prerequisites to successful leadership.

✓ The primary objective of effective delegation is growth and progress.

✓ When delegating effectively, delegate roles not tasks. In so doing ensure that your protégé has the appropriate mix of skills, competency or knowledge, ability, and authority.

CURES - FILTERS TO PRIORITIZE

- Why prioritize?
- Roles Filter
- People Filter
- Issues Filter
- Goals Filter
- Living your sweet spot

13: WHY PRIORITIZE?

The first day back

Adam walked into his office at 7:15 A.M. the first day after the holidays. A quick glance at the flashing phone message light brought back all the resentment he had for the excessive work demands placed on him. Turning his voice mail on he heard, "You have 22 messages." The first message was from his SVP; it said, "Hi, Adam! Be sure to check your e-mail. The Boss has called a lunch meeting to update Q1 revenue commitments. I told him that I thought you will have no problem being ready for that."

After a depressing review of his voice mail Adam turned on his e-mail. He always checked his e-mail and calendar first thing in the morning. He said, "You never know what snakes are hiding in e-mail." As usual a flood of e-mail and back-to-back meetings were forecast for a hectic day.

It was almost 9:00 A.M. when Adam opened his door to get his third cup of coffee. Several people were waiting to see him. In his good humor he yelled, "OK everyone; take a number and don't block the hallway. It's against fire regulations."

Standing in front of the coffee machine he remembered a question Eve Wise challenged him with at the Board of Trade party. She asked, "What important roles do you play in your organization?" His reply was, "I am the corporate controller." She graciously said, "I did not ask you for your title, Adam. I asked you for the important roles." The discussion that followed helped Adam realize that he was a victim of "Title-Imposed Roles."

Adam was a very competent and knowledgeable corporate controller. In his fast moving, growing business he was known as the "go to man". His willingness to take risks gained him a reputation as a troubleshooter. His flexible educational background encouraged others to recruit him as a key member in a variety of committees. Committee meetings often resulted in long "to do" lists that he was encouraged to undertake.

While Senior Management often admired his activities, the operational need of his finance team and his family commitments were frequently neglected. Guilt and frustration added to his *real feeling of overload. In planning for his annual performance review he was quick to realize that some changes would have to happen.*

Adam realized his need to prioritize differently. He would have to focus on roles where he would be most fulfilled and where he would deliver the highest value. He knew that his actions might be counterculture and that he would have to do some tough negotiations with his boss. He did. He was glad he did. His boss and his family were glad he did. When Adam aligned his priorities around what he was best at, the results were the best for all concerned.

The challenge most of us face is not in choosing between the good and the bad. The challenge is filtering, to choose between the good and the best. Developing your own filtering system will help you focus, prioritize, and choose to be the best you can be and do the best you can do.

Filtering is a thinking process to help you prioritize and focus on where you can be most effective and most fulfilled. Most of us prioritize our days based on a "to do" list. This list is often based on the demands and expectations of others. As we fall behind on our "to do" list, guilt sets in and discouragement takes over so we discard our list and start a new one. Others of us seek to prioritize using goals to direct personal and work lives. As we discuss later, setting goals is admirable and very important. Regretfully, goals are often unreasonable and seldom reached leaving us discouraged and unmotivated.

Most of my working career was as a missionary in the third and underprivileged world. There, the needs are huge and the opportunity to do good are endless. It is critical to learn to filter and prioritize how we invest the limited resources and time available to us. It is hard to ignore or overlook the temporal and short term needs of hurting people, but at the same time long term perspective is more critical. I had to keep in mind that maximum impact for good will come when a person is connected to the source of all good and that is God himself. For me personally, I have to go to God for wisdom and direction. He helps me align my personal focus to bring Maximum Impact For Good. **ARNOLD COOK**

Filtering is also learning to avoid bad work and life habits. Most of us develop bad work and life habits not because we desire them, but because we do not have enough motivation or the tools to break them or avoid them. In previous chapters we discussed the challenges and the changes that we hope will motivate you and ignite in you the desire to filter and change. We hope you can see that in filtering there are opportunities to improve your effectiveness and greater rewards. In this section of the book we will review filtering principles and prioritizing tools that you can use to improve your effectiveness by overcoming work and information overload.

The Priority-Based Filtering Framework ™ is a strategic **four-part tool** that provides a thinking process. We believe that given the opportunity to think carefully and the tools needed, most of us can change for the better. Based on our clients' experiences using this thinking tool, you can develop personalized filters that will help you **focus on higher value roles, relationships, issues, and goals.** Then and only then can you create reasonable goals that can empower and direct your activities. The priority based filtering system is a dynamic interrelationship of four critical parts:

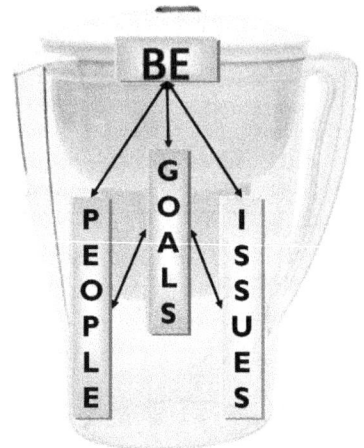

Filtering Framework

1. **Roles:** What are you expected to **be** in the roles you must play? Roles are different from job titles. They are seldom defined in job descriptions. While some job descriptions may sometimes outline areas of responsibilities this does not clearly define the role a person is expected to play. In filtering we encourage you to start by focusing on what you should **be** and let that drive what you are expected to **do** in order to become what you should **be**.

2. **People:** As a knowledge worker, people are your value exchange and knowledge exchange partners. People are also the recipients of your value proposition. Unless the roles you play ultimately add value to people, one must question if they add value at all. With this in view, how you impact people should be **a primary focus.** While all people are valuable they differ in your priority and your life investments. In filtering we encourage you to focus on your **important and teachable people** and avoid the negative impact created by your **draining people**.

3. **Issues:** In any given day many issues call for your attention. The issues you deal with are either obstacles to playing your role or opportunities to help you fulfill your role. Filtering is choosing the issues that you are likely to impact the most by bringing your highest value contribution. In filtering we need to focus on the important issues, not fall victim to the destructive culture of urgency.

4. **Goals:** Goals are the **energizing, driving force** in this filter system. Goals provide a yardstick by which you measure the effectiveness of your role in life. In filtering we encourage you to:

   • Focus on your sphere of accountability
   • Leverage your sphere of influence
   • Avoid the sphere of concerns

![Summary icon] Summary

✓ Today, the challenge you face is not choosing between good and bad, but choosing to focus on what is best not just what is good.

✓ You can filter wisely by redefining and focusing your roles to the people you consider your value and knowledge exchange partners—your important and teachable people.

✓ The issues you choose to deal with are opportunities that help you set goals to fulfill your roles.

14: ROLES FILTER

In the 1600s Shakespeare wrote in *As You Like It*:

> "All the world's a stage,
> And all the men and women merely players:
> They have their exits and their entrances;
> And one man in his time plays many parts"[31]

Shakespeare provides us with powerful imagery that we hope you will keep in mind as we challenge you to filter on high value roles.

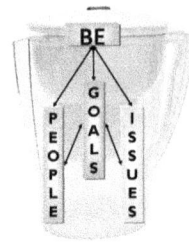

Danger: title-imposed roles

Most of us, when asked about the role we play at our place of work, are likely to provide our title. If the questioner persists, we respond highlighting our functional or organizational responsibilities or work habits. If asked to clarify further, we list all we do. It is easy for us to define our roles based on what we do. Sometimes it feels good to list all we have to do. Most of us are hired into the organization using job titles. These fall short in defining the high value roles we are expected to play and often lead to the risks associated with title-imposed roles.

> Your roles are a reflection of what you can **be**. What you can **be** is a reflection of your character attributes. It is out of the abundance of your character attributes that you are able to **do** what you can for the benefit of yourself and others.

In title-imposed roles, our priorities are based on the demands others place upon us. These demands are based on the varied needs and assumptions and historical experiences of a variety of individuals and groups. While titles may sometimes highlight the area of responsibilities, they leave you open to urgency created by the changing world of the one who is demanding your services.

In our fast changing world responding to urgent demands we are often compelled to fill in the gap of uncertainty responding by saying **"let me see**

what I can do." Each demand, once fulfilled, becomes a de facto part of the job title and is added to the ever-growing "to do" list—after all you did it once so well why not do it again.

Over time what we do defines who you are. In most social settings a common introductory question is **"What do you do?"** We forget that we are called human **beings,** not human **doings.** Title-imposed roles feeds on a longer "to do" list. As the list of what we are expected to do gets bigger we lose our focus and our ability to prioritize on what is most important or what brings the highest value. The cure for Title-Imposed Roles requires us to go back to our sweet spot. In chapter 10 we encouraged you to define your sweet spot by focusing on the key attributes that you need to be. That is what will help you prioritize the roles you are best suited for.

You are on stage

In performing our roles, life presents each of us with three stages on which we play our roles and demonstrate our value. As the Roles Filters diagram shows there is the **Leadership Stage,** the **Project Stage,** and the **Operational Stage.** Like a professional actor our impact and our effectiveness is directly related to our ability to **be** the character roles we need to play. Such attributes equip us to perform different tasks. The stage on which you feel most fulfilled is the one that provides you

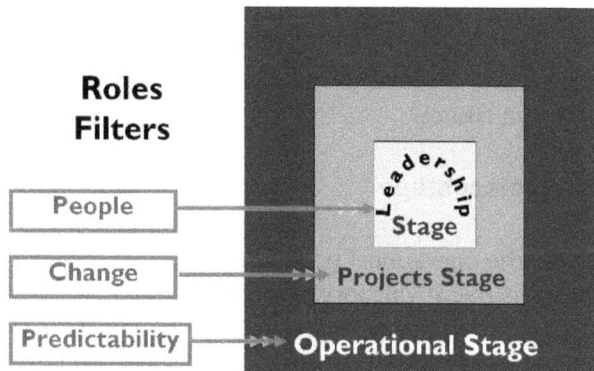

with the ability to **be** your best, to **do** what you are best suited for and to live in your sweet spot. Very often it is on this stage that you are likely to deliver your highest value. Your value is directly related to your ability to focus on your highest value roles and be supported by and provide the needed support for others who share the stage with you.

Like an actor in a performance, you need to take an active part in defining your roles. If you do not exercise that ability, **others will assume roles for you.** They will assume roles that reflect their own priorities. They will impose definitions that are biased by their own expectations, not necessarily by your abilities and limitations. They will impose role descriptions that may be in conflict with your values. Being active in defining your role involves honest communication and negotiation with those who share the various stages of life with you.

The operational stage

Think of a gas station when you think of the operational stage. The gas pump is always ready to deliver with no surprise. On the operational stage we leverage routine and predictability. Things happen in a consistent manner. You leverage commonly agreed upon patterns and behavior. The expectations placed upon us are matched with reasonable guidelines that are not easily changed. On the operational stage you are called to be a service person, a helper, and a resource that is always on demand.

Managers that oversee the operational stage have a mandate to ensure operational integrity and avoid change of standard protocols. Change brings about disappointments to those who play the role of monitors and overseers. As watchdogs they sound the alarms on deviation from normally accepted behaviors or patterns.

On the operational stage some of us are positioned to respond to crisis situations. Since dangers and risks are unavoidable we place resources ready to respond. Some of us feel most fulfilled in the role of firefighters, problem solvers, and troubleshooters. In such roles we thrive on a life that is addicted to adrenalin rushes.

The project stage

Unlike the operational stage where we leverage routine and predictability, change is the driving force on the project stage. Those of us on the project stage look for change and anticipate the impact it brings. Change is inevitable and those who thrive on the project stage see beyond its conflicts and the stress it brings. On the project stage we play specific roles based on project plans and expected deliverables. Those who play the role of project managers or leaders have a great responsibility to use project resources in a manner that brings maximum expected benefits.

Ensuring your ability to deliver maximum value on the project stage hinges on clearly defining your roles and fitting them into the project process. Delivering maximum value on the project stage is directly impacted by your ability to negotiate the role that best suits you as a member of the project team.

Some of the roles you play on the project stage include that of:

- **Project Authority** who is able to arbitrate conflicting priorities and ensure the availability of needed funds and resources

- **resource** who contributes knowledge, competencies, or experience to the project team

- **advisor** who provides answers to critical questions

- **champion** who is able to rally for the support of, or to sell new ideas needed for project success

- **planner** who has the skills needed to articulate realistic tasks and milestones

- **manager** who ensures the proper execution of needed tasks at the appropriate time

A key contributor to project failures is the assignment of the project roles. For project teams to fulfill their high value roles those leading the project must ensure the optimum mix of:

- **Soft skills** to envision alternatives or sell tough ideas

- **Technical competencies** or experience or academic credentials

- **Decision-making** with reasonable measures of **authority**

- **Time** to fulfill the expected role.

One very common mistake project leaders make is to define project roles based on titles or organizational structures. We believe that the only impact organizational structures should play in selecting a project team is in the point of providing the authority needed to make tough choices. Even this should be kept to the minimum.

The Project Effectiveness Framework™

Projects require the participation of committed individuals with clearly defined roles. Your ability to fulfill such a role

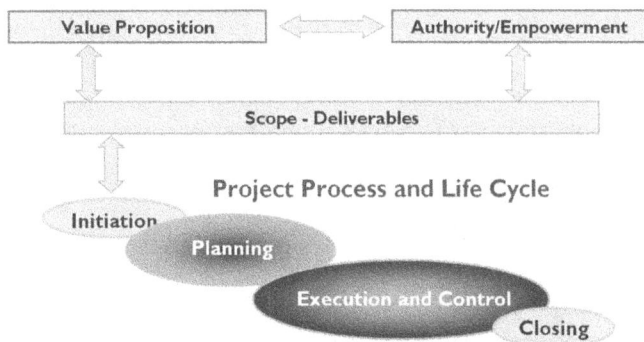

Project Effectiveness Framework™

on the project stage depends on the presence of **key project success factors** illustrated in what we call The Project Effectiveness Framework™:

- **High project value:** Too many projects are started without clearly articulated benefit statements. A benefit statement responds to one simple question, **"Why should we do this?"** Benefit statements clearly define the expected changes and outcome of a project. Benefit statements reflect the tangible and non-tangible benefits that will result from investing efforts and resources in the stated project. Benefit statements serve to mobilize and recruit appropriate players and project participants.

- **Responsible Project Authority:** The Project Authority is the person who has the responsibility of funding the project. Very often it is the person who has the vision to see the high level benefits of the project or who is most likely to receive most of the project benefits.

- **Project scope and deliverables:** Regretfully, far too often we see clients starting a project without a clear definition or agreement on scope, deliverables, or expected outcomes. A clearly articulated scope should highlight what is included and what is excluded from the project considerations. A list of key deliverables must be documented and have the approval of the Project Authority. Any changes to the project scope must be well controlled.

- **Initiation:** The project process starts with the project initiation. The initiation is the clear documentation and communication of the **project value, authority, scope, and deliverables**. Some leading project thinkers suggest that a project does not exist until the initiation is completed or almost concluded with release of what is called the project charter. **The project charter** is a high level document that answers key questions:

1. What do you call this project and who are its key sponsors?

2. What is this project all about?

3. What are the project business drivers and how do they impact key stakeholders?

4. What is the project's scope and what does it cover?

5. What are the key project deliverables?

6. What are the major tangible and non-tangible benefits?

7. What are the major initial and recurring costs?

8. What are the critical success factors and what risks could be encountered?

9. What are the key project roles and who will play them?

10. What, who, and when? What is the high-level action plan?

CHALLENGES, CHANGES & CURES

11. Space for leadership comments, approval, or rejection.

Note: for a project charter template go to
http://www.nomoreoverload.com/templates.html

- **Planning:** A project plan is a clear list of projected tasks. Such a plan defines the interrelationship between the project players. It provides reasonable estimates of costs and efforts. It sets the stage for rational expectations and timelines. It helps in avoiding disappointments and frustrations. The project plan often has multiple overlaying phases that may be dependent or independent of each other.

- **Execution and controls:** In the absence of control and accountability we are all tempted to unacceptable compromises. During the execution phase, control manages unrealistic assumptions and expectations and ensures adherence to proper communication principles and agreed upon protocols and plans.

In this project phase the project leader and key team members control what we like to call **"The Puzzle of Project Constraints."** Project constraints are the interdependence

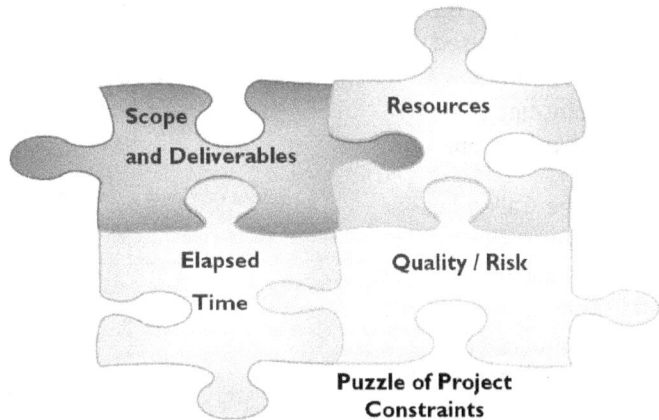

Puzzle of Project Constraints

of project scope, committed resources, elapsed time and related quality expectations, and reasonable risks. As illustrated, like a well fitted jigsaw puzzle any change to one part will require an adjustment to the other part. Nothing comes from nothing.

- **Closing:** Proper closing is almost as critical as project initiation. Whether in successful celebration or regretful disappointment all projects must be closed. It is in this phase that all the documentations are concluded, evaluation of the participants' roles and contributions are clearly acknowledged, and lessons learned are documented and communicated.

The leadership stage

As we view people around us, we see that there are differing types of leaders. Borrowing concepts from Dr. Thom S. Rainer[32] our hope is to help you examine your leadership sweet spots and develop an action plan that will enhance the effectiveness of your leadership roles. As you examine the following leadership type diagram try to identify your leadership sweet spot.

The called leader: Regardless of your title or state in life you are a leader. By your actions, words, or even your silence you are a leader. The problem is that in this you may not be intentional and your leadership is totally dictated by the labels or titles others give you. Your leadership, or lack of, is totally based on the assumption and expectations of others and how they interpret these labels and titles. Title-based expectations are often a cause for unfocused overloaded lives, disappointments, and leadership burnout.

While the Called Leader is totally unintentional, the wise leader examines and seeks to manage the impact of his or her leadership sweet spot. Like a well matched jigsaw puzzle, we can be one or more of the five leadership types as we seek to leverage our strength and that of others who share the leadership stage in which we perform our roles.

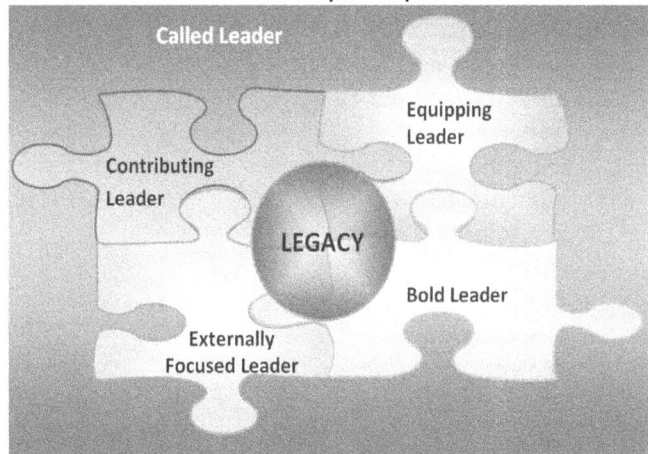

Called Leader

Equipping Leader

Contributing Leader

LEGACY

Bold Leader

Externally Focused Leader

LEADERSHIP TYPE

1. **The contributing leader:** The contributing leader is more focused on delivering tasks based on corporate or personal objectives. These are often associated by specific, relatively controllable performance indicators and benchmarks.

2. **The equipping leader:** When you think of equipping leaders you think of good coaches. They are seldom visible during the game. Their life investment is in the disciplined rigor of knowing each of their team members, planning appropriate rehearsals, and practicing regularly. While you do not hear their voices on the field, their words in the locker rooms echo loud and clear. Their thoughts and attitudes linger in the minds and

hearts of well chosen team players who shine because of their coach's leadership.

3. **The externally focused Leader:** Seeking opportunities and initiatives outside the walls of his or her enterprise is the passion of the externally focused leader. This leader is always in search of new partnerships to collaborate with, competitors to turn into customers, or old enemies to turn into allies and friends.

4. **The bold leader:** The exhilarating rush of joy that comes with big ideas motivates the bold leader. Whether it be opening new business horizons or calling a nation to put a man on the moon and return him safely, such are the visions and risks that energize bold leaders and captivate the minds of those who follow them.

5. **The legacy leader:** Focus on the impact left behind long after he or she has exited the stage of life is the objective of the legacy leader. While organizational loyalty is unquestionable, the legacy leader seeks for an impact that survives normal organizational life expectancy. The legacy leaders intentionally invest their life with a view of what they will leave behind.

As we consider the issue of legacy, it is important to note that in some measure, whatever leadership type we may be, we each leave our own mark and personal legacy. Good or bad our footprints will leave some tracks on the sandy shores of life.

Note:

- We do not imply that one of these stages, Operations, Project, or Leadership, is more important than the other. The priority is totally based on your talents, where you have your best fit, and where you complement others the most.

- As you examine your sweet spot and leadership type, it is important to also note that these are not placed in any order of priority or value. For example, we do not suggest that a bold leader is more valuable than a contributing leader or vice versa. Rather like the illustrated jigsaw puzzle, there are strong possibilities of interdependent relationships between the various leadership types.

While there is no hierarchy of value, there are often great opportunities for personal and corporate growth in moving from one leadership type to another. For example, there is a multiplying value if a contributing leader can expand his or her sweet spot by focusing on coaching or mentoring less experienced team members. Should an equipping leader become externally focused, there are often new opportunities for multiplied benefits in the broader enterprise or community.

Exercise: Roles Filter

The following five-step thinking exercise is designed to help you focus your roles by relating them to your sweet spot which you identified in chapter 10.

1. Using your calendar, examine one or more work weeks that are representative of your work life. Where did you invest your life? Guesstimate the percentage of activities, or time you spent on each of the three referenced stages. In order to live fully in your sweet spot, do you see a need for change in your time allocations? In the following table, write your present and desired allocation along with any comments, and observations for the reason to change.

Stage	Present %	Desired %	Why, Comment, Observations and/or Reason
Operation al Stage			
Project Stage			
Leadership Stage			

2. In chapter 10 you defined your sweet spot using your five key character adjectives and or attributes. Go back and examine these attributes and write them in column 1 in the table below.

Key Adjectives or Attributes	My Most Suitable Key Roles

CHALLENGES, CHANGES & CURES

3. Keeping your focus on your desired stage allocation from step 1 and your key attributes you just listed in step 2, examine the following Sample Roles List and add other roles you may consider missing.

4. Select one or two roles that you consider to be the best match to your key attributes and write them in column 2 beside each adjective or attribute.

5. As you ponder the operation, project, and leadership stages on which you play, begin to ponder and journal your thoughts on what changes you need to make to the roles and responsibilities to help you focus and leverage your sweet spot. Later on we will encourage you to communicate your findings so you can you collaborate and delegate effectively.

Sample roles list

☐ Activator	☐ Enforcer	☐ Overseer
☐ Administrator	☐ Entrepreneur	☐ Partner
☐ Advisor	☐ Facilitator	☐ Peacekeeper
☐ Advocate	☐ Guard	☐ Peacemaker
☐ Arbitrator	☐ Guide	☐ Planner
☐ Authority	☐ Helper	☐ Problem solver
☐ Builder	☐ Influencer	☐ Promoter
☐ Catalyst	☐ Investigator	☐ Prospector
☐ Champion	☐ Interrogator	☐ Provider
☐ Change agent	☐ Leader	☐ Resource
☐ Coach	☐ Listener	☐ Sounding board
☐ Commander	☐ Mediator	☐ Supporter
☐ Counsellor	☐ Mentor	☐ Teacher
☐ Decision maker	☐ Model	☐ Trendsetter
☐ Diplomat	☐ Motivator	☐ Trouble-shooter
☐ Developer	☐ Negotiator	☐ Visionary
☐ Enabler	☐ Observer	☐ - Add other
☐ Encourager	☐ Organizer	☐ - Add other

Note: If this is the first time you are doing such an exercise, you may find this awkward in the beginning. Please do not let this hold you back. **Remember your goal is progress, not perfection.** Later on this will become second nature to you.

I have learned to be more diligent in clarifying my priorities and managing people's expectations of me. You can never please everyone. If you spread yourself too thin, you will please no one.

We live in a culture where we are often valued based on what we do. My advice to the overloaded person is to be brutally honest with yourself and clearly define what is important to you. At the end of the day there are very few things that significantly impact our life. Prioritize aggressively and reprioritize if necessary; this will allow you to keep your commitments. People will respect you more when they know where you stand. **SUSAN MALENICA**

Recently, I was speaking with a Deputy Minister of Health about the mistake we often make of placing people in leadership roles based on their business or clinical skills without giving enough attention to their social and caring qualities. A person's knowledge or competencies do not necessarily ensure that he or she is a good fit for the roles assigned in an organization. **JOHN MCGARRY**

Summary

✓ Filtering is the ability to prioritize and focus more effectively.

✓ While most of us prioritize based on "to do" lists or goals we need to prioritize on roles and what you are expected to be.

✓ What you are expected to be will help you to select the most suitable stage on which you can perform you best roles.

15: PEOPLE FILTER

Over caring leader

Tom and his wife, Sue, are two of the most wonderful people you will ever meet. Just looking at them you can tell that they love people and people love to be with them. Tom had a very diverse career in the upscale home building industry. Overseas assignments developed in him a passion for helping the underprivileged world. As a very articulate communicator he has a unique teaching ability. His natural talent along with the call of God on his life led him to the pastoral profession.

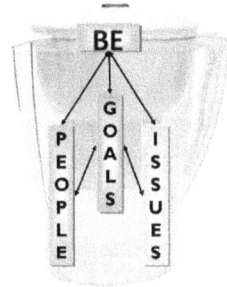

Sue, on the other hand, is the consummate caregiver. Her love for children goes to the extreme end of sacrificial love. As their children moved from infancy to independence Sue started a new career when she received a telephone call from children's aid and social services. Soon they had four therapeutic special needs foster children in their care.

Over time Tom's ministry grew as more and more people sought his help. His life became filled with teachable and draining people. There was the need to teach and preach, counsel troubled marriages, encourage newlyweds, bless little babies, and bury the dead. He did all of this yet his passion for helping the third world did not diminish. Long days and working nights became a regular pattern of life.

Regretfully, the body cannot endure this lifestyle for very long. As Tom neared fifty years of age with a family history of heart disease and diabetes he had to heed the warning that, "You do not drive an old car like you drive a new one." Tom had to accept the facts associated with his lifestyle and work habits. Tom had to change by focusing on the people and groups where he could have the greatest impact.

Change was not easy for Tom. He chose a change of careers and now he feels more fulfilled and more effective as he now focuses on only one of the groups or areas he had been involved in before. He does this in full collaboration with the church where he served for many years. Tom is a wise man.

Regretfully, Tom's story is far too common. Driven by growing demands and their passion to help, individuals engaged in the care and social services profession are at a much higher risk of overload and burnout. Overwhelmed by growing needs leaders and overseers often neglect the care of front line managers, workers, and care givers.

Our value proposition and productivity is directly related to how we impact the lives of other human beings for good. Even those of us who care for animals or natural resources must admit that the final link of what we do is often related to the well-being of humankind. Every one of us who knows how to do good and neglects to do so, is short-changing others and denying the purpose for which we exist. With this in view, we must always take an inventory of our relationships and assess our ability to have maximum impact for good on the lives of others.

Most of us have been taught that all people are equal. Yes, all people are equal under the law and all people are equal when it comes to death and taxes. But not all people are equally important or have the same priority when it comes to prioritizing our personal and business relationships. Our time, energy, and resources are finite and we need to invest them where we can deliver the highest value and where we have maximum impact for good.

Important, teachable, and draining people

In his thought-provoking book, *Restoring Your Spiritual Passion*, Dr. Gordon MacDonald suggests that in our lives we have different types of people.[33] We recommend reading his book along with Stephen Covey's bestseller, *The Seven Habits of Highly Effective People*.[34]

The people filter illustrates three circles based on the impact of three different people groups. They are:

- The circle of accountability holding your Important People
- The circle of influence holding your Teachable People
- The circle of concerns holding your Draining People

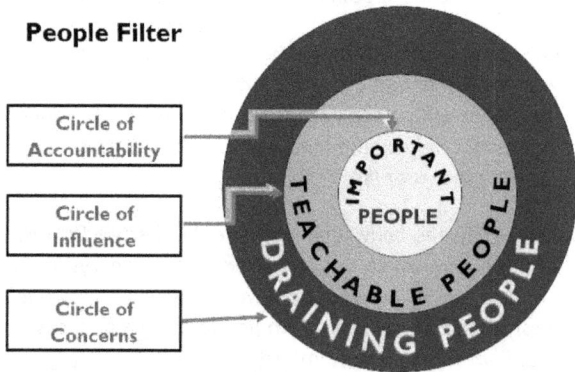

People Filter

- Circle of Accountability
- Circle of Influence
- Circle of Concerns

IMPORTANT PEOPLE
TEACHABLE PEOPLE
DRAINING PEOPLE

I. **The circle of accountability:** While all human beings are important not all of them should have the same priority in our attention or focus. Here we recommend two definitions for your important people:

A. The important people are **the people with whom you have a high level of accountability.** By virtue of organizational disciplines and authority, your primary boss and or key organizational superiors are part of your circle of accountability and should be considered among your important people.

B. The important people are **the people who help you define your roles and the people who are critical to the achievement of your goals**.

On the stage of life the **people who help you define your roles** are important people because they appreciate and understand the roles you need to play. They are individuals with whom you have a strong, open relationship that allows them to provide input into your values and character. They are people who are committed to your success and/or whose success is highly dependent on your success. In many cases they are individuals to whom you are accountable or those you ask to hold you accountable. The important people may include special family members, key people in your business organization, and others you consider mentors or great influencers on your values and thoughts.

We hasten to say that some of the important people who have helped us define our roles are writers. Through their writings and ageless wisdom they have impacted many for good.

The people who help you define your roles may be different for each role. But at all times keep that number to a mere handful; otherwise you may be faced with the confusing task of prioritizing conflicting opinions.

Also, the **important people are those who are critical to the achievement of your goals**. High value goals are often achieved through interdependent relationships with others. Such people often, directly or indirectly, derive benefit from your success. These people may include your children, colleagues, key customers, and/or suppliers of the products and services you need.

Once again, you will find that as you grow in your roles and value contribution you will need to prioritize and reduce the number of people who are critical to achieving your goals. If you do not do this, you run the risk of diluting your impact and relationships.

As you take inventory of your important people, do not overlook counting yourself in that list. Your values, character, and attributes are the most critical factors in helping you define your roles. Your health, talents, and abilities are most important assets in helping you achieve your goals.

To me, the important people are not limited to those in authority over me. Important people are those who help shape my roles and are interested in my personal development. Important people include family members and friends. On the opposite side, draining people often have a negative impact on the achievement of my goals and on how I feel about the roles that I undertake. It is important to limit exposure to draining people in order to avoid their negative impact. One way to limit exposure to draining people is to make encounters with them more structured and controlled. In that way you can still get their contributions to issues. **DOUG STIRLING**

2. **The circle of influence:** This circle holds the teachable people who are influenced by your character and/or your attitudes. They admire your behavior and your life values. They consider you a model in certain aspects of your life and wish to learn from you. Teachable people are in your circle of influence by their choice and your invitation. With them you have a mentoring, coaching, or leadership relationship.

The teachable people are committed to you and you invest time and interest in their growth. You seldom expect tangible or monetary rewards from your teachable people. However, as they grow you are energized and rewarded by seeing them progress and do well. Sometimes your teachable people are the people to whom you can delegate some of your roles and responsibilities as you move on to higher value roles, goals, and activities.

I organized the time I spend with my key employees as they are among my important and teachable people. While my team knows that they can come and see me any time, I have structured regular one-on-one meetings to discuss work and personal issues. This has reduced the number of interruptions I get and has enhanced my relationships with my staff.

I also learned that I need to block one-on-one time with myself. For me, life can be quite hectic. I need processing time to "think" without the interruptions and distractions of others around me. The most important advice I can give to an overloaded manager is to block regular processing time to think. This is invaluable in the long run. **JOELLE PEREZ**

CHALLENGES, CHANGES & CURES

The teachable person is someone who is open for new challenges and is prepared to take some risks. A teachable person is someone who brings a desire to learn with some level of fear; they recognize and are willing to admit that they don't know everything. A teachable person is one who is a bit timid about trying something new, but comes along with an attitude of "I'd like to do this but I am not sure I can; I'd like to try, would you guide me?" When I find a person like this I jump at the opportunity to coach him or her.

Among my team there were many who simply fulfilled their work assignments day in and day out and they did it very well. But there were others who I could sense as being keen to get involved or take responsibility for the next new initiative.

I believe in the workplace we have lots of great teachable people. The problem is that leaders are often too busy managing operations and do not take the time to identify or support their teachable people. So what happens to such people? They leave or their passion gets stifled and dies. **LYNN NAGLE**

Let us see how this works. Suppose you realize that you are on too many committees and you want to free more time for your family. You approach one of your teachable people who can benefit from the experience of being on such a committee and help him or her decide to take your role. As you do this you move to a new role in his or her life. You may become a coach or an encourager. As you watch him or her fulfill a new role you are satisfied and fulfilled by the progress. At the same time you are freed to pursue higher value roles, goals, and activities.

Your teachable people are the legacy of a life on life investment—the legacy you leave as you move on life's journey. Your teachable people are the ones who will most likely have the fondest and best memories of the impact you have had on their life.

One very simple and key way to help you identify your teachable people is the energy exchanged as you spend time with them. After meeting with your protégé you feel energized, encouraged, and fulfilled.

3. **The circle of concerns:** This circle holds the draining people. These are the people who do not fit in the first two categories. People concerns are the most draining of life experiences.

    A. Draining people are individuals whose behaviors and attitudes bring you concern and overtax your emotional wellbeing while resulting in little improvement on their part.

B. Draining people repeatedly face the same problems, complain about the same issues, but seldom take action to change eventual outcomes.

C. Draining people are often critical of others, disruptive in meetings, and are seldom proactive in facing life challenges.

D. Draining people often deal with superficial symptoms and are seldom ready to confront the root causes.

E. Draining people enter our lives in a variety of forms. They come in the form of individuals, as well as in the form of negative media reports, editorials, or TV programs that promote violence and negative behavior or lifestyles.

In dealing with the draining people you need to avoid them, reduce or control your exposure to their draining behavior or remove yourself from their life circumstances. Fortunately, if you focus on your important and teachable people your life will be so full that the draining people will find it hard to have access to your life.

Sometimes, for the good of all concerned, you have to confront draining attitudes and behavior. In his excellent book, *Caring Enough to Confront*, David W. Augsburger points out that the primary motivation for confrontation is that you value and desire to protect an important relationship.[35] It is out of loving concern for the person that we need to confront draining behavior. If you do that wisely you may win an important or teachable person.

As a Christian minister, the model of Jesus Christ impresses me and I try to follow His example. He prioritized His life around people. He knew His important people and focused on them. He spent much time praying and talking with God and that helped Him define his important roles. At the same time, he focused on those who needed his teaching and healing ministry, as they were critical to the achievement of his goals.

Early in His ministry He identified twelve teachable people and focused on them. And within that group he identified Peter, James, and John in whom he invested extra effort and time. They eventually became among the first to carry his legacy of impacting the world for good. **ERNEST LaFONT**

Draining people come in a variety of forms and shape. The people that I find most draining to me personally are:

- People who need constant, almost daily praise and affirmation.
- People who are not easily teachable—who struggle with the same problem over a long time and do not seem willing to change when given options to do so.
- People who do not grow in spite of your efforts to help them.

Working in a caring relief agency, I must confess that we may go overboard in accommodating draining people on our staff. This is a risk that caring managers and leaders face regardless of their profession. But I believe there comes a time when we have to "bless them and release them." Here you need to encourage such persons to seek other places that may be best suited for them. It is always helpful to have a frank and honest discussion for the benefit of both parties. **DAVE MCCOMISKEY**

Regretfully, as we work with clients in our workshops we see one common observation. Most business leaders spend far too much time with the draining people; they seldom identify their teachable people and take the important people for granted.

A question we are often asked is, "Can important people be **draining people as well?" The answer is yes.** To explain, the following are four illustrative stories that Baha often shares in our workshops.

My precious daughter

Like any father my firstborn, Rebecca, was the apple of my eye. Many parents will relate to the sudden change that happened when my precious girl became a teenager. My very important person became one of my most draining people. She told me that she did not need parents anymore.

Fearful and anxious, I struggled with this sudden change. While she became one of my draining people I could not abandon my role as her parent. What I had to do was limit my exposure to her destructive moods swings, avoid confrontations, and find common ground for reasonable communication.

Today, Rebecca is in her thirties. While still her parent, my goals and relationship have evolved. Rebecca has become one of my delightful, teachable people.

My only client

During a year of economic recession and poor business I had one very large client— my only client. All eyes were focused on how we were doing with this very large and complex piece of business.

As the key relationship manager for our company, my key contact at the client site was a very draining and volatile woman with a very bad temper. She was my very important and very draining person with whom I had to have almost daily stressful encounters. The more desperate I was for the business, the more abusive this client seemed to be. Motivating my account team was becoming impossible.

One day, after a very volatile exchange I had to express my inability to cope with this abusive attitude and offered to resign and even cancel the whole deal. In anger she left the office as I began to think about what might be the end of my career.

The next day she called a meeting with my boss during which she apologized for the way she had been dealing with my team and me. With emotional sincerity she complimented me for my integrity and the value of the trust she had in me. My very important, very draining person became one of my best business friends for many years thereafter.

My negative boss

Through my thirty-eight year career I have had many bosses. Some were excellent; others not so good. Let me tell you about "Joe" (not his real name). Joe used to say that he "liked to play the role of the devil's advocate." Any time I had a good idea he would say, "Let me be the devil's advocate." Then he would proceed to point out all the rational and irrational reasons why things would not work out and why I would surely fail. He was very skilled in uncovering all the negatives and making the brightest day dark. One day when Joe commented, "Let me be the devil's advocate," I had enough of this attitude. In frustration I said, "You know, I never liked the devil and I do not want to work in hell."

Joe was one of my important and draining people. I had no chance of changing his attitude. My only option was to look for another job and I am glad I did.

My very dear wife

Newly married, my wife was my most important person in my life. We were attracted to each other by our opposite qualities. Regretfully, the caring spirit that she loved in me became an overprotective, controlling, and highly draining culture that I could not see. Yes, in my love for her I had stifled the individuality of this very talented woman and I had become one of her most draining people.

Though she tried to confront my draining behavior I was not teachable. Fortunately, we were both open to the external help of a family counselor who helped apply principles that have become a part of our married life for over thirty-five years.

Here you have four examples of challenges faced with important but draining relationships. Four different cures you can use are: avoid, confront, change what you can, and/or seek external help.

> Leaders have a huge, critical role in setting and impacting culture. By their models leaders have a huge impact on organizational effectiveness. The tone comes from the top. Whether it be by the way they carry themselves in the hallway or how and when they send e-mail they send a message of the expected behavior to the rest of the organization. If my leader is always frantic and stressed, I will act the same. If my boss regularly sends me e-mails on the weekend and late at night and expects immediate responses, I assume that I should be regularly working on the weekend and late at night too. **PETER NEUFELD**

Exercise: People Inventory

1. Take time to list five important people in your life. Indicate reasons why they are important to you. Write them a note or send them an e-mail with your thoughts.

2. In a similar manner list five teachable people in your life. Again, indicate why you consider them teachable and the progress you have observed in their lives. Write them a note or send them an e-mail with your thoughts.

3. If you wish, list draining people in your life. Again, indicate the reason why they are draining to you as well what you need to do to control their draining relationship.

Note: If this is the first time you are doing such an exercise, you may find this awkward in the beginning. Please do not let this hold you back. **Remember your goal is progress, not perfection.** Later on this will become second nature to you.

I = Important T = Teachable & D = Draining People ⬇		Indicate role important people play in your life and reason why
Person or Organization	I T D	Reason for Importance

Summary

✓ Your life's value is directly related to the impact you have on the people you encounter on the various stages of life.

✓ Life provides you with three different circles holding three differing groups of people.

- **The circle of accountability** holds your important people who help you define your roles and are critical to the achievement of your goals.

- **The circle of influence** holds your teachable people who learn from you and grow through your influence on their lives.

- **The circle of concerns** holds the draining people who bring extra concerns to your life and are seldom impacted for good by your relationship.

✓ As you focus on the important and teachable people you will have little time for the draining people.

✓ People may be important, draining, and teachable at the same time. Take an inventory of your relationships to enhance your impact and reduce the risks of negative exposure.

16: ISSUES FILTER

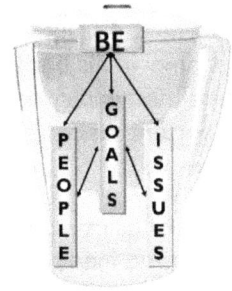

Thoughtless leaders

"Ready for lunch, Janet?" asked Penny. "No I can't go. I have to finish this urgent report for my new boss. He sent me an e-mail late last night and he wants to have it before his one o'clock marketing meeting. This guy is report hungry. Every one of these reports is a major project. I don't think he has any idea of how much work this is. Plus I don't believe anyone reads them. Stuff like this drains me and makes me sick."

"Have you asked him why he needs this report?" "No," Janet replied, "I am afraid to. Plus, I have been here for ten years and I think the information is meaningless because most of the marketing people know all of that anyway and do nothing with it. I shouldn't be hard on him; he is new."

Penny looked at her with pity and said, "Oh, you are too kind. He's been here for a year. You have to talk to him. He can't keep springing stuff like this on you all the time. Plus it is month end and you will be in another panic mode like every month with all of these reports he keeps demanding."

Janet is correct. Her new boss recently joined the company from an organization where data mining and reporting tools are standard. He does not appreciate how much work is involved. If he did, he would be more reasonable in his expectations. Her assumptions that few use the results of her hard work are fair. In the culture of urgency we do not ask the key questions that help us filter the urgent from the important. Janet can help herself and add significant value to her new boss by filtering out the urgent and focusing on the important. In so doing they can both be more effective and control the negative impact of work and information overload.

It is very likely that Janet's boss is a very bright and caring person. His critical problem is that he does not have the time to think and prioritize. He is thoughtless. In this overloaded world Janet has a unique opportunity to help him filter and prioritize by filtering the issues that come her way.

What are the issues that impact your roles? If we carefully focus our roles and relationships then the issue we encounter become opportunities to play our roles supported by the important and teachable people who share the stage of life with us.

Regretfully, most of us fall victim to the tyranny of the urgent. In so doing we sacrifice what is often more important. Defining your high value issues and subjects will help you develop an information infrastructure that supports you as you perform your high value roles and achieve your high value goals.

Issues are an important part of our work and personal life. How we filter them and prioritize them has a direct impact on our effectiveness and the value we deliver. Today it seems that our personal and business cultures are driven by urgency. On a given day most of us are confronted with what appears to be urgent matters that call for immediate attention. They force us to change our priorities, disrupt our plans, and cause more stress than we can afford. Charles Hummel in his booklet, *Tyranny of the Urgent*, writes, "But in the light of eternity their momentary prominence fades. With a sense of loss we recall the important tasks that have been shunted aside. We realize that we've become slaves to the tyranny of the urgent." [36]

Some of us can cope with the tyranny of the urgent better than others. At the same time medical and scientific research confirm that living under a prolonged state of urgency causes more stress than our bodies can tolerate. The results are seen in compromised health and emotional wellbeing. The objective of this chapter is to help you take control and prioritize life issues and to filter on what is important and not what is merely urgent.

Importance and priority category

Authors like Merrill and Donna Douglass [37] as well as Stephen Covey have used diagrams similar to this illustrated issues filter with four different grouping of issues. As illustrated, our daily issues can be placed in four categories and plotted against an axis of urgency and an axis of importance. When we do this, you will note the following **four categories on a four point scale**:

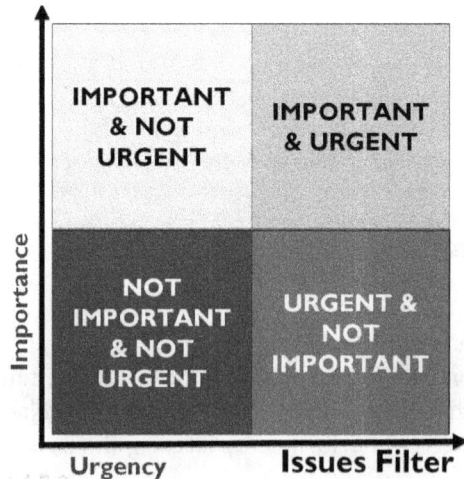

1. **Not important and not urgent:** These are time wasters and should be avoided and totally eliminated from your life. These

are often driven by the unhealthy motivation of giving in to external temptations. An example of this would be giving in to the strong impulse of having a big hamburger after you finished a healthy dinner, watching a senseless TV program, or spending time reading the "For sale car ads" when you have no intention of buying a new car.

2. **Urgent and not important:** These should be avoided whenever you can. Most often such urgency is imposed by an external source and is based on someone else's priorities or anxiety. An example of this would be persistent telemarketing phone calls that disrupt your quiet, family dinnertime. Others would be e-mail sent by draining people labeled URGENT with no apparent reason for that urgency or someone coming to your office when you are focused on a critical project and insistently seeking your help for something he has failed to do on time.

3. **Important and not urgent:** These are the important activities that are often neglected or overlooked. These often require an act of strong will and disciplined self-control based on convictions and commitments. Examples of such activities include thinking and planning, coaching and mentoring your staff, engaging in quality conversation with your spouse or child, paying tribute and saying thanks to a faithful client, acknowledging the goodness of a friend, or taking time to energize your body, mind, and spirit. While these are of highest value they are often the most neglected or compromised.

4. **Important and urgent:** These deserve your attention. They could be the result of events beyond your control, poor planning or the fast changing world in which we live. An example of this would include a child falling off a bike and needing immediate medical care, your bank account running on overdraft, or a disruption of your supplier's operation that requires an immediate change to your just in time manufacturing processes.

While the above examples may be simple and clear, often what we confront is not as simple and as clear. As a result, many of us fall victim to the urgent and overlook what is important. "General Eisenhower is quoted as saying, 'The urgent is seldom important, and the important is seldom urgent.' Too often life is controlled by the 'tyranny of the urgent.' We put aside higher and more worthy issues to put out fires." [38]

IMPORTANT AND URGENT—IDENTIFYING THE DIFFERENCES

While most of us accept the issues filter illustrated here, we are often asked how do you differentiate and know the difference. The following are four principles or tips that you may find helpful:

1. **Important and Draining People:** Earlier we discussed the value of filtering on people. We suggested that in your life you have important people and draining people. In daily activities you will find that the important people are more likely to feed you important issues while draining people are more likely to present you with urgent issues.

    The important people understand your important roles; they are engaged on your stage and are interested in your success. As a result of that commitment they protect your priorities and filter out the distractions that come from unnecessary urgency. On the other hand, the draining people are not as committed to your goals and less likely to appreciate the price you have to pay as you respond to their urgent demand. The draining people are not as involved on your stage of play; they are driven by the demands of different priorities or stages. So as you focus on your important people, you will most likely reduce your exposure to urgent matters that plague our culture today.

2. **Feelings and thoughts:** The second filter is to examine your feelings and thoughts in response to the issues presented to you. Urgent matters activate your feelings. They cause you to feel anxious or stressed or perplexed. They compel you to act based on your emotions. They may cause you to feel guilty, nervous, and/or frustrated. Important matters activate your mind and call you to think in a rational way.

    When confronted with an urgent matter, do not respond emotionally. Do not make commitments before thinking of the alternatives and the consequences. We recommend that you practice project-like thinking. Ask yourself:

    A. What is the worst that could happen if this urgency is neglected?
    B. Is there any real value in what is being presented?
    C. What commitments need to be delivered?
    D. What actions need to take place in response to this demand?
    E. What sacrifices and costs need to be incurred?
    F. What is the impact this urgent matter has on my important people?

    Our suggestion is that when you are presented with an issue that results in negative or stressful feelings, bring it under the control of your mind before making any commitment. If the issue is presented by one of your important people, negotiate for alternatives. By so doing you add great value by enhancing the thinking capacity of your team.

3. **Reactive and proactive:** Urgent issues often call us to react, and place us under the influence of individuals or conditions outside our control. Important matters call us to be proactive and controlled. **Remember, you cannot start anything without stopping something**. There is very little wisdom in giving up something important in favor of something that is merely urgent. Important matters or issues fit within a plan that is forward thinking and balanced.

4. **Permanence:** The issues that have longer impact or duration deserve higher priority. Issues that impact longer term relationships should have higher priority as well. To help illustrate this point picture the following scenario. Supposing you are a married forty year old professional with small children. On your desk place four pieces of paper. On one paper write **your name** (reflecting your physical, emotional and spiritual health). On another write **your job title.** On the next write **your spouse's name.** On the last write **your children's names.**

Now, place these four papers in a priority order. Which one should be top priority, second, third, and fourth? What do you think? Following the permanence principle the correct order should be **yourself, your spouse, your children, and** then **your job.** Please let me explain:

- **Yourself:** this is the most permanent relationship you will have in this world and should have the highest priority. You will live with yourself until you are placed in a box six feet underground. Out of your good physical, emotional, and spiritual resources you can provide maximum impact for good for all the other three priorities. This is the one area you are likely to have most control over and for which you are most accountable.
- **Your spouse:** this is the second most permanent relationship you will have in this world. You are to live with your spouse until death. Out of the strength of this relationship you can parent your children, be most effective in your job and deliver maximum impact for good to your community.
- **Your children:** the primary objective of good parenting is developing your children's independence until they are ready to leave the nest as responsible self motivated adults.
- **Your job** is the least permanent of all. Whether you remain with the same organization or not, your career is a rapidly changing forum to support you in being the provider for the needs of the first three priorities.

Permanence is a vital prioritizing principle. It is very easy to put your job first or yourself last. Compromising the permanence principle often results in compromised health, broken homes, and eventually, regretful lives. On the flip side, how can we trust individuals who cannot manage their personal lives where they have the most control, to manage the business world where they have little control?

The permanence principle can be applied to dealing with other family, social, and business relationships. It can be applied to processes, milestones, and conflicting project priorities.

5. **Is it operation or project?** At the core of urgency are unrealistic expectations. It is fair to assume that most of the people we deal with are rational and sane. Unrealistic expectations start from miscommunication, misunderstanding, or compromised thinking and planning. In the opening story of this chapter, there are several communication gaps between Janet and her new boss. There is one that we consider very critical. Referring to the reports Janet said *"Every one of these reports is a major project."* She also said *"I do not believe anyone reads them."*

Janet's boss is a victim of the overloaded world. The fact that he sends her e-mail late at night is an indication that he is short on thinking time. He assumes that his request is a simple operational report that should be part of the normal operational output. Regretfully, in our changing world such reports are seldom routine or operational. This is the reason why they fall in the project category. Janet is wise. By her thinking capacity Janet can add value to her boss by asking project-oriented questions such as:

*   What are the key questions that need to be answered by this report?
*   Who are the recipients of the report and what are their key hot points?
*   What is the best content and format that will enhance the discussion and decision-making process?
*   What level of detail and supporting material will add credibility to the discussion?

Once Janet is able to dialogue with her boss on the above questions she will be able to set a reasonable project plan and activity list with reasonable timelines for delivering a quality, high value report that multiplies the effort and energy of her boss without taxing her workload.

When confronted with urgent issues, take control by bringing what may be perceived as urgent operational demands into the project thinking mindset. Negotiate for alternative lower cost options. If you focus on the important issues of life, you will most often be able to negotiate out of the lower priority, urgent issues. Our message is before you react evaluate the price you have to pay, should you respond to it.

Maximum impact for good plays to the issues of effectiveness versus efficiency. We often talk about the goodness of a strategy and the issues invoved; this calls us to keep in mind the sustainability for the long term impact on people, environment, and global long term issues. Maximum impact for good often requires a long term and broad view. Regretfully, under economic pressures many organizations tend to be short-term and narrowly focused. **PETER NEUFELD**

Exercise: Issues Inventory

1. Examine the issues that you are often confronted with. Your e-mail file is a good place to start.

2. Using the following template, sort and prioritize your list based on:
   - **Source of issue: Use people category** (I=Important People, T=Teachable People, D= Draining People)
   - **Category: Use the issues category priority scale** (1=Not important and Not Urgent, 2= Urgent and Not important, 3=Important and Not Urgent, 4= Important and Urgent)

Issue	Source of Issue	Category 1,2,3,4

My mission statement gives me a yardstick to help me evaluate what is important and what is not. It is sad to see how much time people invest in what is not important. In our fast moving world it is easy to allow what is urgent or what may seem urgent to crowd out the important parts of our life. In the book, *First Things First*, Stephen Covey presents research showing that executives in high performance organizations spend:

- 25% of their time on what is important and urgent.
- 70% on what is important and not urgent.
- 15% on what is NOT important but urgent.
- Almost no time on what is NOT important and NOT urgent.

Executives in average organizations reverse the time spent in categories 2 and 3, getting caught up in things that are urgent but not important at the expense of things that are important but not urgent. **BRUCE MCALPINE**

It is very easy to let professional roles overtake personal life. Recently, I stepped back and examined my roles as a young mother, wife, and manager. I quickly realized that children, by virtue of their dependence, seem to take priority in my personal life. This, coupled with professional demands, made it easy to overlook the needs of my spouse who seemed independent and self-sufficient. Now I am paying more attention to my role as a wife and the critical importance of developing my relationship with my spouse. **DONNA JOHNSTON**

In the business world, whether you are a senior leader or junior manager, priority based filtering is a key success factor. Having roles that are clearly aligned to corporate objectives is vital to personal and business effectiveness. One of the key roles of a leader is to rely on experience and filter away urgency from his people. This will help them focus on what is important and not be distracted by urgent demands. When talking to overloaded people I often find that as much as half of what they are doing is working on the wrong thing or spending too much time on things that do not deserve so much time and should be put aside. **JIM WRIGHT**

Some time ago I read a quote about this wise person who when asked about his life priorities said, "My priorities are God, family, then my job. They are in that order because when the job disappears I want to have something left to fall back on." The advice I give to an overloaded person is that the job is important but it is not the most important thing in your life. Make your time at work as productive as you can (work all the time you are at work), but remember to leave and go home for what is more important and what gives you joy and satisfaction there. **KAREN MACDONALD**

I am convinced that as individuals and corporations we need to take a broader and longer term view when we examine the need to bring maximum impact for good. We need to always ask how we are making the world a better place. It is critical that we take a strategic view of our programs and not only respond to short term crisis which are many. **DAVE MCCOMISKEY**

Summary

✓ Your life's value is directly related to how you respond to the important and urgent issues you face every day.

✓ As you filter, avoiding the urgent and focusing on the important, note that:

- Important people are likely to feed you important issues while draining people may be the source of most urgent issues.

- Important issues engage your thinking while urgent issues activate your negative emotions.

- Important issues cause you to be more proactive while urgent matters cause you to be more reactive.

- More permanent issues are more important.

- Project oriented thinking engages your rational thinking helping to add significant value to your team.

17: GOALS FILTER

Winning goals

Adam Smith is a corporate controller at a fast moving company. Eight of his direct reports are young, eager university graduates. The last employee engagement survey gave him lower scores than he expected. That was a disappointment for Adam. In addition, the staff reported that there was little emphasis on team and staff development. Lately, Adam had been reading about the value of mentoring and coaching relationships in the workplace. So he decided that his goal for the coming year was to spend more time coaching his junior managers. His boss complimented him on this admirable objective and asked that it become part of his performance evaluation plan.

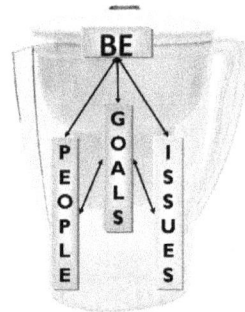

Sometime in early March his boss asked him how he was coming along with his coaching goal. Adam expressed disappointment that he was not sensing any progress on the part of his team members. He said that his team members were not responding to his availability and open door policy as he expected.

In search for further help Adam read some books about great coaches. He pondered their qualities and character attributes. He decided that as a coach he wanted to be known as knowledgeable, available, disciplined, and results oriented. These are qualities he admired and thought he could easily be. Going further, Adam put a simple plan together that would help him translate these attributes into objectives and reflect each of these objectives into goals.

What are the goals that direct your life priorities? Goals energize you and direct your progress. Once you define your high value roles it is critical that you articulate specific goals that help you prioritize your activities and track your progress.

While roles define what you are expected to **be,** your goals define, focus, and direct what you are expected to **do.** Living without goals leads to an aimless life. The old saying is true "If you aim at nothing, you will surely get there."

Accepting a role without defining clear objectives and goals could lead to unrealistic expectations of yourself and others. This often results in disappointments and/or overloaded lives. Unless you actively participate in developing your objectives and goals, others will assume them for you.

The power of objectives:

It is very helpful to translate your roles and what you want to be into clear objectives. Objectives are statements of faith that reflect your vision of what you wish to see happen at a future point in time. While they do not need to be specific they should be reasonable, rational, and sensible. While they may not have the support of all involved they should reflect significant value that justifies the cost of change or investment. Objective statements serve to ignite the passion for change and motivate you and/or others in committing to the needed work to make the change happen. An easy way to write an objective is to think of a short sentence that starts with an active verb and communicate one of the attributes you want to be.

Example: Adam Smith, realizing that he wanted to be **knowledgeable, available, disciplined, and results oriented,** wrote the following objectives:

A. **Knowledgeable:** Develop my personal coaching skills
B. **Available, disciplined:** Dedicate adequate and consistent high value time to coach my team

The power of SMART goals

Objectives are the forerunners of goal-setting. While objectives can be vague and high level, goals must be more specific and clear. Goals are stepping stones to the realization of our objectives. In the excellent book, *Strategy for Living*, Ted Engstrom and Richard Dayton say that, "goals have the power to change you as they motivate and keep us focused."[39] Someone has suggested that we all have goals. Some are clear goals; others are fuzzy goals. Some are good goals and some are foolish goals. Regretfully, many seldom achieve their goals for one simple reason their goals are not **specific, measurable, agreed upon, realistic, and time dependent.**

Specific: Goals need to be specific. In sports a goal is a very clearly marked point. We suggest that a specific goal is one that can be verified by one of the five senses or can be confirmed by scientific measurements. If you were to say that your goal is to be a good coach then this is subjective and open to interpretation. It is highly based on the image you and others have of what a good coach is like. But if you were to say that you want to coach five people in e-mail etiquette, then you have a more specific goal. Specific goals are smart goals because they communicate value that justifies the discipline and effort required to achieve them.

Measurable: Socrates wrote that an *unexamined life is not worth living*. Goals are a measurement tool to help us evaluate and measure our progress toward maximum impact for good. Having a measurable goal allows you to gauge your progress towards reaching it. So if you were to say that your goal is to find five people to coach, then you can measure your progress as you find the first, second, third, fourth, and fifth person. Measuring progress is a very critical self-motivator. Measurable goals are smart goals because they help you make appropriate and timely changes to your action plans when necessary. The more specific the goals the more measurable they are likely to be and the more likely to succeed.

Agreed upon: Before you embark on any goal you must be sure that your goal is agreed upon by those who have an important stake in it. Unless you and the five individuals you have targeted for your coaching role agree on their need for your coaching, you have no chance of achieving your goal. In other words, agreed upon goals are smart goals because they are backed by the support of other people who are committed to the same outcome. In addition, the support you receive will bring along with it an element of healthy accountability that will keep you motivated and encourage you when you are tempted to give up.

Realistic: A common mistake encountered by most of us is that we underestimate the effort and the investment required by most goals. One thing that has helped us very much is to **"aim high and goal low."** It is good to set high and lofty visions or objectives but it is wise to set realistic goals. Setting realistic goals that can be easily achieved will encourage you as you progress to higher value goals and activities. Realistic goals harness the expectations of others and set you up for the possibility of over achieving your goals.

Time dependent: Like any drama on a stage a smart goal has a starting and a finishing point. Goals with endless timelines lead to frustration and apathy. As an example, in our story of Adam Smith, one of his goals could read, "to coach the five members of my team in corporate governance requirements over the coming three months." Time dependent goals are smart goals because they help you avoid the natural temptation to procrastinate. The shorter the time horizon, the smarter the goal and the more likely it is to succeed.

The stage of accountability, influence, and concerns

It is important to note that no goal is one hundred per cent assured. Objectives and their related smart goals are statements of faith—faith that is compelling and reasonable. We live in an imperfect, often uncertain world. Fear of failure may hold some back from setting goals. Do not let the desire for perfection and risk aversion restrain you from determining goals. **The three stages of accountability, influence, and concern** illustrate this point.

Focus on Accountability

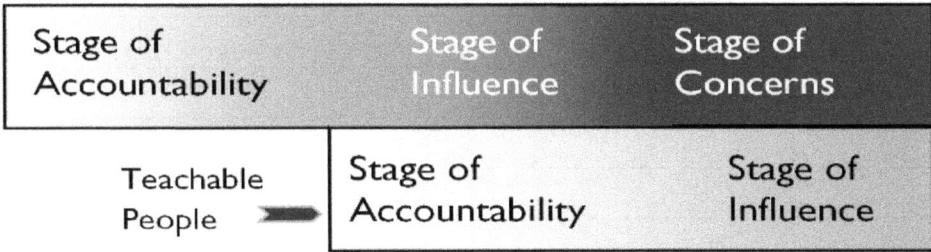

Stage of Accountability	Stage of Influence	Stage of Concerns

Teachable People ➤	Stage of Accountability	Stage of Influence

A. **The stage of accountability** is the area of responsibility where your goals are least impacted by what others can or cannot do. Remember, you cannot be responsible or accountable for what you do not control. So keep your goals focused on your stage of accountability.

B. Define objectives for your stage of influence and delegate the responsibility of related goals to your teachable people. In this you assume the role of monitor and/or overseer.

C. List appropriate assumptions associated with your goal. Where appropriate build contingency plans to mitigate reasonable risks.

D. Avoid the temptation to meddle or get deeply involved in the stage of concerns. The stage of concerns is the area where you are least likely to have any impact. If there is any possibility of positive influence this should be delegated at the discretion of your teachable people.

E. Remember, goals are outward expressions of your roles. If you do not set them clearly, others will assume them for you.

Exercise: Goals Inventory

1. Consider one of your most important roles. It could be one of the roles you listed in the exercise in the previous template. Supposing like Adam it was the role of a coach with the attributes of being knowledgeable and available. Use the template on the following page.

2. List your role and related attributes.

3. Write appropriate objectives that relate to each attribute. These are the accomplishments that will reflect the fact that you are living your character attributes.

4. Write SMART goals so you will know that these objectives are being fulfilled or realized. These are the stepping stones that are associated with each objective.

5. Indicate the target completion/action date for each goal.

Role / Attributes	Objective – What? What do I want to happen? (Accomplishment)	SMART Goal, How? How will I know it happened? (Actions)	By When? Target date

Exercise: Filter at a Glance

Filter at a Glance is a simple dashboard that you can create and keep handy. You may wish to print it and keep on top of your desk or hang it on your wall or create it as a screensaver. It highlights the most important elements of your filtering systems.

Referring back to previous filters and exercises build the following table:

6. List your key **attributes** from your roles filter (no more than five).

7. With each attribute list one to three **people** that are most impacted by your character attribute. Your people filter and inventory should help you in your selection.

8. As you examine the people you listed, what are the most pressing **issues** that you share with them?

9. For each issue write a key **objective** statement reflecting what you wish to see happen.

10. For each objective list one or two most critical **goals** and relate each goal to a specific issue that would be impacted by it and by the objective you wish to accomplish.

Attributes	Important People	Issues	Key Objective	Critical Goals

Please note: If this is the first time you are doing such an exercise, you may find this awkward in the beginning. Do not let this hold you back. **Remember your goal is progress, not perfection.** Later on this will become second nature to you.

Over the years I learned that it is very important to set realistic expectations of others and myself. As a leader there will always be more to do than you are able to do. It is very easy to fall victim to unrealistic self-imposed expectations. There is always more that you wish you could control than you really do control. You must learn to say no, so that you can say, "Yes" to the truly important priorities. Another important lesson I learned is that you cannot be responsible for things over which you have no control. It sounds simple, but so often we get caught up in trying to manage things that are really not ours to manage or we are held accountable for results in areas over which we have no control. Both approaches lead to stress! As a result you cannot assume responsibility for what you do not control. Accepting such reality has had a great impact on my work-life balance. **KAREN MACDONALD,**

A life well lived requires planning. I have found it helpful to set objectives in all areas of my life, including spiritual, relational, physical, career, educational, and financial. These I track and monitor regularly. I confess that sometimes it may go too far. **BRUCE MCALPINE**

Summary

- ✓ Your high value roles must have meaningful outcomes associated with them.
- ✓ If you do not lead in defining your goals, others will assume them for you.
- ✓ **SMART** goals are **S**pecific, **M**easurable, **A**greed upon, **R**ealistic and **T**ime dependent.
- ✓ **SMART** goals are the best way to define what you are expected to **do** on the various stages of life.
- ✓ Define your goals by writing what you want to see happen as an accomplishment. Then list the actions you need to take towards achieving your accomplishment along with the target completion date.

18: YOUR MISSION STATEMENT

A model with a mission

Today we have a lot of information. We are a very learned society. Yet we fall far short in applying what we know. The world needs models, coaches, and mentors.

Dr. Arnold Cook is a model to many of the people he impacted throughout the world. It has been said that success is measured not by what we do or make but by what we leave behind. Even in his late seventies he is one of the most focused and successful men I have ever met. Since the age of twenty-two Arnold has traveled and served all over the world, not for material wealth, but to touch people's lives for good. Dr. Cook has a simple mission statement: maximum impact for God and maximum impact for good.

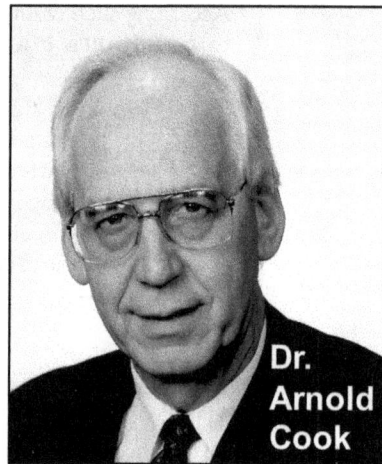

Lest he forget, his mission statement is written on his car license plate. His e-mail address is AcookMIFG@...com. This is a reminder also that holds him accountable in his communication with others. Even at this age, Arnold lives every day focused on his mission.

Young or old we can learn from such a highly-focused man. I am challenged by the lives of people like Dr. Cook. Those of us who reached the ripe age of maturity have a unique role to play. More than ever we can focus on being models, mentors, and coaches.

Do you need a mission statement?

In chapter 10 we discussed finding your sweet spot. Living your sweet spot requires focus. Organizations large and small develop mission statements to help them focus and communicate who they are and what they do best. A mission statement gives you focus in the face of conflicting opportunities and demands. Here are some tips to guide you in developing your mission statement.

CHALLENGES, CHANGES & CURES

Corporations interact and communicate with a vast number of individuals and other corporate entities. Corporate leaders are confronted with a multitude of demands and often conflicting opportunities. To help them prioritize their investments, develop their resources, and focus their activities they rely on mission statements supported by clear objectives and operating practices. These helpful tools serve to energize and focus corporate efforts on what they can best be. Further, mission statements help corporate managers prioritize conflicting demands in the face of limited resources.

Investing time to develop your mission statement, or what is sometimes referred to as a purpose statement, will help you articulate clear, concise answers to the following questions:

1. What are the core values or character attributes that describe you?
2. What individuals or groups of people do you want to impact the most?
3. What are key accomplishments you want to be remembered for?

If you have invested time in defining the filtering system described in the previous chapters you are well on your way to developing your mission statement. Let us take a moment and see how the Roles, People, Issues, and Goals filter can help you develop your Mission Statement.

- **What are the core values or character attributes that describe you?** Stated differently, what inspires your imagination, dreams, and desire to excel? What delivers the greatest moments of fulfillment, satisfaction, and joy in your life? As you think of these moments try to understand why they seem to be so precious and valuable to you. Picture the stage on which you performed these roles. Try to identify the roles you played during these encounters or situations and describe them clearly. As you do this you most likely keep coming back to your character fit to the best you can be. Be sure to write your impressions.

- **What individuals or groups of people do you want to impact the most in life?** The important people are the people who help you define your roles and are critical to the achievement of your goals. Who are these individuals that impact your character and cause you to be your best for them? Who are the people that energize you, either by their character attributes or the compelling needs and opportunities they present to you? Now that you have identified these individuals or groups ask yourself a very important question, **"If asked about me, what do I wish these people would say about me?"**. If given the opportunity to pay tribute to me, what commentary do I wish they would give? Write down your thoughts.

- **What key accomplishments do you want to be remembered for?** If you have completed the issues and SMART goals inventory, you have done most of the work. You now see how you can highlight the tangible and non-tangible deliverables that you deem important. Now you have a very clear picture of the endeavors that are deserving of your life investments. Don't forget to write your thoughts clearly.

A mission statement is **primarily a statement to you**. It does not need to be perfect but it must be clear, motivating, and an honest reflection of what you are or want to be. The answers you wrote to the three points above will give you all the information you need to write your own mission statement.

Most of us do not fully embrace the mission statements of corporate employers, social, and religious organizations. This is especially true in large multi-national bodies where the mission statement serves senior leaders well but loses its impact as it filters down to regional or departmental organizations and individuals. In such cases it is helpful for the regional or departmental leaders to take time in modifying the corporate mission statement so that it relates most fully to the roles, goals, and functions of the departments and individuals they lead.

Exercise: Write a mission statement

1. Block two to three hours of uninterrupted time when you can think clearly.
2. Find a quiet place that you consider a favorite thinking spot.
3. Bring laptop, blank paper, a pencil, or eraser to write your thoughts and change them, with ease.
4. On separate sheets write each of the following headings:
    A. My core character attributes and values that motivate me are:
    B. The individuals or groups that I want to impact the most by my accomplishments are:
    C. The key issues and accomplishments that I want to be known or remembered for are:
    D. The tribute I wish these people would say about me would be:
5. Once you have completed the above statements try to summarize your thoughts into short sentences that tie them together and have the most meaning for you.

Note: If this is the first time you are doing such an exercise, you may find this awkward in the beginning. Do not let this hold you back. **Remember your goal is progress, not perfection**. Later on this will become second nature to you.

Having a mission statement keeps my focus in the midst of growing demands and perplexing priorities. My mission statement has evolved over the years. It started with a passion to help people in the underprivileged world which energized me through a 40 year missionary career.

My mission statement is simple. It is Maximum Impact for God. As a Christian my highest point of accountability is God Himself and the expansion of His love and care for the world is my top priority. I find it critical to keep that as my constant focus. I tend to be a bit fanatical about my mission statement, so much that my children gave it to me as a gift license plate for my car. Now I use it as part of my e-mail address. Maximum Impact For God has been the theme and the evaluation criteria that helped me in making most of my career and personal life decisions. **ARNOLD COOK**

We all can fall victims to roles overload. I prioritize my roles by focusing on my mission statement. My mission statement provides me with an umbrella that guides me and helps me focus on my reasons for existence. Based on who I am and what I want to be as well as based on understanding my strengths, beliefs, and passions, I developed my mission statement that says:

"I will use all the talents I have been given in the service of others to increase their self-worth, reduce their suffering, and uncover their virtues. I will make a positive difference in each life I encounter." **KAREN MACDONALD**

Having a mission statement is important to me because it allows me to maintain both balance and focus. As Stephen Covey says, "It is easier to say NO when there is a deeper YES burning within."

My mission statement serves to motivate me and keep me focused on the priorities I have for my life. Founded in my faith my mission statement is "I will live a Christ-centered, balanced life with joy and integrity, enjoying a high quality relationship with my God, my wife, family, friends, and business associates and empowering those within my sphere of influence to do so as well." **BRUCE MCALPINE**

Summary

✓ Corporate leaders rely on mission statements to communicate and prioritize.

✓ Personal mission statements motivate individuals to prioritize and excel in what they value and in what they want to be known for and remembered.

✓ Leveraging your priority based filtering system can develop a mission statement that is tailored to your specific needs and potential.

✓ When writing a mission statement be sure that it communicates clearly and honestly to you personally. It is personal.

✓ If you are part of a large organization modify the corporate mission statement by relating it to your own values and distinctions.

19: SELF DIRECTED COACHING

Coaches are not people who can do things better than you can but they are people who can encourage you, support you, and hold you accountable. Some of us are self motivated and may not need much coaching. On the other hand, like high performance athletes who rely on coaches to win championships, you too may need a bit of coaching when it comes to the tough issues of life priorities.

The material we shared in this filtering system and the controls we will suggest in the coming section are highly countercultural. For this reason we encourage you to hold your self accountable in a self-directed coaching process. The coach you will need to find is someone whom you trust to hold you accountable.

To avoid conflict and/or disappointment, it is critical to define the role of your coach. In addition to holding you accountable to the disciplines you promised yourself, depending on his or her skills and competencies, your coach may play one or more of the following roles:

- **Sounding board:** To provide honest reactions to ideas, opinions, or points of view to reflect the measure of their effectiveness or acceptability
- **Advisor:** To provide educated opinions or specific answers to questions
- **Counselor:** To recommend appropriate actions on specific subject
- **Empathizer:** To support by providing identification with and or understanding of specific situations, feelings, and/or motives

While a good coach has your best interest at heart, a good coach must not be seen as a parent, friend, or point of authority. A good coach must be disciplined in availability and how the time invested serves towards achieving change and progress. If no progress is being achieved then the coaching objectives are not being realized and the coaching relationship should be terminated.

Progress Dashboard

The objective of the following self-directed dashboard is to help you:

- Maintain focus amidst increasing demands and conflicting priorities.
- Gauge individual progress towards fulfilling personal objectives that are supported, where possible, by clear measurable progress indicators.
- Document encouraging achievements that are often ignored or forgotten.
- Highlight issues, concerns, and critical communication with important people or groups.
- Provide a clear communication tool and support healthy accountability.
- Reduce the administrative burden and possible conflicts that are often associated with performance review.

Exercise: Self Directed Coaching, Progress Dashboard

The end of this chapter provides a Progress Dashboard template and description. Depending on your need you can update this weekly, biweekly or monthly.

1. How are you?

How you are being is more important than how you are doing. Personal and family health affects our being and impacts our performance in all our roles. This **health check** is very subjective and totally depends on how you are feeling at a particular moment. Rate the spiritual, physical, emotional, and financial health of yourself and your family. In a similar manner, if you oversee others take the pulse and record the health of your team. While this is an indicator of your perceptions it serves as a good touch point, and where appropriate a discussion opener between caring individuals.

The focused attributes refers to the character attributes that you or your team committed to focus on as you live your roles among those in your circle of accountability.

2. How are you doing?

A. **Key Objectives and Milestones** are what you wish to accomplish or a summary of the objectives you listed in your objectives exercise. For progress tracking indicate this period and the previous period percentage of completion.

B. **Key Indicators** are measurable yardsticks, outcomes, or the evidence of accomplishment for your stated objectives. These must be specific. As yardsticks they indicate progress as well as a possible shortfall towards the end line.

C. **Notable Achievements and Communications** are important to record especially if they are not measurable. They may be the result of effective communication or rewarding relationship building.

D. **Issues and Concerns** highlight risks that may call for special or extraordinary actions. In this space record issues and concerns that are within your circle of accountability and where you are empowered to take corrective action. Persistent concerns that are brought forward from a previous period should also be recorded so they are highlighted and not overlooked.

E. **Recommendations or Requested Action** document issues and/or concerns that may impact your progress **but may be out of your circle of accountability.** Here you call on the support, or intervention of others who share the leadership stage with you.

F. **Received by/Date** is a record, if needed, of when this review was received or discussed by your coach or organizational leader.

Note: Make copies of the following page for your personal use. This is to be prepared by you, not by your coach. Above all else, it is for your own benefit. File it for future reference and year end consolidation.

If you are using this as a tool to help you coach your team, make sure that **they prepare it carefully** for their individual benefits. At your individual progress review or coaching session ask open ended, evaluative, encouraging, and supportive questions. For future reference and accountability write your observations and/or advice on the back page for future reference and/or year end performance review.

Note: For an MS Word copy of the following template please go to: http://www.nomoreoverload.com/Data/Templates/ProgressReport.doc

My advice to an overloaded person trying to address the problem is to be determined but also patient with themselves. The required behaviours to address overload are counter-culture to most of the work world today, and one can expect to face some resistance and criticism that may shake one's confidence. Therefore the change will take time. Both determination and patience are required to not give up early due to frustration. **DOUG STIRLING**

Progress Dashboard

Prepared by: _____   Date: _____

1. HOW ARE YOU? HOW ARE YOU BEING?

Indicate your opinion on a scale where 5 = Excellent, 4 = Very Good, 3 = Good, 2 = Fair, 1 = Bad

Health Check	Spiritual	Emotional	Physical	Financial	Focused Attributes
Personal/Family					
Those You Lead					

2. HOW ARE YOU DOING?

a. Key Objectives and Milestones	Planned Completion Date	%Complete This Period	% Complete Last Period
1.			
2.			
3.			
4.			
5.			

b. Key Indicators Where Possible Relate to Objectives, Goals or Budget	Target or Budget	To date Value / %	Balance Remaining
1.			
2.			
3.			
4.			
5.			

CHALLENGES, CHANGES & CURES

c. Notable Achievements and Communication This Period
1.
2.
3.
4.
5.

d. Issues and Concerns This Period or Brought Forward from Previous Reviews
1.
2.
3.
4.
5.

e. Recommendations or Requested Action This Period or Brought Forward from Previous Reviews
1.
2.
3.
4.
5.

Received by	Date

CHALLENGES, CHANGES & CURES

CURES—CONTROLS TO IMPROVE

- Controlling the sources of overload

- Controlling e-mail overload

- Controlling telephone overload

- Controlling meeting overload

- Controlling interruption overload

- Controlling paper overload

20: CONTROLLING SOURCES OF OVERLOAD

It's your life. Take control !

Kam is a senior executive in a multi billion dollar corporation. He heads a large organization and reports to a Senior Vice President. He was in a kind of complaining mood when we met for our one-on-one coaching session. Pointing to the stacks of files on his desk he said, "Look at this mess; every one dumps this stuff in here asking me for what I think. Who has the time to read all of this?" When do you do your reading? I asked "When I am bored in meetings I attend." "Between this and conference calls and e-mail I hardly have time to breath." During my two hour visit with Kam I counted at least:

- 8 telephone rings, fortunately he was brave and did not answer except one from his boss, when his assistant came to tell him, "You have to take this one."
- At least 10 tones from his Outlook e-mail notifier
- 3 people who politely knocked and said "Sorry, Kam, can I have a minute with you later?" This is in addition to the many that came, looked through the glass partition, hesitated and then politely left.

Trying to help Kam see that he has to take more control of his life was not easy. With every suggestion I gave he seemed to have a reason why it would not work or why others would not allow him to change. In a way I felt sorry for him and wanted to find a solution to his problem. From my vantage point I knew he could not go on like this, and he knew it.

So I had to come with a new way of getting to him. That was the moment when I had a thought; I wondered how Kam handled his personal finances. "Kam, can you give me 20 bucks?" I said. He looked suspicious and as he opened his wallet pulling out a crisp twenty he said, "Why?" "Don't worry," I said, "It's OK."

Putting the green bill in my pocket I said, "I see you have another twenty there. Give it to me please." "No way," he objected "you have to tell me why." I said, "Trust me, Kam, and give me that twenty." "No way," he said, "you have to tell me why." Sympathetically I looked at him *and replied, "Kam you fight me and grill me over a twenty dollar bill while you allow everyone total access to your most valuable resource - your time. Is that fair?"*

"Kam, my friend," I said, "I am glad you grilled me abut the twenty bucks. At least I know you handle your personal finances better than you control access to your time and life. If you did not, I suspect you could end in bankruptcy."

Before we lean too hard on Kam, we each need to look at the mirror and ask who holds the key to our most important vault. What controls access to our life priorities? If we cannot manage our most valuable assets—our life—how can we be trusted to manage and control the assets of others?

In a knowledge-based economy, leaders and knowledge workers face a highly interdependent relationship between work overload and information overload. Information overload and its sources often rob you of the priorities established by your filtering systems.

Here, our objective is to help you identify the sources of information overload and control them. We believe that as you control the sources of information overload you can be more effective by controlling work overload as a natural by-product. Here we will deal with the controls you build in your work habits.

As knowledge workers, information enters your world in various ways. The most common are: **e-mail**, **meetings, telephone, and other mobile technologies, paper, and interruptions**. In the coming chapters we will provide some thoughts and tips on how to deal practically and easily with each of these.

Just as with previous sections of this book, we are presenting a set of building blocks. Select what is most appropriate for you and what you can adapt to suit your own needs and style. There will always be exceptions to every rule. Do not let concerns for the exceptions direct and limit your thinking or your personal search for solutions.

Thinking strategically about the overload problem, we need to look beyond the symptoms to the root causes, which I think are social in nature. I think they have a lot to do with personal identity in a group and with self-esteem. Dealing with these underlying causes makes a lot more sense to me than struggling with consequences. **RICK FENTON**

The power of your mind

Martin Luther once said, *"I cannot keep a bird from flying over my head. But I can certainly keep it from nesting in my hair or from biting my nose off."*[40] In a similar manner you may not be able to control the environment that creates overload but you must be able to control how it takes residence and crowds your mind robbing you of valuable mental energy and resources.

Our minds have an amazing capacity to capture images, events, and information. Our minds can be likened to a digital camera that is always on. Everything that comes into our world through our senses is captured and stored indefinitely. The more we focus on an issue, data, or image, the deeper it is ingrained in our minds. Each of these exposures consumes mental energy and occupies storage space in our brain.

As another illustration, our minds are also like a disk drive on a computer. Scientists believe that even before our birth the mind captures sounds and memories of the world around us. This continues without ever deleting anything. Over time our data storage becomes crowded and overloaded. Regretfully, science has not found any delete buttons allowing us to purge our brains of unnecessary clutter.

One of the symptoms of information overload is difficulty in recalling people's names and details. While aging may be a factor, a key reason is our overcrowded minds. Just like accessing data on a heavily loaded disk drive or finding a document in a disorganized filing cabinet, recalling details from the vast quantity of data stored in our minds takes time and mental energy. This explains the reason why small children can recall details faster than older people. This happens primarily because their storage banks are still uncluttered by the huge amount of exposures accumulated with every passing year.

> The greatest cause of stress in the workplace is not so much the amount of work or demands placed upon you but the sense that you are losing control of your priorities.

Mobile technology and access controls

Now you can run but you cannot hide. Present mobile technologies have created unique cultural and environmental conditions and expectations that cannot be ignored and must be controlled. The always on mind set can be emotionally draining. The expected urgency often leads to compromised quality. The on demand mindset is often a cause for misplaced priorities. We cannot over stress that while technology provides access to the leader and knowledge worker, control is and must remain a personal responsibility.

CHALLENGES, CHANGES & CURES

Technology has had a very positive impact on our lives. Over the coming years I expect we'll see significant advancement in information and communication technologies that will have a considerable impact on connectivity and mobility. From a technological prospective this appears to be very helpful. On the flip side, such advancements will allow us to be accessible 24/7. This will call for better personal mechanisms allowing us to differentiate between work life and personal life.

Those of us who do not learn now to set personal control mechanisms will be on a slippery slope that will certainly impact negatively on our quality of life. **ANDREA SEYMOUR**

Tips for controlling information overload

Just as you can prevent flying birds from making a nest in your hair you can prevent information exposure from settling in your mind **by tackling it at the source**. Our strategy for controlling the information overload is to control the sources of unnecessary information before they cement their exposure, taking more space and mental energy.

In the coming sections we will give tips for each of the five information sources we referred to earlier. But before we do this, let us share five common tips that apply to all of them. Later, we will highlight these common tips giving you examples of how they apply in your day-to-day life.

- **Define your communication protocol** and communicate it to your important people. A protocol is an expected code of conduct or behavior that governs our interactions. For example, when you meet someone in the morning you expect him or her to give a greeting such as "Good morning." If you meet in the evening the expected greeting is different. In years past, when you called someone's office you expected a person to answer the phone. That was in the past. Now, the protocol has changed. Today, you expect to leave a message on a telephone answering machine hoping that your call will be returned. If there is no answering machine you feel disappointed or frustrated because your communication protocol has been violated. You may be taken off guard if the person you are calling answers the phone. By doing so he has actually violated your expectations.

From the preceding examples, you will note that in the absence of agreed-upon standards or social norms, protocol is largely defined by the expectations of the originator. Such expectations may not be compatible with your circumstances and life priorities. Therefore, it is important to define a **personal communication protocol** compatible with your high value roles. This protocol should be based on reasonable priorities and expectations. To avoid any misunderstanding this protocol should be clearly communicated to your important people.

- **Seek the support of your important people for your new communication protocol**. If you have ever tried dieting or losing weight you know that this requires commitment and discipline. You also know that success in such disciplines is made easier when you have the support of the important people in your life. Overcoming overload in an overloaded world is countercultural and is not easy. Overcoming information and work addiction will require changed attitudes, priorities, and work habits that are easier if you have the support of your important people.

Your new communication protocols will most likely result in changed behavior. Change is often difficult especially if it requires modified behavior on the part of others. With this in view, it is critical that you negotiate for the support of your important people believing that such changes will bring long term higher value for all concerned.

- **Batch process because this is more efficient.** Years ago computer memory and processing power were very expensive. Programmers were very careful not to waste system resources. As a result, systems were programmed and used in a batch-processing mode. As technology became more abundant and cheap we moved to a high demand, multitasking processing environment. This is often wasteful and less efficient in terms of system resource utilization.

Regretfully, our human mind has a finite capacity. Being stretched and overtaxed we need to move back to a more efficient processing model—batch processing. Try it. You will like it.

The concept of "batch processing" is to group similar functions into one common, easy-to-administer process. This common process helps you concentrate on one type of activity at a time. This, by nature, allows the mind to focus and be more efficient. As you practice batch processing, you become better at estimating the amount of time required to complete such groups of activities. You become better at completing tasks on schedule. This will enhance your confidence and your effectiveness. In the following chapters we will give you examples of how to batch process e-mail, phone calls, paper, and even meetings and interruptions.

- **Make it a habit; it becomes easier.** Those of us who commit to an exercise program know that once it becomes a habit it becomes much easier to keep and maintain. Habits, good or bad, are hard to break. You

CHALLENGES, CHANGES & CURES

will also find that others are less likely to challenge you or tempt you to return to your overloaded behavior. People admire and respect disciplined individuals. Good habits communicate consistency and stability that result in an element of security and self-confidence. Good habits will help you feel more in control and reduce the feeling of anxiety that result from our overloaded world.

In the coming sections we will encourage you to develop habitual routines to batch process your e-mail, voice mail, paper, and even meetings. Developing a pattern of behavior is healthy and less stressful for you. As a side benefit, you will become more predictable to your team and to those who interact with you regularly.

The one thing that has contributed greatly to my effectiveness is becoming committed to what I call quiet reflection periods during the day. Such a time period allows me to process, sort, discard, and organize. Having practiced this for some time now, I realize that giving myself this precious quality time reduces my stress and gives me more control of my priorities. Now when I come into the office in the morning I am not rushed, I have time to greet my staff nicely. This is good for the overall atmosphere in the office as well.

The one advice I give to an overloaded person is give yourself "periods of think time" during the day. Providing such periods of reflection, thinking, and processing is critical to help you process, prioritize, and improve your effectiveness in a busy workday.
GERRY BARANECKI

- **Ensure processing capacity.** We explained earlier that as knowledge workers our value contribution is directly related to our ability to take information in and digest it through the thinking capacity thus converting it into meaningful knowledge.

To illustrate this, please consider your small computer and its processing capacity. As you know it can do simple calculations very fast. Your computer is also capable of handling large data tables to be manipulated by complex algorithms. The only difference is that it will require more time to do such complex functions. Given finite memory and processing power the only variable is time. The same applies to our finite minds. The more complex the issues we deal with and the larger the amount of information we must digest, the more processing time we must allow.

Summary

✓ There is strong interplay between work overload and information overload. As you control the sources of information overload you will become more effective by managing work overload.

✓ We suggest five common tips for handling information sources:

- Always seek to define your personal communication protocol and communicate it to your important people.

- Seek the support of your important people for your new protocol.

- Batch process your information input; it is more efficient and uses less mental and emotional resources.

- Whenever possible, make your input processing habitual. This will make the application of new disciplines easier.

- Ensure adequate thinking time.

21: CONTROLLING E-MAIL OVERLOAD

I hate that ding dong!

As I sat across from Eve's desk I frequently heard a familiar ring tone. With every ring Eve would glance at her notebook monitor.

"Eve," I asked, "Why do you keep your e-mail notifier on?"

"Well," she replied, "I hate it. But I look at it in case someone sends me an **urgent message.***"*

"Then, what do you do?" I asked.

"I often leave it till the evening. I do most of my e-mail after I put the kids to bed. **My husband hates this.***"*

During our 55 minute visit Eve received 11 interrupting and distracting ring tones. Based on this, I estimate that she receives about 100 e-mails a day. While e-mail may be a very efficient communication tool, in the urgency- driven culture created by this technology, e-mail is by far the least effective communication medium. The negative impact of e-mail misuse is seen in miscommunication, distractions, reduced productivity, **and even legal liability***.*

> **Email overload,** is not having too much e-mail, rather it is the resentment we feel from the misuse or abuse of this tool and how it robs us of valuable time and resources.

E-mail has become a very important communication tool. E-mail availability, ease of use, and low cost make it the most common communication tool. E-mail misuse has become a most destructive communication tool. Regretfully, e-mail has often become a replacement for voice communication as well as the all-important personal face-to-face interaction.

At the same time there is a significant downside to this impressive development.

Participants in our **Overcoming Overload** workshop often refer to e-mail as the greatest cause of information overload. Some managers spend as much as three hours a day dealing with the flood of e-mail. Studies indicate that e-mail can be a leading cause of reduced productivity, increased stress, poor communication, and increased corporate and/or personal liability.

Today what we call an e-mail system has become a multi purpose, often complex, tool. Most e-mail systems are used in three distinct functions:

1. Communication medium by which we share information and/or request specific action
2. Time and task management tool
3. Information storage or filing system

In this section we will deal mostly with the first element. In other parts of this book we will deal with the management of our life and how to prioritize our activities as well as filing electronic information.

Today, there are many new forms of business communication that did not exist in the past, for example, e-mail. This communication tool, while helpful because you can quickly and easily send messages to a number of people at once, has also established an expectation that we provide an equally rapid response. The sheer volume of e-mails to process can make you feel as if you are an air traffic controller! To me, it is important to have in my inbox only the items that I need to action. The rest, after scanning, are immediately moved to an appropriate file in my reference filing folders. Less clutter = less distraction. **CATHY WARD**

The personal and corporate risks associated with e-mail misuse were highlighted in a survey of large corporations which found the following:

- 28% of employers have fired workers for e-mail misuse for the following reasons:
  - Violation of any company policy (64%)
  - Inappropriate or offensive language (62%)
  - Excessive personal use (26%)
  - Breach of confidentiality rules (22%)
  - Other (12%)
- 66% of employers monitor Internet connections
- 24% of employers have had e-mail subpoenaed by courts and regulators
- 15% have battled workplace lawsuits triggered by employee e-mail[41]

In seeking to harness the benefits of this powerful tool, individuals need to develop a personal e-mail policy that is compatible with their high value roles.

At the same time, organizations that fail to establish a clear e-policy leave themselves wide open to misuse and even legal liabilities. The corporate e-policy should be tailored to reflect the corporate culture, business needs, as well as its unique legal requirements.

E-mail Effectiveness Framework™

The illustrated E-mail Effectiveness Framework™ is a topical collection of thoughts and tips that can help you in developing a personal e-mail protocol. In addition, it holds most of the elements needed for developing a basic, yet effective corporate e-mail policy. This framework illustrates three gears that work together to bring maximum benefits to individuals and corporations. Bringing these gears together along with a commonsense etiquette can enhance your effectiveness as you seek to implement appropriate policies and protocols:

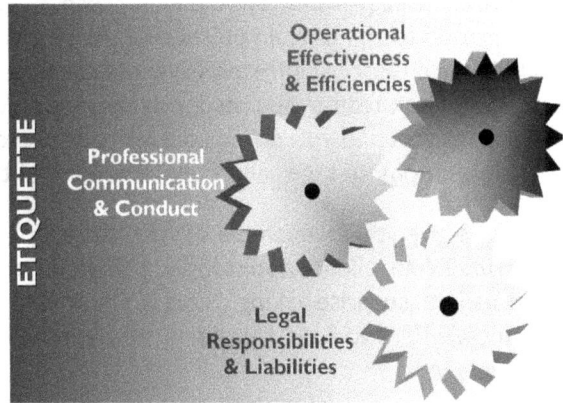

E-Mail Effectiveness Framework™

- **Operational effectiveness and efficiencies**: Too much of a good thing can be counter productive. Your e-mail policy should serve to limit undisciplined use that results in wasted time, energy, and corporate resources.

- **Professional communication and conduct:** Easy access to computers has resulted in careless communication habits. Fueled by a culture of urgency and unrealistic expectations, e-mail has become the cause of reduced communication quality that reflects poorly on the image of individuals and the corporation they represent. Studies indicate that in effective communication our words offer only 10%, our tone adds another 30% while body language plays the lion's share at 60%. When rushed, regretfully, words run out of our fingertips often void of tone. E-mail recipients driven by their own rushed, emotionally charged lives are more likely to superimpose their own tone and personal understanding on your intended message. Your e-mail policy should support reflective, effective communication.

- **Legal responsibility and liability:** E-mail is a communication gateway between individuals and corporations. With this in view, it brings issues, rights and responsibilities. Legal minds have not fully articulated what these rights and obligations are. Today, there are many court cases indicating that e-mail presents employees and employers with significant issues and risks.

Even if your corporation does not have an e-mail policy, it is important that you develop a personal and corporate e-mail policy that protects you as an individual as well as the interests of the corporation you represent.

Tips for controlling e-mail

Whether your organization has an e-mail policy or not, you **are responsible for what you can control.** Here are some tips[42], [43], [44] that you can consider and tailor to your own needs:

- **Develop your own e-mail protocol and communicate it to your important people.** Your e-mail protocol defines how and when you respond to the e-mail you receive. As you consider your important roles, what are reasonable responsiveness expectations? If you are a firefighter on a help desk team, your responsiveness is different than if you are a coach of a sales group. If you do not define your protocol, you will be subject to the assumptions and unrealistic expectations of the sender.

  Let us give you an example of why this is important. One morning we had a 10:30 A.M. client appointment. When we arrived the secretary looked at us with surprise asking, "Didn't you know that the meeting was cancelled?" "No," we replied. "I sent you an e-mail this morning," she said.

  The problem was that our e-mail protocol was different from her expectations. As consultants and speakers, we are out of the office frequently. So our e-mail protocol is to process e-mail only once, at the end of the day. We failed to communicate this to our friendly secretary who is used to her protocol where her system notifies her the moment any e-mail arrives in her inbox. Her expectations were that I was subject to a world similar to hers—a world where e-mail is an instant communication tool. Regretfully, due to the miscommunication of our protocol that morning we wasted a lot of time.

- **Seek the support of your new e-mail protocol.** Remember your important people are committed to your success. If you explain that your protocol provides for reasonable responsiveness expectations, they are likely to support you. This will make it easier for you to follow through with your implementation.

- **Define and communicate your e-mail protocol.** The following is an example of an e-mail you can use for this purpose:

TO: (LIST) Important and teachable people

SUBJECT: Action Requested – My e-mail handling protocol

It is my desire to improve my effectiveness in handling the flood of e-mail I receive. Towards this goal I have set up my e-mail system to give priority to e-mail directed to me from important people like you. Therefore, e-mail you direct to me personally will be given higher priority and I will do my best to respond to it in **XX working hours**.

All other e-mail and e-mail where you have copied me will be considered for information purposes or given lower priority. I will seek to review such e-mail in **X working days**.

To reduce my e-mail and electronic filing requirements I will assume that the originator always keeps a copy. **Therefore, I may not have to keep one.**

Thank you for your support.

- **Don't let your inbox define your day**: A common work habit or trap is checking e-mail first thing in the morning. The reason is "in case there is something urgent." In doing so, we mentally open our mind to a culture where the urgent takes priority over what is important. If you have your day well planned and controlled, this habit feeds a culture where the urgent overrides the important. If you clearly communicated your e-mail protocol, then issues that are important and urgent will be communicated to you via the phone or other way. What we recommend is that you set your e-mail system so that when you first open it, it displays your calendar and "to do" list. This gives you the ability to remind yourself of your day's plans and activities.

- **Batch process your e-mail at a regular time in the day**. Set regular times to review your e-mail. For example, it may be after lunch and again, at the end of day.[45] By so doing, your communication partners become accustomed to your processing cycle and are less likely to impose other expectations on you. So, block this processing time in your calendar as an important meeting with yourself. You may call such appointment a **"processing meeting."** Be sure to provide adequate time. Start by estimating approximately three minutes for each e-mail message you need to process. So, if you need to process twenty e-mails a day, plan at least half an hour in the midday and another half hour at end of day.

- **Read, Think, Respond, File**: As you develop the habit of batch processing, your mind will get used to a simple routine.

It is like giving your mind a simple process but to do this you need to give it the processing time which we recommend to be about three minutes on average. E-mail items that require longer processing time need to be set aside and rescheduled at a later time as we will explain later in this chapter. You can see how by doing this, at the end of any day, your inbox will always be empty.

- **Apply the "OHIO"—Only Handle It Once**—principle. This is an old, wise piece of advice that is easier said than done. However, if you allow enough e-mail processing time it will be easy to do as you apply the **4 Ds** described in the following steps:

  - **Delete it now.** Most e-mail you receive you never asked for, and you do not need. Your first questions should be, "Why should I even open it?" "Why not **delete it now?**"

  - **Deal with it now.** If you have blocked adequate time for your e-mail processing you have the time to deal with now. If the e-mail at hand can be processed in **three to five** minutes **deal with it now**.

  - **Delegate it now.** If processing such an e-mail will help one of your staff or teachable people grow, **delegate it now**. For example, if you receive an e-mail with a forty-page attachment or study that may be important, ask one of your teachable people to examine it and provide you with a synopsis and recommendations.

  - **Diarize it now.** If the e-mail requires more than five minutes to process, make a processing appointment with yourself to deal with it later. Be sure to **diarize it now**. The way you do this is simple. Highlight the e-mail in question and drag it to the calendar icon. This will activate your calendar which will give you the option to set up an appointment with yourself to deal with the issue at hand. Another option, is to drag the e-mail to your task list and assigning the start and end date for this task. In either case, your e-mail will be noted in your appointment or your task list waiting for you to take care of it according to your predefined protocol.

- **Turn off your e-mail notifier!** The thing that bongs and calls your attention every time you get an e-mail. This is a wasteful distraction. If you have committed to batch processing your e-mail at regular intervals, you do not need it. If you do not need it, turn it off. We understand there will always be exceptions, especially when you are anxiously waiting for important e-mail.

- **Use rules-based filtering aggressively.** Most e-mail systems offer rules-based filtering tools. Rules are a set of conditions, actions and/or exceptions that process and organize e-mail messages. These rules are applied to

CHALLENGES, CHANGES & CURES

incoming e-mail to help reduce e-mail clutter. Further, rules organize incoming e-mail into predefined folders based on predefined processing priorities that are compatible with your most important roles. To learn more about the rules tools in your e-mail system go to "Help" in your e-mail and search on rules or wizards.

It was depressing to open my e-mail and find a flood of several pages that are more than I can ever go through. People are wrongly using e-mail as a replacement for face-to-face communication. They often copied me on e-mail without thinking of why they were sending this to me. I made a commitment to take control of my e-mail problem. I use the rules-based filtering to sort and prioritize my e-mail and focus on my important people. I also apply the OHIO and the 4 Ds principles. Now I go through my important e-mail much faster than ever before, leaving me valuable time to focus on my important roles. More than any other factor, this has helped me become more effective and have more work-life balance. **KATE AGNEW**

For me personally, I am always in search of good tips that would impact my work habits. For example, in my role a lot of the information I get and the decisions I make are via the e-mail system. I learned that it is important to filter and act wisely when it comes to e-mail. I have a simple system that helps me do this. I learned to batch process my e-mail at regular time of the day and I have a sticker attached to my notebook computer that reminds me of my commitment to "Read, Think, Respond, File." This along with keeping a good filing system helps me keep my e-mail and information clutter under control. **GEORGE ABATE**

- **If you get too much e-mail, unsubscribe and get off e-mail lists**. It takes time to delete all those messages, even if you don't open them.

- **Group all your accounts**: If you have more than one mail account have them all forwarded or merged in one presentation tool. For example, if you have your business e-mail account and a personal account have them all appear in one inbox if your e-policy allows this.

- **Don't print that mail**. Unless you have a need to study and make notes, try to avoid the temptation of printing e-mail. Printing e-mail doubles your filing effort and creates more paper clutter.

- **Before reading, prioritize;** first prioritize by reading e-mail that is from important people, then important subjects.

- **If e-mail requires action on somebody else's part before you can deal with it**, move it out of your inbox into a "Waiting" folder or flag it for follow-up. You should make a note in your calendar for appropriate follow-up.

- **E-mail messages with important attachments can be deleted after you save the attachment** in your own electronic file or hard disk. In this case, give the attachment your own file naming structure based on how you think, so you can find it easily.

- **Set up a "Reading" folder.** File e-mail newsletters or discussion groups in a "Reading" folder for an assigned time to read later. Much educational material is now sent via e-mail. The time you dedicate to this can be considered high value professional development time. Remember your professional growth is directly related to your effort and the quality of your professional development resources.

- **Save administrative messages from mailing lists**. When you subscribe to an e-mail newsletter or e-mail discussion group you usually receive a welcome message with information about your subscription, policies about mailing to the group, answers to frequently asked questions, etc. Copy all this in a document or set up a "Mailing Lists" folder to file such messages so you remember what to do if you wish to unsubscribe from a list at a later time.

- **Use Auto Archive and Auto Delete to reduce the size of your e-mail file**. This will reduce your filing and maintenance overhead and will help your system run faster or more efficiently.

- **Learn the tool**. Most e-mail systems have more in them than what you can ever remember. Take time to learn the parts that are most helpful to you. Buy a book that offers tips and tricks that relate to the system you use. Write yourself a simple cheat sheet of parts you use less frequently and keep that handy. But never feel guilty about not knowing everything. In other words, use what you need and avoid information overload.

E-mail etiquette

The following is a suggested list of e-mail etiquette that could enhance your communication quality. Select the ones best suited for your role and the culture of your organization:

When creating e-mail

- **Before all else, think of the recipient(s) first**. The quality of your e-mail is impacted by what the recipient will think when he or she receives your e-mail much more than what you think when you type your e-mail. Remember the tone you communicate is highly impacted by the recipient temperament and the kind of relationship you have with him or her.

- **Never write e-mail when you are angry or to let off steam**. This could be very damaging.

- **Define a clear objective for your e-mail**. If you can, include your objective in the subject line. For example:

  - Action Request, Expenditure Approval or

  - FYI Only, Vacation Plan

- **Limit each e-mail message to one subject**. It is easier to understand and file, if needed.

- **Define a clear goal or goals for your e-mail and introduce this at the beginning of your e-mail**. To make your communication specific start your goal with a **verb**, for example:

  Dear Joe:

  - Examine my department YTD budget and approve the expenditure of $3,500 for new furniture

  - Advise on how many more $$ I should plan for next fiscal year

- **Write to express, not to impress**. Use simple, easy to understand language to communicate effectively. Bulleted points are easier to read than long paragraphs.

- **Avoid using e-mail to discuss confidential information**.

- **If you must send sensitive material add an appropriate disclaimer or a legal liability phrase**. As an example:

  IMPORTANT NOTE: This e-mail may contain confidential information intended solely for the use of the individual or entity to whom it is addressed or to others authorized by them. If you have received this communication in error, **please** notify us immediately by responding to this e-mail and then delete it from your system. This is your rightful and legal responsibility.

- **Think of all the supporting information** that you need to include in your e-mail. Use only that is helpful to the recipient in taking proper action.

- **Start your e-mail with a proper salutation and end it with a proper signature**. It adds structure and clarity.

- Make sure the tone of your communication including the typeface and font support the e-mail objective. As an example:

  - **BOLD FONTS AND CAPITAL LETTERS are more aggressive.**

  - Normal fonts and simple sentence structures are friendlier.

- **People like the sound of their name**; use it in a reasonable manner if you want to be more personal.

- **Use abbreviations and acronyms carefully**. Make sure the recipient understands them.

- **Avoid slang words.** They introduce cultural conflicts and may be offensive.

- **Do not ramble.** Write specific points in short sentences.

- **Use proper sentence structure and layout**. Keep your language gender neutral. Do not use only masculine pronouns when writing to a mixed audience.

- **Before sending your e-mail read it once or twice**. Check it for content, quality, spelling, and proper grammar.

- **Before sending your e-mail consider formatting issues**. The recipient's e-mail may have certain limitations that cannot receive the fancy formatting you employed.

When sending e-mail

- **Send e-mail to as few recipients as possible**. It will enhance your ability to focus the objective of your e-mail and improve your chances of success.

- Set personal e-mail protocol and responsiveness expectations that are compatible with the most important roles you play. Communicate your protocol to your important people and ensure that you can support their reasonable responsiveness expectations.

- **E-mail is not an "immediate" communication tool**; be realistic in your expectations. It is not intended to replace the phone or the all-important face-to-face contact.

- **Avoid frequent use of the Urgent or the High Priority.** It's like "crying wolf" or giving a false alarm too many times.

CHALLENGES, CHANGES & CURES

- **Avoid the "E-mail tag game"** when answering e-mail. Anticipate all questions and answer each of them clearly.

- **Avoid the use of the "REPLY TO ALL" feature**. Unless requested, give the e-mail sender (originator) the privilege of deciding who should receive your reply.

- **If you are sending a mass mailing, personalize your e-mail** using mail merge. This way you avoid distributing other people's e-mail addresses.

- **Do not request "Delivery" or "Read" confirmation** unless necessary for important confirmation purposes.

- **Avoid forwarding e-mail or attachments without permission**. Others may misinterpret e-mail intended for you. Forwarding it carelessly may put you and the originator in potential liability.

- **Do not overload the recipient's e-mail** by sending unnecessary attachments.

- **Forwarding e-mail containing defamatory, offensive, racist or obscene remarks will put you in a compromised position**. Do not do it, even if you think it is funny.

- **Do not engage in the SPAM game**. Do not ever forward or reply to SPAM.

- **Careless people may send you "hoax" type messages**. Do not forward any hoax or virus warning before validating its claim through a reliable source.

Learn how to use your tools

Among the resources we recommend in our workshops are:

- *Total Workday Control Using Microsoft Outlook: The Eight Best Practices of Task and E-Mail Management* by Michael Linenberger [46]

- *Take Back Your Life!: Using Microsoft Outlook* by Sally McGhee [47]

- *Lotus Notes Domino 8* by Tim Speed, Dick McCarrick, Bennie Gibson, and Brad Schauf [48]

- In addition, the help function of your own e-mail offers great how to resources.

Whatever you do, make sure that you do not become an e-mail processor. Take time to learn only the parts that support your filtering system. As you learn the tool make sure that what you are learning will help you:

- Play your high value role.
- Equip you to manage your high value relationships.

- Provide the information you need to deal with your important issues.

As communication director in a geographically diverse organization, e-mail is a very important resource for my roles. E-mail has become the primary method of communication in most organizations like ours. Allowing e-mail to build up in your inbox makes it an unmanageable communication gateway. To harness the power of this tool, I have a simple filing system. Everything I get is filed either by an "action required" file or as a reference item into my reference file. Now I seldom have more than five items in my inbox. E-mail is not a problem for me anymore. **SHELLEY FLETCHER**

Summary

✓ Define an e-mail communication protocol that is compatible with your most important role and communicate it to your most important people.

✓ Seek the support of your important people for your new e-mail protocol.

✓ Batch process your e-mail applying the **OHIO** (**O**nly **H**andle **I**t **O**nce) principle as well as the **4 Ds** (**D**elete it now, **D**eal with it now, **D**elegate it now, **D**iarize it now).

✓ Apply a simple routine (Read, Think, Respond, File)

✓ Apply rules-based filtering aggressively.

✓ Apply good processing habits to reduce effort and clutter.

✓ Apply good e-mail etiquette and teach it to others.

22: CONTROLLING TELEPHONE OVERLOAD

When Alexander Graham Bell invented the telephone in 1876 he launched a communications revolution. In his wildest imagination Mr. Bell could not have imagined the impact his invention would bring. The telephone has become the most common communication tool in the world. Ease of access and good quality have made it a favorite with young and old alike.

Today we are all expected to have at least one phone at home and at work. Even in remote communities the use of mobile phones has become commonplace. In the office world the telephone is a prerequisite for every knowledge worker. Additional features such as call forwarding, conferencing, call waiting, and message waiting add flexibility and complexity of a system that has become mandatory for business communications. Regretfully, few individuals take time to fully learn the effective use of this common tool.

> Telephone communication is far more effective than e-mail or instant messaging. Phone overload is not receiving too many phone calls, rather it is the resentment we develop towards phone calls that are void of clarity and purpose or create unrealistic demands and expectations.

Today business leaders spend 10 to 50 % of their time in communicating on the telephone. These **phone meetings** are as common, if not more common, as face to face meetings. Business managers have an average of three telephone numbers. Along with paging systems each of these is associated with voice mailboxes that need to be checked and maintained on a regular basis. The incessant ring of the telephone demands your attention diverting your concentration from important projects or important conversations with your important people.

Coupled with text messaging and instant messaging, telephone anxieties are common complaints in social circles. Alexander Graham Bell invented a tool to serve modern society. Today the servant tool has become a taskmaster that is driving many to distress and distraction. Let's take back control.

> While talking on the phone I often found myself tempted to do other things at the same time. I thought I was being more productive by say, answering my e-mail or reviewing correspondence. I must admit in doing so I was not giving due attention to the other party on the phone.
>
> It shocked me to realize that, whether by the clicks of the keyboard or the number of times I asked them to repeat what they said, this distraction was noticeable to the other parties and understandably, offensive. It became obvious to me that this common behavior is not appropriate. So I made a simple change that removed this temptation. I placed my computer on the desk in front of me and my phone on the table behind me. This simple change has had a very positive impact on the quality of my phone communications. I highly recommend this. **ANDREA SEYMOUR**

Tips for controlling the telephone

Whether your organization has a phone policy or not, you are responsible for what you can control. Here are some tips[49], [50] that you can consider and tailor to your own needs:

Defining and communicating your phone protocol

- Keep your recorded greeting clear and brief. Clearly include your name, as well as your voice mail handling protocol. Indicating the conditions that govern your reply will help set realistic expectations for the caller and will avoid disappointments on his or her part.

- Unless your organization dictates, we do not recommend that you include the date and your planned activities. Not too many people care what you are doing that day. In addition, daily changing your voice message is one more administrative task that you are likely to forget and if neglected leaves a poor first impression that you cannot afford.

- Encourage callers to leave a message that requires a specific response or action. Explain that if they do, you will give their message priority. If a caller explains specifically what is expected, you will be better prepared to respond and may avoid phone tag or back and forth phone calls.

CHALLENGES, CHANGES & CURES

- If you are going to be away for more than a day, tell callers that you will have limited access to your voice mail and you may not be able to respond in a timely manner.

- Be sure to speak at a speed that enables the caller to record needed details.

- For security reasons, avoid telling callers you are **"out of town."**

- **Define and Communicate your Phone Protocol:** The following is an example of an outgoing voice mail message that you can modify to your role and corporate culture.

> Thank you for calling **(state your full name)** of **(state organization).** Please tell me how I can help you so I can give your call priority.

> I try to return my priority calls within **(X)** working hours. If you need immediate service, please call **(state alternate and phone number).**

> Thank you.

Batch processing your return voice mails

- Whenever appropriate, screen all calls and return phone calls en masse at a regularly planned time each day. Remember your outgoing voice message has set the caller expectations. Try to keep your commitment.

- If possible, use the auto reply feature on your phone system. This feature leads you directly into the caller's mailbox where you can leave a message and avoid lengthy discussions. This could save you one to three minutes per call.

- As you listen to the incoming message, write a brief note in your notepad along with your expected reply.

- Remember **"OHIO"—"Only Handle It Once",** if you can.

- Apply the **4 Ds—D**elete it now, **D**eal with it now, **D**elegate it now, and **D**iarize your planned or expected action. In this case be sure to let the caller know your expected action date.

- When you receive a batch of voice mail messages, prioritize them. Focus on your important people first. Avoid responding based on urgency only.

- Place your call right before lunch or at the end of the day if you must call a known "chatterbox." This will keep the conversation brief.

Reducing time spent on telephone calls

- Have a mini agenda for your call. This could save you at least five minutes per call. This agenda should have:
  - One primary objective and if you must, a secondary objective. Avoid putting too many objectives or conflicting objectives on one phone call for this will dilute your focus. A clear statement of objective should start with an active verb. (For example, confirm the need for a meeting.)
  - State clear outcome expectations or what is to be accomplished. Start these with an active verb as well. (For example: 1) Discuss alternative to meeting, and 2) Agree on follow-up activities)
- Leave a clear time expectation for the callback or response.
- If receiving a call, help the caller identify the agenda quickly by asking "What can I do for you?" or "What is the most important point you want me to learn?"
- Keep the conversation focused. Use your agenda to bring the conversation back to the subject under discussion.
- If you have a need for constant communications on small matters with the same individuals, use a sheet or a log in which you record thoughts that you need to discuss with such people. Jot down your thoughts as they occur to you. This will form an agenda for your next phone call and reduce the number of calls you make. This will not only save you considerable calling time but will reduce the number of times you need to interrupt the other party. If you train the other party to do the same this will reduce the number of times he or she interrupts you.
- Try standing up when you talk on the phone. This keeps you "on your toes" and will reduce your call time.
- Watch your voice quality and tone. If you are stressed, the caller will detect that in your voice. The person will keep you on the phone longer, demand more detail, and may call you back for reassurance. A warm, crisp tone will make the caller trust your competence and shorten the length of your call. Smiling and lifting your voice at the end of a question will help.
- End the phone call by talking in past tense. Begin by summarizing the call and the follow-up action and promises. Then say, "It was nice to talk with you! Thank you, good-bye!"
- Unplanned phone calls can be classified as interruptions. Handle them firmly and politely. Ask to schedule a time convenient to both of you.

CHALLENGES, CHANGES & CURES

- Make the best of your voice mail. Don't let the phone dictate the priorities of your life. Feel free to let your voice mail pick up the call or screen your calls via the digital display.

Leaving a good voice mail message

- Think about your message before you call. In today's business you are more likely to get a voice mail than the person you are calling.

- Your tone of voice is three times more important than the words you say. Remember it is not what you say but how you say it that counts. If your message is void of the tone you desire the receiver is likely to superimpose his or her own feelings on your words.

- Always be prepared by having a clear agenda before you dial a number. This agenda will have:
  - Appropriate professional greetings using the recipient's name.
  - Identification of yourself and your organization, if needed.
  - Day and time of call, if needed.
  - The objective of your call starting with an active verb.
  - Brief explanation or expected action or request.
  - Summary of point discussed or objective.

  - In closing, state your name and end with your phone number. Remember that the **listener needs time to process the information and write it down.** Be sure to provide a half second pause as you are saying your telephone number. "My number is 212 (pause), 123 (pause), 3456."

- Avoid telephone tag. Give the listener options. Tell him or her when you can best be reached to prevent frustration.

- Where possible, provide the person you are calling with the option of not returning your call. For example, indicate that if you do not hear from them by a certain time you will assume a certain reply. (For example, "Jim, if I do not hear from you by 8:00 A.M. I assume our meeting is confirmed as planned for 1:00 P.M.)

- Do not ask for a return phone call unless you have a very compelling reason for your call to be returned. Always assume that the person you are calling is very busy. Ask yourself, **"Why would he or she want to call me back?"** Be sure you have a good answer that is not only based on your needs or wants.

- Don't leave repeat messages. Your second call is no more likely to be returned than your first. Try sending e-mail instead or speak to someone else in the organization.

- Telephones distort high frequency sounds such as "f" and "s". Pronounce word endings and do not swallow syllables.

- Watch your tone. Without other non-verbal cues such as body language, your tone is all you have to communicate with. Put vitality in your voice. A monotone lacks enthusiasm. Stand up and smile as you leave your message. Standing will increase your energy, and people can hear a smile over the phone. Smiling conveys warmth. Avoid sarcasm and irritation if you want your call returned. Keep an even temper and state your request.

- Modulate your volume. A voice that is too loud is irritating. A soft voice will not always be heard and the listener will miss vital information. Stand or sit up straight and speak directly into the receiver. Do not cradle the phone in your neck or use a speakerphone.

- If you are angry or have something bad to say, do not leave it on a voice mail. Face-to-face dialogue is more effective.

Summary

✓ Define a phone communication protocol that is compatible with your most important roles and communicate it using your outgoing voice message.

✓ Seek the support of your important people for your protocol.

✓ Batch process your incoming voice mail applying the OHIO—Only Handle It Once principle as well as the **4 Ds**—**D**elete it now, **D**eal with it now, **D**elegate it now, **D**iarize it now.

✓ Reduce the time spent on the phone by having a good reason for the call and a well-planned agenda.

✓ Leave voice mail messages that define expectations and reduce the possibilities of prolonged phone tag and miscommunication.

✓ If you want your phone calls to be returned you must have a very compelling reason for your call to be returned.

✓ Phone calls lasting more than fifteen minutes should be considered virtual meetings with preplanned objectives and goals.

23: CONTROLLING MEETING OVERLOAD

Who pays for this meeting?

It was 6:47 P.M. when Sue walked out of a marketing meeting feeling angry. As she stuffed her laptop into her case she mumbled, "This was a waste of time. I'll pay for it by working late tonight."

Sue had calculated that on average she spends at least 56% of her time in meetings to which she is invited. She believes that such meetings bring little value while she pays the price in long, uncompensated, overtime work at home. Time taken from her three small children.

Someone has suggested that some meetings are like a funeral, in that it is a group of people wearing uncomfortable clothes who would rather be somewhere else. Yet, there are a couple of differences. All funerals have clearly defined objectives whereas few things are ever buried in poorly run meetings.

> **Meeting overload** is not having too many meetings; rather it is the resentment we feel towards ineffective meetings that rob us of precious time and cause compromised work and personal priorities.

Joking aside, everywhere we go people complain about meetings. They tell us they are overloaded with meetings. In a simple survey among some of our clients **86% agreed that they have too many meetings in their organizations.**

We must admit that there are good social and economic reasons for these meetings. There are also what we call environmental causes that lead to having many meetings, for example, the level of integration and complexity in our workplace has made the decision-making process far too convoluted resulting in more and more meetings. The pace of life in our offices often calls for meetings without carefully examining their need, the cost associated with them or other practical alternatives.

> The thing that bugs me most is having too many people in a meeting. Invariably, if you have too many people in a meeting you can be sure you do not have the right people in the meeting. If you have too many people in the meeting there is a high likelihood you will have a weak agenda and little follow-up. Our organization has a very high commitment to this. We always expect a good agenda with appropriate pre-read. We try to hold people accountable with follow-up. It is not perfect but we are always working on it.
> **GEORGE ABATE**

We are not advocating that you should have fewer meetings. On the contrary, we encourage you to have more meetings. Face-to-face communications are far more effective than e-mail or voice mail. It is a well established fact that our communication is a mix of words, tone, and body language. Studies indicate that in effective communication our words offer only 10% effectiveness, our tone adds another 30% while body language plays the lion's share at 60%. In other words, it is not what you say that matters but how you say it. Since a picture is worth a thousand words your body language speaks louder than words. While e-mail may be the most efficient communication and lowest cost tool the phone can help communicate tone. Face-to-face meetings—and to some extent—video conferencing are the only way to communicate your body language. This is especially important with today's increasingly complex issues.

In spite of all the good reasons for our many meetings we must confront the fact that the price for **"meeting overload"** is way too high. Studies report that today's managers spend an average **forty percent** of their time in meetings. In a study of our clients we found that

---

Your personal costs

If an average person with a burdened hourly rate of $50 spends 50% of his/her time in meetings with 50% effectiveness in these meetings:

- Works 1920 hours per year
- Spends 960 hours a year in meetings
- Loses $24,000 in lost productivity
- Loses $24,000 in lost opportunity costs
- Loses up to $48,000 of wasted life.

How about you? How much of your life are you losing?

---

that amount may be as high as **ninety percent** of a regular work day.[51] Some studies suggest that as much as **thirty to sixty percent** of the time we spend in meetings is unproductive but we have found that this amount may be as high as **72 percent**.[52] The price is often paid in long work hours and compromised personal life.

Exercise: Gauge your life cost

At the end of this chapter you will find the Meeting Effectiveness Calculator template. Take any seven days that are representative of your average business week. For each day:

1. Add all the hours you spend in meetings including:
    *   Travel, preparation, and follow-up time
    *   "Impromptu" meetings or interruptions
    *   Conference calls and long phone conversations lasting more than fifteen minutes
2. "Guesstimate" how effective or productive you feel these meetings were. On a scale of 100 indicate your feelings. Record your answers.
3. Calculate your effective time (Total Time X Effectiveness %).
4. Add total Time Spent (1) and Total Effective Time (2).
5. Calculate Lost time and % of Average Effectiveness.
6. Calculate Lost Productivity (A), and record Lost Opportunity and Lost Live Value (B).
7. This will give you Total Loss or Lost Life Value.
8. If this is your Lost Life Value in one week what does it mean in a whole year?

Solutions

What is meeting overload? Meeting overload is the resentment of time and life wasted in ineffective meetings. Whether it is in conferences or corporate events, most of us can recall days full of meetings that left a sense of meaning, fulfillment, and longing for more. At the same time you may recall a half hour conversation that left you drained and unproductive. So as we encourage leaders and knowledge workers to increase their meeting participation we want to provide a solution that guards against ineffective and lost productivity.

As we search for meeting effectiveness we must first define what a meeting is. Examining leading dictionaries we can see that a meeting can be defined as a **process** of **people** meeting together for a **purpose**. There are three key words in this definition; they are **PROCESS, PEOPLE, and PURPOSE**.

The objective of the illustrated **Meeting Effectiveness Framework**™ is to help you enhance the effectiveness of your meeting participation and could help you become known as a person who leads good meetings. For ease of information flow we will deal with these in reverse order using an illustration of three gears that leverage each other with a measure of oil to reduce friction.

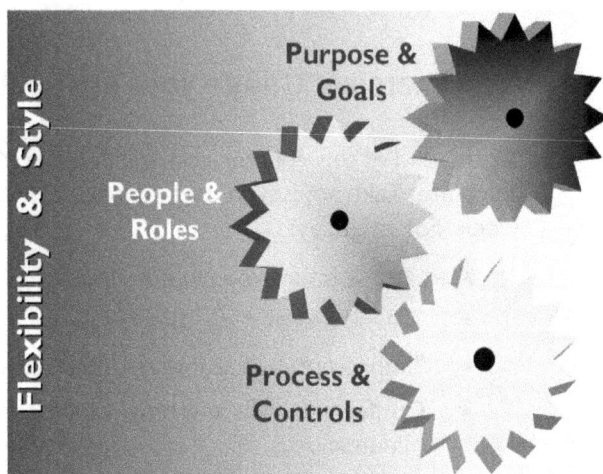

Meeting Effectiveness Framework™

First gear: Purpose and goals

Often, when invited to a meeting we ask a simple question. "**What is the objective of the meeting?**" A response we often get is one or a combination of the meeting title, a list of the attendees or other explanations of the circumstances for which we need to be there. All of this is fine but it never clearly defines the purpose or the objective for having the meeting.

Tips for controlling meetings

Define a clear meeting objective. While the meeting title may be needed as a labeling or scheduling tool, a meeting purpose communicates the high value that justifies having the meeting. This is the springboard that justifies the investment and commitment needed for a well run meeting. Every meeting and meeting invitation should have a meeting purpose in an objective statement. An objective statement is a high level expression of what the leader expects to see happen as a result of having this meeting. With this in view, the objective statement should be:

- **Clear:** Starting an objective statement with an active verb like, Analyze, Evaluate, or Agree. These reflect expectations of high value that justify the investment of time and energy.

CHALLENGES, CHANGES & CURES

- **Short:** Few concise, descriptive words

- **Limited:** Having too many objectives sets unrealistic or even worst, conflicting expectations. This can lead to confusion and disappointment. It is important to set a primary objective. If need be, a secondary objective that is supportive of the first objective may be helpful.

- **Reflected in the meeting goals:** The meeting goals are different from the objective statement. The meeting goals are the stepping stones that will lead to fulfilling the meeting objective. Meeting goals are the agenda items and should be specific, measurable outcomes that the meeting participants are expected to achieve before the end of the meeting. As meeting goals each agenda item should be:

  - **Simple:** Starting with an active verb it should define the expected deliverable from this agenda item.

  - **Allocated a specific and limited number of minutes:** Preferably no more than 30 minutes indicated as (from _ to _)

  - **Assigned to only one person:** who is capable and accountable for ensuring that the expected goal or deliverable is met

Meetings are about leadership: Defining a clear meeting objective is the primary responsibility of the meeting leader. The highest contributor to meeting ineffectiveness and meeting overload is the lack of clear objectives and goals. Until you have a clear objective and a list of expected goals inviting people to meetings will reflect poorly on your leadership ability.

As leaders, we waste too much time. As director of a very active sales organization, meetings occupied most of my day. Meeting overload was a reality of my life. Many of our internal meetings lacked clear, high value objectives. Often key stakeholders were not present or their roles were ill defined.

I managed to reduce my meetings by **about 50%** by simply asking for clear meeting objectives and expected outcomes at the outset. I carefully question the need for my participation and see if a phone call or a one-on-one visit may be more effective. I also apply this strategy for my staff and with my superiors. This approach has reduced the number of internal meetings that involve my staff, so that they are able to spend more time with their clients. They too now have become more careful in clarifying the objectives and outcomes they expect from their client meetings. This has helped my staff derive more value from their client meetings and allowed them to make more productive use of their time. **SUSAN MALENICA**

Second gear: People and roles

A meeting is by nature a process that involves people playing differing roles. Remember what Shakespeare said, "All the world's a stage, and all the men and women merely players." Shakespeare gives us a valuable illustration of how a meeting should run. When you are invited to a meeting you are **"on stage."** Whether you initiate the meeting or not, you are now on stage and you have a responsibility to ensure that the play is well done. By choice or implication you are now part of the team on the stage.

It has been said that how you participate in a meeting is the most important factor by which others form an opinion about you. This is true because this is a place where you communicate with your words, tone, and body language. In a meeting you are communicating the three most important success factors—**character, competency** and **connection**. Character and competency are what you bring to the table. Connection is the way you are able to relate and collaborate in effective dialogue to add value and ensure the success of the meeting.

While developing the objective statement is the primary responsibility of the meeting leader, ensuring the participant's proper role is the responsibility of every participant. To ensure your success in a meeting you must be sure that you have a well-defined role that adds value in light of meeting objectives. So when invited to a meeting you should ask:

- **"What do you expect me to be and do in this meeting?"** A good answer will reflect and help you illustrate your role. Based on the answers you get, be sure that you further define that role:
  - Using adjectives try to define what you are expected to be. Adjectives describe the soft skills and talents you bring to the stage.
  - Using verbs try to define what you are expected to do. Verbs reflect the competencies, experience and/or the authority you bring. Verbs are easily translated into actions you are expected to demonstrate. These can be related to the meeting goals and agenda items as well as the time when your presence is needed.

A clearly-defined role will help you:

- Capitalize on your skills and competencies to bring the highest value to the stage where you are needed the most
- Enhance your relationship by complementing others on the stage of a meeting
- Estimate the time and effort you are expected to invest in your role. Remember, **you can never start something without stopping something**. Carefully calculate your time and the sacrices you have to

CHALLENGES, CHANGES & CURES

make. To justify your role and your investment we recommend that you ensure that the **tangible and non-tangible benefits you deliver are more than two times your hourly pay for every hour you spend in such a meeting**.

Tips for participating in meetings

1. **Define a personal meeting participation protocol** that is compatible with your role and communicate it to your important people (see example on next page).
2. **Seek the support of your important people for your protocol.**
3. Next time you are invited to a meeting **make sure that the meeting objectives are clear** and reflect high value worthy of your time. Be sure that you can contribute to the successful outcome of specific meeting goals (Agenda Items). If you are not sure, make some positive suggestions for change or ask to be excused from the meeting or part of it. Remember, it is your life you are investing or wasting.
4. **Be clear in your understanding of the role you are expected to play before, during and after the meeting.**
5. **Be careful to ensure that you have the skills**, competencies, authority, and/or time needed to deliver your role with excellence.
6. **Do not fall casualty to a role misfit**. It may be an honor to be asked to attend an important meeting. Before you agree, please remember:

    A. By seeking to define your **important roles** you will save yourself and others the risk of being a misfit on the stage that could jeopardize your credibility.

    B. By asking the hard questions of **objectives and goals** you are seeking to use your time with care and wisdom.

7. **Take careful notes** of the commitment you undertake. Be sure to record the expected target date of any commitments. See the example of meeting notes in the template provided. The last page in this chapter provides a practical tool that you can use for recording your concise thoughts, commitments, delegations, as well as follow-up actions. The use of this template is not limited to meeting notes. It can be used as a general notes tool for most of your communication needs.

8. **Take a love hate inventory** of all the committees and meetings you are committed to attend regularly. List the ones you love, the ones you hate, and the ones in between. Examine the ones you hate and the ones in

between and define the value you add to such meetings. Prioritize these meetings based on your role and the value you contribute. Remember, to be effective, you need to focus on higher value roles, goals, and activities. Ask to be excused from committees or meetings so you can use your time for better value.

9. **Define and communicate your meetings protocol.** The following is an example of an e-mail note you can modify and send out to your important people.

TO: (LIST) Important and teachable people

SUBJECT: Requested – My meeting participation protocol

Greetings:

My commitment is to improve my effectiveness and focus on meetings where I can add maximum value. With this in view, I ask for your support in helping me practice the following disciplines:

- I will attend and make maximum contribution to a meeting where my role is clearly stated on the agenda or I have specific responsibility, or where I can add significant value.

- Please excuse me from meetings, or portions of meetings, where my value contribution is small or where I am not clear on what **I am expected to be or do**. At such meetings please consider my attendance optional so I may delegate my role to others.

- I will give maximum preparation to my defined roles in a meeting provided the meeting agenda is circulated at least **3 working days** prior to meeting time.

- . I will exercise maximum effort to deliver on all action items assigned to me during a meeting, provided I receive clearly documented minutes within **3 working days** after the end of any meeting.

I believe this will help me be more effective and serve you better. If you have any thoughts or questions regarding this, please call me.

Thank you for your support.

10. **Meetings are about leadership.** While we believe ownership of playing an effective role is the primary responsibility of each meeting participant, it is equally true that inviting the participant is the responsibility of the meeting leader. Meeting leaders are investment managers. It is their responsibility to assign roles that deliver the highest return in the least amount of time invested.

Third gear: Meeting process and controls

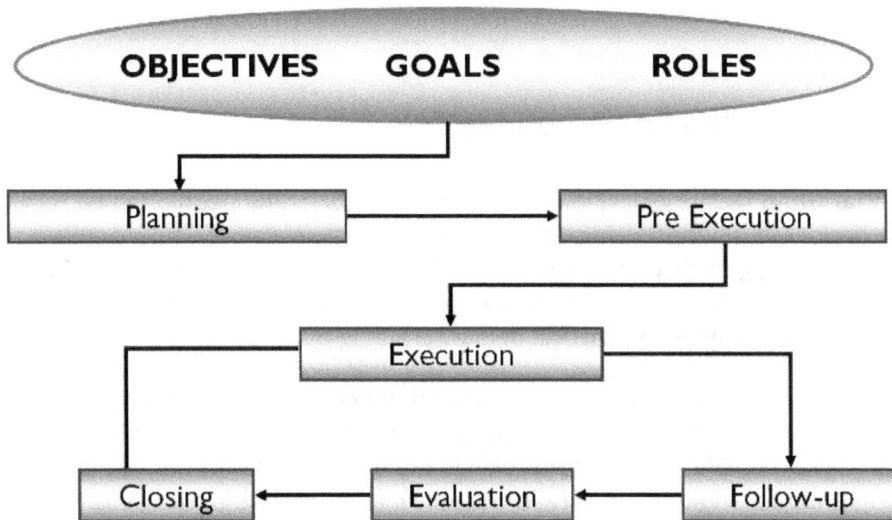

Meeting Effectiveness Process

A meeting is a process, not an event. This is a key factor that must not be ignored. Most of us view meetings as an event, not a process. An event is something that happens at a point in time while a process requires a plan over time. An event sometimes happens outside our control while a process is a series of events that can be controlled. Meeting process and controls are the sole responsibility of the meeting leader. As a meeting leader you are entrusted with controlling and managing the process as you lead the participants in their committed roles. The meeting process is an integral part of making sure that the meeting outcomes are achieved.

I attend a lot of meetings. Meetings can waste a lot of time. I have learned that it is very important to take time before a meeting to think and plan for my roles and expectations. Being organized instills a feeling of confidence and control. I have learned to carry only one binder that is the source of all critical information. In this same binder I have VIP sheets in which I record and sort notes and details that relate to my important people. The same binder also replaces my diary for general note taking purposes.

Controlling overload can be like trying to boil the ocean. It may appear impossible. Choose the areas that are likely to bring you the greatest value or benefit. Focus on these and be committed to make change happen. You will be glad you did. **KATE AGNEW**

Tips for leading meetings

I. **Planning:** Defining clear meeting objectives, goals, and people can be considered the most critical part of the planning process. Some meeting experts suggest that until this is done you should not schedule a meeting. But if this is well done then the planning is a process of confirmation and setting the stage with logistical details.

    A. **Location:** The meeting location and the environment it offers must be compatible with the meeting objectives. This is very important and often ignored. We are emotional beings and the environment affects how we interact with each other. For example, consider the impact of lighting especially if your meeting includes visual presentations.

    B. **Supplies:** Meeting supplies enhance preparation and environment. One of the more common supplies, especially in long meetings, food and drink. Be sure that the supplies that you provide will enhance effectiveness. Plan for audio and video supplies and equipment.

    C. **Draft agenda:** Your draft agenda should be circulated as early as possible. And should include:

        a) **Headings:** Meeting title, date, time , location

        b) **Objective:** A short high level statement starting with an active verb reflecting the high value of the meeting.

        c) **Goal:** Goals must be **SMART, that is Specific, Measurable, Agreed upon by your key participants, Realistic, and Time dependent**. In time dependent each agenda item should be assigned a specific time (From – To). Again, we recommend that you start every goal or agenda item with an active verb. One of the most common pitfalls of planning is poor time management. We recommend that you limit each agenda item to a maximum of thirty minutes. If one item requires more than thirty minutes, try to break it into more than one goal. This will help you keep things on track. Remember, "The mind cannot absorb more than the seat can endure."

                CHALLENGES, CHANGES & CURES

d) **Participant:** Each participant's name must be associated with the role he or she is expected to play such as presenter, leader, advisor, observer, participant, Minute Taker.

Note: In our templates Web site we provide an example of a template. You may find it at: http://www.nomoreoverload.com/templates.html

2. **Pre-Execution:** In our changing world, the best of plans can be vulnerable to unpleasant surprises. In the pre-execution stage you confirm and try to avoid last minute surprises. This is the time when you confirm the participants' readiness and ensure the availability of all support resources.

   At the end of the pre-execution stage you publish your meeting agenda. It is essential that your agenda be sent in a manner that gives your participants one last notice to prepare for their role. With this in view, we recommend that you adopt the **three-day rule.** Your final agenda should be issued at least three working days before the meeting date.

3. **Execution**: As a meeting leader you have a complex and demanding role. You are a **host, a conductor, a guide, a facilitator** and much more. Most of all, **you are an investment manager**. Your participants are investing a valuable portion of their lives in your hands. Your focus should be to ensure that all roles are performed with excellence. Be gracious but firm. Control the process not the mind. Encourage wherever possible. When appropriate, summarize the participant's contribution and confirm future undertakings or follow-up actions. Ensure that the minute taker is left with no ambiguity or misunderstanding.

4. **Closing:** Closing is often neglected in the rush of seeking a quick exit. As a meeting leader you have the vital responsibility of complimenting the participants on their achievements and contribution. As an investment manager it is your responsibility to articulate the valuable outcome and the returns from the investments made by your participants. As an activity manager it is your responsibility to summarize and confirm any commitments made as well as any expected actions.[53]

5. **Evaluation** and **feedback:** Seeking evaluation and feedback are critical to staying on track as well as ongoing improvement. At the end of every meeting a leader should request the participant's candid input. Here is an example of a simple feedback and evaluation tool that you can use. When tabulated it gives indicators of effectiveness and as well as needed improvements.

Meeting Evaluation and Feedback							
Meeting Title:			**Date:**				
Your candid evaluation is very much appreciated. To what extent do you agree with the following statements?		**I Totally** **Agree ←← →→ Disagree**					
1. The meeting objectives were very clear and fulfilled.		**5**	**4**	**3**	**2**	**I**	
2. All the participants played their roles very well.		**5**	**4**	**3**	**2**	**I**	
3. The meeting pace and time invested were reasonable.		**5**	**4**	**3**	**2**	**I**	
4. I am very glad I took part in this meeting.		**5**	**4**	**3**	**2**	**I**	
OPTIONAL: Comment or suggested improvements:							
Please Call Me:	**Name:**		**Phone #:**				

Note: In our templates Web site we provide an example of a longer template. You may find it at: http://www.nomoreoverload.com/templates.html

6. **Follow-up:** Follow-up takes two forms. **The formal follow-up** comes in the form of minutes. Publishing the minutes of the meeting should not take longer than **three working days** after the end of the meeting. Minutes published long after the meeting are based on diminished memories and their quality is often questionable. Meeting minutes should list the participants and the roles they played. The minutes should summarize any resolutions, decisions made, requested actions, and commitments.

In a separate section of the minutes, discussion notes can be added where needed. The format and the extent of these notes depend on the nature of the discussion as well as the maturity of the relationships among the meeting participants.

It is very helpful that the minutes include the tabulated results of the meeting evaluation and feedback. This adds an indication of the value the meeting leader gives to the participants' evaluation. It also encourages the participants to focus on their roles for follow-up meetings.

The meeting leader is responsible for what we call **the informal follow-up**. As a host and a resource manager you have a responsibility to support and ensure the proper feelings of those who have participated in your meeting. Meetings can be stressful environments where offensive words or actions take place. The informal follow-up is the time when support, encouragement, or corrections are made before the next meeting. A phone call or a follow-up visit may be needed to ensure that residual effects are well handled.

Flexibility and style

Like a well run set of gears, meeting leadership and participation require a measure of flexibility. As a meeting leader remember, **"Blessed are the flexible. They never get bent out of shape."** The degree of flexibility required is based on three factors:

- **The meeting style:** Some meetings are constituently established and tend to be very heavy on process and adherence to well-documented details. Project management meetings are heavy on goals and expected outcomes and may be less rigid in participation requirements. Staff meetings and team building meetings place higher value on relationships and on the chemistry between the participants. The amount of flexibility injected in a meeting is directly related to the meeting style. The expected meeting style should be clarified and communicated to the participants as part of the invitation to join.

- **The leader's style:** Your leadership style and participants' temperaments are critical factors in determining the amount of flexibility required. Your natural temperament will cause you to favor meetings that are best suited to your leadership. The amount of flexibility a leader needs to eject in a meeting is also impacted by the temperament of key participants and cultural differences.

- **Meeting objective:** The meeting objective also can highly impact the amount of flexibility a meeting leader must use. Lighter and less complicated objectives can accommodate more flexibility than topics that are stressful and challenging.

  While flexibility is important, it is very important to note that too much flexibility leads to ineffectiveness. A wise meeting leader constantly evaluates meeting effectiveness. If your experience or perceive elements of stress or if you think that you need a meeting tune-up ask yourself:

  - Are my meeting objectives clear and do they communicate high value?

- Do the agenda items represent SMART goals?
- Are the assigned roles clearly communicated and are the participants best qualified for their assigned roles?
- Is the meeting process clear, agreed upon, and easy to follow?

Tips for being a meeting leader

1. Control is not a bad word. **Control the meeting process**.
2. As a meeting leader you are accountable for the outcome and for providing favorable returns for the time and effort invested in your meeting.
3. **Take time to plan carefully.** Remember to state high value objectives and goals for your meeting.
4. **Chose only those participants needed for the important roles in the meeting.** Do not select participants based on their titles. Select them to provide the optimum mix of skills, competencies and authority.
5. **Send the meeting agenda three working days before the meeting time.** Your pre-execution phase impacts your agenda more than you think. It is critical for healthy communication and confirmation. Do not overlook it.
6. **During the execution phase you are on a stage.** You are observed as a director of a well-rehearsed drama. Control the process but not the mind. Be sure to end the meeting graciously on time and ask for evaluation and feedback.
7. **Do not neglect needed follow-up.** Meeting minutes should take no longer than three working days after a meeting date. Do not neglect informal follow-up, if needed.
8. **Use flexibility wisely.** Let your natural leadership style help you shape the needed meeting atmosphere for maximum effectiveness.[54]

To help us change work habits that contribute to overload as a management team we introduced a buddy system. I have a buddy. We meet regularly, discuss overload challenges and progress, as well as hold each other accountable for disciplines to which we commit. **DONNA JOHNSTON,**

Summary

✓ Meetings are critical to the success of our collaborative social and business interactions.

✓ For leaders and knowledge workers, the amount of time spent is likely to keep growing.

✓ As a meeting participant, your effectiveness is highly impacted by:

- Engaging in meetings that have high value objectives and SMART goals

- Playing appropriate roles that complement and support other meeting participants

- Encouraging adherence to a meeting process that provides reasonable control and flexibility

✓ You can become known as a person who leads good meetings if you follow a simple meeting process, filter your leadership through appropriate style, and temper your experience with flexibility.

Meeting Effectiveness Calculator

DAY	Total Time Spent	I rate this day's meetings overall effectiveness % as Poor ←←←←←←←←←←→→→→→→→→→→ Excellent										Effective Time
DAY 1		10%	20%	30%	40%	50%	60%	70%	80%	90%	100%	
DAY 2		10%	20%	30%	40%	50%	60%	70%	80%	90%	100%	
DAY 3		10%	20%	30%	40%	50%	60%	70%	80%	90%	100%	
DAY 4		10%	20%	30%	40%	50%	60%	70%	80%	90%	100%	
DAY 5		10%	20%	30%	40%	50%	60%	70%	80%	90%	100%	
DAY 6		10%	20%	30%	40%	50%	60%	70%	80%	90%	100%	
DAY 7		10%	20%	30%	40%	50%	60%	70%	80%	90%	100%	
TOTAL	(1)											(2)

Lost Time = (1) – (2)   % Average Effectiveness = (2) / (1) %

A – Lost Productivity = Lost Time X Burdened Hourly Rate	B – Lost Opportunity Cost = Same As Lost Productivity	Your Total Loss or Waste to Your Life = **A + B**

Communication and Note Taking Sheet

⊞

Today's Day _____ Date _____ 20____

Meeting Title: _____ Meeting Location. _____

Attendees: _____, _____, _____, _____, _____, _____, _____, _____,

Time				Action Requested		Priority
Type	Name / Subject / Thoughts	Response / Tips		From	Due Date	ABC

☛ Encounter Type: P: phone   V: voice mail   M: meeting   C: correspondence   E: e-mail   O: other

24: CONTROLLING INTERRUPTIONS

Do you have a moment?

Sam is a very competent business manager in a fast growing organization. In a period of three years the size of the team he leads has grown from 4 to 11 managers. He believes in an open door management style that makes him very popular.

It was 7:30 P.M. when he walked into his home exhausted. Empathetically his wife said, "You look like you have had a full day!"

To that he replied, "Not at all! I did not accomplish a thing all day. Today I was supposed to finish my budget project but most of my day was shot answering questions from about eleven people who kept coming to my door asking, "Do you have a moment?" It seems as if people can't think for themselves."

My current business role requires me to be very responsive on a very short time basis. In a way my current role leaves me highly exposed to interruptions and external, urgent demands. I learned to accept that and adapt to it. For this reason, I had to develop my own screening mechanism to give me some measure of control. At times when I am working on projects, it is important that I do not allow interruptions to distract me. To accomplish this, I find it helpful to turn off the phone or instant messaging or find a remote location where I cannot be easily reached. Another way to overcome the bad habit of constant urgency is to ensure the support of a good team or family members.

If you are like me living in a world where interruptions and urgency are a way of life, my advice is to learn to prioritize. Accept the fact that you cannot do everything. Focus on the two or three things that you are really good at and do not feel guilty about the rest. **DALE MCERLEAN**

Studies suggest that as much as 30 % of your workday can be wasted due to interruptions.[55] Constant interruptions lead to irritability and frustration. As you try to prioritize your daily activities and focus on important roles, goals and activities, interruptions take control of your life and prevent you from doing what you had planned. We suggest that there are two types of interruptions, **externally initiated and self inflected.**

- **Externally initiated interruptions**: Interruptions come from a variety of sources and take a variety of forms:

    - **E-mail notifier**: Whether by ring or synthesized voice calling "You Got Mail" this most irritating technology can divert your attention and cause you to waste valuable energy. So what can you do? Turn your e-mail notifier off and batch process your e-mail based on your reasonable communication protocol that is compatible with your roles and has the support of your important people.

> Interruptions are a normal part of life and should be expected as long as it is justifiable.
>
> Regretfully, most interruptions are driven by a culture of urgency that brings more harm than good.

    - **The phone** has become an accepted source of interruption. Its persistent ring seems to give it the right to override all other priorities. Whether you are focusing on an important task or engaged in an important conversation the ring of the phone demands your attention. So what can you do? Forward your calls to your voice mail and batch process your calls based on your reasonable personal communication protocol that you communicate through your outgoing voice message.

    - **Instant Messaging**: If you are part of the emerging world order you may be expected to be **always on.** Through instant messaging products friends and foes have access to your ears and eyes as long as you allow them. So what can you do? Turn off this feature or restrict access to a very select few only when you are prepared to receive interruptions in response to very important situations. Use appropriate filters to control this most invasive technology.

    - **"Do you have a minute?"** This common request that faces a busy manager can be most irritating when it comes repeatedly from the same draining people. Before your inner soul is able to say **"No"** the visitor has already entered your office and is comfortably seated in your chair. So what can you do? Avoid the draining people. Coach your important and teachable people in batch processing interruptions into well-planned meetings. Even managers with an open door policy should have the privacy of protected time and focus. Do not hesitate to close your door or put a "do not disturb sign" at your cubicle. On our website you will find a sign that you can print and use for this purpose. You can find this at: http://www.nomoreoverload.com/templates.html

- **Self-inflected interruptions**: This is the way the self-inflected interruption plays out. As you are working on something important that requires your focus, a thought comes into your mind. You remember something you need to share with another person. In fear of forgetfulness, you rush to relieve your mind from the burden of carrying this thought. You pick up the phone, send an e-mail or get up and drop by the unsuspecting other saying, **"I was just thinking…"** This not only destroys your concentration but also inflicts unwanted interruptions on others.

My advice to the overloaded person is to turn off the electronic alarms in your life - whether it be the sound that notifies you of a new e-mail, or the meeting reminder that buzzes you every ten minutes of a coming meeting, or the persistent ring of a phone when you should not be disturbed. These are distressful distractions that can drive you to despair. Take control over them; turn off what you do not absolutely need. **ANDREA SEYMOUR**

Tips for reducing interruptions

1. **We recommend the habit of using a "VIP Paper."** At the end of this chapter you will see this simple tool that will help you capture important thoughts and record important tips. Further, it will help you organize your thoughts and set the stage for focused one-on-one meetings with your important and teachable people. You can download a copy of this template from: http://www.nomoreoverload.com/templates.html

   VIP always stood for "Very Important People". Here we like to call it a **"Very Important Paper for a Very Important Person"**. The following template provides an example of a simple sheet to help you capture your thoughts for future discussion with your important and teachable people.

   This is how it works. Keep a separate VIP sheet for every one of the important people you communicate with regularly. Place these in a divided ring binder. As you are working or even while you are in some meeting when you remember or receive a valuable thought that you wish to share or discuss with one of your important others resist the urge of calling them, e-mailing them or going up to see them. Instead, write that thought down in the "Thought" column of the VIP sheet you labeled with this person's name. Save that thought till the next time you meet.

2. **Focus on one-on-one meetings.** One of the great ways to enhance your relationship with the important and teachable people in your life is to have regular, pre-planned, one-on-one meetings with them. Depending on the relationship and the need, such appointments should vary in duration and frequency. It is during such a meeting that all the thoughts you recorded can be brought up and discussed. You can then note the response in the "Tips or Response" column. What you have indirectly developed is an agenda for your one-on-one encounter. As you collect these sheets they become a progressive record of the items you discussed, an appropriate reminder for follow-up, and a non-offensive tool for ongoing accountability. Most importantly, you have reduced the interruptions you are causing yourself and others.

Now is your chance to be a coach. You can see that if you train the people who interrupt you frequently to follow the same approach you will also save most of the interruptions they cause in your life. This will save you even more time and energy.

You may be presently using regular notebooks for a similar purpose. This is fine. One key advantage of using the approach described above is that as you keep your sheets in a divided binder you are sorting your thoughts as you go along. Keep a sheet or section for yourself as well. This would serve as your "one place for all notes." Periodically, say once a month, take out a section, label it, staple it and put it away for your records.

Note: There will always be times when things cannot wait. That is fine. Be flexible to respond to reasonable emotional or practical needs. Remember, "Blessed are the flexible, they never get bent out of shape."

3. **Gently confront draining behavior.** This system may not work with highly impulsive or draining people. Let us give you an example that happens far too often. A draining person who often interrupts your day comes to your door asking the same question, **"Do you have a minute?"** Before you are able to say no, he or she starts talking. Here is what you should do. Shortly after the first few sentences ask, **"What would you like to see happen as result of our visit?"** You see, you are politely asking for a clear, visible outcome. You are helping him or her define an agenda for your meeting. A draining person is not likely to have thought so far. By this statement you are helping the draining person think and take some responsibility for the outcome of the meeting. If no agenda was thought of or if he or she says, "I am not sure" ask him or her to return when they

have defined one. If the person has thought of a clear outcome, suggest that for best results you would be glad to schedule adequate time in the future. In so doing you are coaching the draining person in the value of proactive thinking and planning. You are respectfully allowing them appropriate time based on your controlled calendar.[56]

4. **Work where you cannot be easily reached.** In order to focus there is no substitute to hiding in a relaxed place where you cannot be reached.

5. **Please do not disturb**. With agreement among your important people use a simple do not disturb sign.

I lead a large team plus I have other senior leaders that I call my important people. My life is full of activities and demands that are hard to sort and organize. I had to find a tool to ensure that nothing falls through the cracks. Having a VIP binder was the tool I needed.

My VIP binder has a tab for each of my important people. As thoughts or "To Do" items come to mind, I automatically record them in the section relating to the particular person. It also has a section for notes for myself. This provides me with an easy tool for organizing and delegating responsibilities to the appropriate roles among my team. This, by far, has had the greatest impact on my effectiveness. **PAUL KIM**

The most important tool that has helped me take control of my urgency driven world is a simple binder in which I record all the important thoughts that cross my mind or the important communications and commitments I make. This binder is organized by sections reflecting my important people as well as the important details I need to remember. During the day I take time to examine and process what I have entered in my binder. Some items will lead me to block additional time in my calendar when I can work for longer, uninterrupted periods. This has been most helpful to me. **DALE MCERLEAN**

Summary

✓ Interruptions can waste as much as 30% of your day, frustrate you, and destroy your effectiveness.

✓ Interruptions often result as a response to urgent situations and impulses.

✓ Most items that cause interruptions can wait for a future time and a future response.

✓ Interruptions come via e-mail, phone, instant messaging, or impromptu meetings.

✓ Batch process your important thoughts by using regularly scheduled one-on-one encounters with your important and teachable people.

✓ Use the **VIP sheet** to develop thoughts to guide your one-on-one meetings with your important people. This will also serve as a record of follow-up and accountability.

✓ Become a coach helping others to follow your lead and example by not interrupting you.

✓ By example and simple questions train the draining people to think before they interrupt.

VIP – Thoughts and Tips

Prepared For Discussion With: *Name*

Time		Action Requested		Priority
Date		Due Date	From	ABC
Name / Subject / Thoughts	Response / Tips			

25: CONTROLLING PAPER OVERLOAD

The paperless office is a myth that may never happen. Consider the following:

- A 2006 Statistics Canada report smashes the myth of the paperless office, finding instead that paper consumption has doubled over 20 years even as Canadians adopt new technologies. Per capita consumption of paper for printing and writing from the years 1983 to 2003 rose 93.6 per cent to 91.4 kilograms—about 20,000 pages per person.[57]

- In 2003 Christina Cavanagh, a notable professor and author, wrote that "Experts have tabulated that North American office printers spewed out 1.2 trillion sheets of paper in 2001; an increase of 50 percent since 1996."[58]

Most people feel they need more office and desk space. This is primarily due to having too much paper cluttering their work environment. Paper in your office has a strong visual impact. As your eyes glance at what you have on your desk or on your shelves your attention is diverted from what deserves your focus. Cluttered filing spaces often result in lost documents and/or high maintenance overhead. While you cannot live without paper in your office, you must work very hard at keeping it under control.

> The paperless office may never happen. A clutter filled office not only hinders your ability to focus and concentrate but also it creates a very negative impression of your control and organizational ability.

As a general principle, document originators have the responsibility of maintaining copies of all documents they create. With this in view, you need to always examine the reasons for which you create documents or file documents you receive from others. The following are some tips that have helped many of our clients. Tailor them to your own needs. Apply them to simplify your life and they will give you great benefits.

Tips for controlling paper

Whether your organization has a document handling and retention policy or not, you are responsible for what you can control.

- **Develop your own paper handling protocol and communicate it to your important people**. This protocol defines in general terms how and when you will respond to the various types of documents you receive. While there will always be exceptions, exceptions should not dictate and drive your rational processes. If you do not communicate your protocol and gain the support of your important people you will always fall victim to the varied expectations others establish for you. These are often based on their agendas and personal priorities.

- Define and Communicate Your Paper Protocol

  > **TO: (LIST) Important and teachable people**
  >
  > **SUBJECT: Action Requested – My paper handling protocol**
  >
  > Greetings:
  >
  > It is my desire to improve my effectiveness in handling the flood of paper I receive. Towards this goal I ask for your support as I adhere to the following disciplines:
  >
  > - I will access my paper inbox only once a day at **(state time of day).**
  >
  > - I will give priority to items sent to me personally from important people like you and I will seek to respond or act on them within **(X) working days**. All other mail and mail where you have copied me will be considered for information purposes and given lower priority.
  >
  > - To reduce my paper filing requirements I will assume that the originator always keeps a copy. **Therefore, I will not have to keep a copy**.
  >
  > Please do not place any incoming mail anywhere except in the inbox.
  >
  > Thank you for your support.

- **Seek support for your new paper handling protocol.** Remember, there will always be conflicting priorities. Items that others may deem important may only be merely urgent. Your important people will help you withstand the pressure of urgency if they understand and support your paper handling protocol.

- **Batch process your paper mail at a regular time in the day**. Set regular times to review your inbox. This could be first thing in the morning or maybe midday. If so, block this time in your calendar as an important appointment with yourself. You may call such an appointment a "processing meeting."

- **Keep your inbox by the recycling box**. This encourages you to discard most of your mail before you take it into your office.

- **Apply the "OHIO"—O**nly **H**andle **I**t **O**nce principle. If you allow enough paper processing time, you can apply the **4 Ds** described below:

  - **Delete (Discard) it now.** If you have not asked for it or it is not clearly labeled to be from one of your important people, your first question should be why even open it. Why not delete it now?

  - **Deal with it now.** If the item at hand can be processed in three to five minutes deal with it now.

  - **Delegate it now.** If processing such a document will help one of your teachable people grow, delegate it to him or her. So delegate it now. For example, if you receive a forty-page report or study that may be important, ask one of your teachable people to examine it and provide you with a synopsis or recommendations.

  - **Diarize it now.** If the document you just received requires more than five minutes of your time make a processing appointment with yourself to deal with it. Be sure to diarize it now.

- **Keep your inbox out of sight**. This will help you avoid the temptation for distraction every time someone places an item in your inbox. This is a wasteful distraction that you can avoid.

- **Keep a delete box**. This is a box where you place items that you wish to discard but fear the possibility of needing it some time soon. Avoid the temptation to open such items. Instead, place it in the Delete box so you can retrieve it if the need arises. If the need does not arise within a reasonable period, say a month or two, discard it permanently.

- **Keep your outbox handy**. If your outbox is within reach you can place items in it easily and access them any time you are leaving the office or passing by the mail drop box.

- **Unsubscribe from magazines and periodicals**. When you get them, clip what you need, place in your reading file, and discard the rest.

Paper overload has been one of my critical problems. I seemed to be overrun with paper, charts, and reports that built and accumulated on my desk. To improve my effectiveness and cope with the increased demands placed on me I had to take control of this part of my business life. My starting point was to design a filing system that reflects my roles and how I operate. It was important to make sure that the headings on the files are easily understood and make sense to me, reflecting the way I think. Now I have a cabinet that contains my key issues or key items. I also have one drawer that deals with my staffing issues and my relationship with them. During the day I move a lot to different meetings. Now I carry a small binder that holds all the current critical data that I need to refer to often.

Having an organized filing system and keeping my desk clear did not only help me feel in control of my world but has also saved me a lot of time. Now I do not waste too much time looking for what I need. **GERRY BARANECKI**

Summary

- ✓ The paperless office is a myth that may never happen.
- ✓ Most documents in our offices are not needed for normal business life.
- ✓ As a general principle, the originator of any document is responsible for maintaining it. Always ask why you should keep a copy.
- ✓ Develop your personal paper handling protocol, communicate it, and gain the support of your important people for it.
- ✓ Batch process your mail. Handle it only once applying the 4Ds.
- ✓ Keep your inbox out of sight and your outbox handy.
- ✓ Use a delete box to help you discard items that you are afraid to destroy.
- ✓ Unsubscribe from magazines and periodicals. When you get them, clip what you need, place in your reading file, and discard the rest.

CURES: DE-CLUTTER TO SIMPLIFY

- More than meets the eye
- The way librarians file
- Designing a clutter-free system
- Building a clutter-free system
- Maintaining a clutter-free system

26: MORE THAN MEETS THE EYE

Does this photograph look familiar? It's the office of a highly respected medical professional with impressive academic credentials who held a responsible position in one of the most acclaimed institutions in the field. As a leading forensic pathologist, the weight of his testimony had the power to put people behind bars or set them free.

The caption that accompanied the picture in the National Post read "Pathologist's disorganization a serious problem: inquiry".[59] The highly publicized inquiry of his work confirmed that his faulty findings and report led to the imprisonment of several innocent people. We are not here to pass judgment on the work of Dr. Charles Smith, but to point out that clutter and disorganization can give a strong impression of poor work quality. If a picture is worth a thousand words then this picture cried out "How can you trust a man whose office is so disorganized?"

We have no doubt that, like most of us, Dr. Smith was a very busy person. Like most leaders and knowledge workers his life was flooded with both meaningful and meaningless information. Like most of us he seldom had time to sort through, organize, and de-clutter his office and his life. Like most of us, Dr. Smith experienced the complexities that accompany a cluttered world.

We all can fall victim to information clutter and the very high price it can take. Most of us have experienced the anxiety that accompanies the loss of an important file. Many of us have faced the panic of a lost document just before an important meeting or event. Whether it is in our electronic world or paper files, the majority of us have faced the frustration of how long it takes to find what we need. If you are not sure whether your filing system needs help or not, maybe the following questions can guide you:

- Are your filing systems simple and logical so your boss or associate can find important information within three minutes?

- When rushed or short of time, do you find it hard to recall where you have stored an important report that you need right away?

- When you walk into your office, do you see files, papers, or magazines that you have not used in the last few days?

- When you look at your desk, is most of it covered?

- When you open your e-mail inbox, is it full of old and new, read, and unread messages?

If you answered yes to the above questions, you are not alone and you need help before things get much worse. More than ever before, today's knowledge workers are suffering from information indigestion and cluttered filing systems.

A Reuters News Service study of 1300 managers found that:

- 38% waste substantial amounts of time looking for information

- 43% could not make important decisions because of information overload[60]

Regretfully, the information glut is not likely to improve. The volume of information thrust upon us is expected to increase with every passing year. The time has come to take control and organize information in a manner that reduces the physical and mental burden that comes from too much information.

The cure or solution is designed to help you simplify your filing system so you can find what you need when you need it.

This solution is made of two interdependent parts:

- **A filing methodology** we call the Frequency of Use Filing Methodology™. As a methodology it is a method of simplified thinking that we borrow from our observations of how libraries are organized. So we say "file the way librarians file."

- **A filing structure** we call Roles-Based Filing Structures. This structure is based on the simplified filtering system we encouraged you to use to prioritize your roles. Building a simple roles-based filing structure will help you ensure that the knowledge you collect becomes an infrastructure to help you fulfill your role rather than information clutter that burdens you and wastes your time and energy.

27: THE WAY LIBRARIANS FILE

I hate to file!

"I hate to file," said Michelle as she looked at the piles of papers covering her desk and spilling on the floor around her. "I fear that if I file anything I will not remember where I put it. Plus it is hard to figure out where to put everything."

Adam opened his e-mail to see 2,128 items in the inbox. "I feel overwhelmed and I do not seem to be able to stay on top of all of this," he said.

James, his desk mostly covered by paper believes that "Out of sight is out of mind." "I use a pile system with yellow sticky notes to highlight priority items." A file in one pile had a date that is ten months old.

"I do not throw anything away," said Janice. "There is always a chance someone will ask me for it. My only problem is that I have nowhere to work."

Confronting the fear of filing

Before discussing a simple solution we should confront three fears some of us face about filing.[61]

- **Fear of making a decision:** Where should I file it? What should I call it? If you don't know what to call a piece of paper, you will call it nothing. If it doesn't have a name, it won't have a home. Such papers end up in unnamed stacks or piled on your desk or inbox. To confront this fear you need a simple, clear naming or indexing convention that simplifies this decision-making problem. We will lead you in a simple process to document your filing index. Keep this index handy and it will help you overcome the fear of making filing decisions.

- **Fear of discarding anything:** What happens if I need it someday? About eighty per cent of filed papers are never referred to again.[62] In our fast changing world the shelf life of most information is very short. So any documents you file today will likely become obsolete in a short time.

Remember, if it is important the originator will most likely keep a copy and will be glad to provide you with another. So, take a risk. When in doubt, discard it. The rewards are worth it.

- **Fear of not finding it when it is needed:** How can I trust the filing system? Your filing system needs to be simple and easy to maintain. Such a system will reduce the risks of misfiling and will help you find what you need, when you need it.

I am no longer afraid to file. Before I organized my filing, I used to spend a lot of time debating what I should do with the flood of paper and electronic documents I receive. Now I have one simple filing system that reflects my leadership roles, my project roles and my operational roles. I no longer debate. I have researched my records retention requirements, organized a department db that houses project information and reduced the need to personally file documents. I also have a simple process that allows me to review what I need and discard what I do not need to retain. My files are cleaner and neater. I believe this has improved my effectiveness by at least thirty percent. **JOELLE PEREZ**

Librarians are entrusted with more books, files, and records than any other profession. Yet professional librarians use a simple filing system that is easily understood by a small child. If you visit a local library you find what we call **Frequency of Use Filing Methodology**™. Illustrated in this diagram we recommend a simple system of three main categories plus some supporting time dependent boxes:

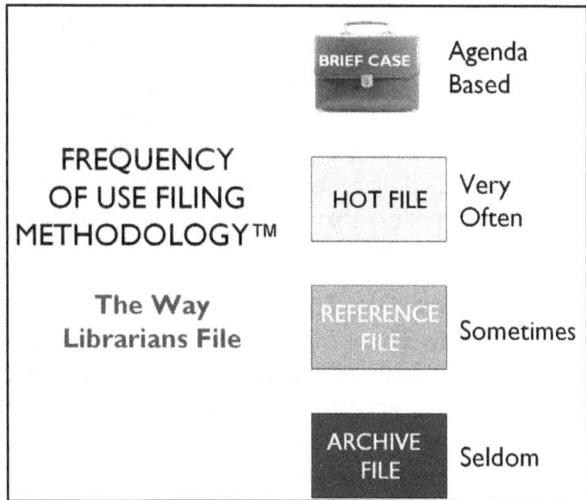

- **The first category** holds items that are in high demand. These very often used items are placed in close proximity to the librarian's desk. We like to call this the Hot File. This collection is usually small and kept clutter free. Often, only the librarian accesses and maintains these books or files.

- **The second category** holds items that are used less frequently. These are placed in the stacks of the main library floor. We call this category the Reference File. This collection is sometimes referred to and is usually much larger than the first. While still well organized, access requires a longer retrieval time.

- **The third category** holds items that are seldom used. These are placed in the archives. We call this the Archive File. Access to this collection is far less frequent and often requires an even longer retrieval time.

In addition, we will describe in more detail, three other parts of your ideal filing system; they are your briefcase, inbox, outbox, and delete box.

- **Hot File:** This file holds items that you are presently working on, items you need to reference often or items that require regular updates or follow-up attention. This file needs to be crisp, small, and clutter free. Your ability to retrieve a document from such a file needs to be at short notice requiring quick access. As a matter of fact, the benchmark for retrieving a document from this file should be less than 60 seconds in the paper file and 30 seconds in the electronic file.

Why 30 seconds for the electronic file? Suppose you prepared and sent an important management report. Shortly after sending it, you received a concerned call from a senior executive who had some questions regarding your report. You have an immediate need to engage in this dialogue. You need to have the report in your hand for this important discussion. If you are not able to have a printed copy of this report very quickly you can be assured that your stress level will increase, your effectiveness in the discussion will deteriorate, and the patience of the caller will be challenged. We hope you see the need for this file to be easily accessed so you can retrieve what you need very quickly. An additional benefit is that keeping this file small will reduce the maintenance time and effort it requires.

- **Reference File**: This file holds items that you have completed or need less frequently. These may include recently closed projects, annual budgets, and corporate policies and bylaws. This file needs to be well-organized and available for access with limited effort. Your ability to retrieve a document from such files may require movement from your desk. Since you access this file less frequently you may choose to have it outside your office, freeing valuable office space for more useful activities.

In some cases it may be advisable to designate a common reference file for a department or a team of knowledge workers. The maintenance responsibility of the reference file, paper or electronic, may be delegated to a special person who takes ownership of it on behalf of the group. This will reduce duplication of records as well as ensure the effective use of this common resource.

Depending on the work you are doing at any given moment you may need to bring items from your reference file into your Hot File. An example of this may occur if you are working on the annual budget preparation or a new policy development project.

- **Archive File:** This file holds items that you are far less likely to need, but that you must keep for legal or historical reference. While such files still need to be organized their access is far less frequent than the Hot or Reference files. Such files should be available in common storage and may even be delegated to an off site location or media.

Sometimes, depending on the work you are doing, you may need to bring items from your Archive File into your Hot File. An example of this may occur if you should be called for a tax audit, a mortgage renewal, or a court case of some kind.

Note: Depending on your roles and needs, you may prefer to combine the reference and archive file. This is perfectly fine especially when you are designing with the e-mail and electronic files, since there are many search engines and tools that can facilitate the search and retrieval function.

- **Briefcase:** The briefcase represents the information you are likely to need in fulfilling your role when you are away from your office or workstation. Your briefcase should hold information you have taken from your Hot File. Most of us tend to take more papers to a meeting than we need. Mistakenly, we fear saying, "I do not know" or our motto is "Always be prepared for the unexpected." But, in fact, this can cause you more stress and reduce your effectiveness.

Before a meeting, take time to review the meeting objectives and meeting agenda. Examine your file and bring only the most important documents you need from your paper, electronic, or e-mail system. Organize your briefcase in the order of your meetings and related agendas. This will help you to reduce clutter, distraction, and frustration. In addition, you will appear to others to be more organized and in control. This is very valuable. Few things are more damaging to your credibility than frantically thumbing through a stack of papers looking for information while all those around stare at you.

- **Inbox:** Your e-mail and paper systems must include an inbox. This is the input point to the batch processing principles we recommended as part of your control systems. Once the information in your inbox is accessed and processed in the batch mode, we recommend it be closed to avoid distractions and present urgency that hinders your effectiveness. For example, once you check your e-mail close your e-mail system keeping only your calendar open, if needed. In a similar manner keep your paper inbox out of sight and access it only once or twice a day.

- **Outbox:** Your paper outbox needs to be handy and easy to access. As you periodically move from your office you can take the contents of your outbox and deliver them to the intended destinations. This is another way of batch processing. We recommend the same for your e-mail outbox. You can do this to configure your e-mail to hold your outgoing mail until you click the send and receive button. This allows you the option to give your outgoing mail one last consideration before you release it to its intended recipients.

Note: As a general rule, for most business reasons the originators of a document or e-mail are responsible for keeping a copy of all items they create. Be sure to archive your outgoing documents and retain them long enough in compliance with your business needs and retention policies.

- **Delete Files:** Since a lot of the material you receive you never ask for or are unlikely to need, we encourage you to be aggressive in deleting items as they arrive and to do this before even opening such items. Most computer and e-mail systems allow the option to retrieve deleted items within reasonable periods. You can set the parameters for this with the user or administrator options in your systems. Realizing that you can retrieve an item that you have deleted within a reasonable period will help you be more aggressive in deleting items that do not appear to be of high value at first glance.

You can adopt a similar delete file in your paper world. This is how it works:

1. Designate a conveniently located box or drawer as your delete box.
2. When you receive a document that does not fall within your Hot Reference or Archive priority mark it with the date received and place it in the Delete box.
3. If, for any rational reason, you need to recover that deleted paper document you still have the option to easily do so within a reasonable period such as two or three months.
4. Periodically, once a month as an example, take the oldest batch in that file, possibly three months old, and get rid of it permanently. Granted, there may be a slim chance that you may need what you have discarded. In this case, the originator should be willing to provide you with another copy. Let me assure you, the benefits of reduced clutter and stress will far outweigh the risks.

Roles-based filing structure

Your filing system should be a simple, easy-to-administer resource that supports you in fulfilling your roles and achieving your goals. It should be structured along the same lines as the roles you play. You may recall in discussing your roles we

CHALLENGES, CHANGES & CURES

suggested that each of us play different roles on three differing stages we call the Leadership stage, the Projects stage, and the Operation stage. Based on this, we recommend that your Hot File, Reference File, and Archive File should be structured in three different categories, Leadership, Operation, and Projects.

- **Leadership Files:** Here you store items that relate to your interaction with specific individuals or groups where you play a leadership role or who play a leadership role in your life. This is an ideal location to store items that relate to your direct relationship with your important people, teachable people, boss, or family, and items that relate to you personally.

- **Operation Files:** Here you store items that relate to regularly planned patterns such as expense reports, administrative monitoring, billing cycle, and management committee's minutes. This is a good place to file reading material that you have regularly scheduled time to review.

Roles Based Filing Structure

- **Projects Files:** Here you store items that relate to projects where you play specific roles as a member of a project team or a project that you are undertaking by yourself.

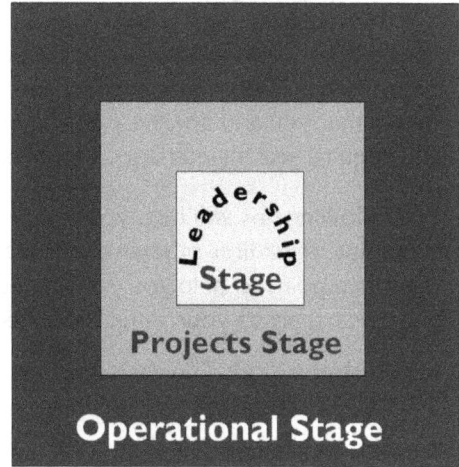

The team I managed was involved in numerous projects. My files were previously organized alphabetically by project name. At one time, I was asked, "Donna, are you managing the projects or the people running the projects?" This led me to examine my role and the impact my filing system had on how I behaved. I began to file by the name of the person managing the project. Every time I opened my filing drawer, I could visualize how I should be managing my team, not the project. This had a very positive impact on the type of information I collected, as well as how I managed my relationship with my staff. **DONNA JOHNSTON**

Tips on choosing subject headings

One of the key fears we face in filing is the fear of making decisions. Where can I file this? What should I call it? This fear can be relieved if you have a simple filing index to follow.

For librarians, choosing appropriate subject headings is a very important part of designing the library filing system. Our advice is to keep your filing system so simple that you and anyone else can find appropriate information easily. It will also require less maintenance and overhead.

The following tips will help you chose appropriate subject headings. As you read these tips, think first of your paper files. The paper files give you a tangible reference point to help you get started. Later you will find that the same principles apply to your e-mail and electronic files as well.

- **Alphabetical:** The easiest way is to file in alphabetical order within a subject category.

- **Broad categories:** These can represent sections, drawers or cabinets. (Example: Hot Files, Reference Files, Archive Files). Then move to smaller categories. (Example: Leadership, Operation, and Projects). Then add sub-subjects. (Example: Project A, Project B, Project C)

- **Generic headings:** These are better than hard to remember words, e.g., "Organizing" rather than "Time Management", use "Financing" rather than "Loans, or Venture Capital".

- **Nouns:** A single noun is the ideal type of subject heading because it is simple in form and the easiest to understand and remember.

- **First words are important:** Rarely use an adjective, adverb, date, or number as the first word (unless it's a proper name or "tag" name). For example, a direct mail firm filed a set of hot mailing lists under the heading "New Lists" but some time later the word "new" was forgotten. The lists remained lost in the "N" section of the file for over three years.[63] A better way would be to file it under "Lists" followed by a secondary heading such as "New" or "Date", etc.

- **Avoid using "Miscellaneous":** "Miscellaneous" lets you avoid making a proper filing decision! Also these files have a tendency to grow out of control, (not to mention that you will probably forget what you put in this file anyway).

- **Easily understandable:** Using easily understood categories can give you options to provide subcategories, e.g., use "Banks" then you can add sub categories as "ABC Bank", then "Savings Account".

- **Comprehensive headings:** These let you include a substantial quantity of documents.

- When naming folders and subfolders, keep it simple. Making a folder name sophisticated will ensure that you won't remember what you called it.

- Think of each hanging or main folder as the family name. This will help you think of subfolders as children and grandchildren in that family.

- Merge similar materials into relatively few "fat" folders, subdividing only when the folder becomes physically unwieldy, say approximately two to four centimeters thick.

- **Cross-reference:** Adding a "See Also" note in a visible place.

- **Subject index:** Create a list of your filing system and keep it handy. It will simplify your decision making process, minimize duplicate files, and coordinate the use of shared files. This will also enable others to retrieve files in your absence.

Take time and type the **subject or index list** of your new filing system. You will need this when we move to the next step - building your filing system.

As you consider your filing methodology and structure, it is important to apply the same principles to your paper files, e-mail files, electronic files (hard drive or shared drives), and even the information you collect through your Web browser. Very often we see clients using different filing systems for each media. Recalling and maintaining three filing systems leads to confusion and increases the mental burden associated with your information management. For best results use one system across all media.

In the following chapters we will help you design and build a simple clutter-free filing system, followed by a simple maintenance plan to keep your filing system from deteriorating over time.

In my role and the type of work I do it was easy for me to become an accumulator of paper and documentation. In the taxation world the government has the ability to create and distribute more information and paper than most of us can cope with. The result is that it became difficult for me to easily find what I needed when I needed it. Some change had to happen. I decided to take control of information overload. Today, my office is clutter free. I am able to prioritize, delegate, and handle documents more promptly. I have very few outstanding issues.

It is interesting how this has impacted my staff. Following my example, they in turn have become more organized. In an organization where document retention and timely access is critical to effectiveness I now seldom hear anyone complaining about not being able to find a document.

As we keep the discipline to prioritize and organize our document handling and processing I believe that our effectiveness will be improved by at least 50%. **ROSS GRAHAM**

Summary

- ✓ A cluttered office reflects poorly on management competence and credibility.
- ✓ Information clutter has a very high price in lost time and productivity.
- ✓ The simple Frequency Of Use Filing Methodology™ includes:
  - o Hot File for items most frequently used
  - o Reference File for items needed less often
  - o Archive File for items seldom required
- ✓ Supporting this methodology is a simple roles-based filing structure where you store information based three types of roles: **leadership, operation, and project.**
- ✓ Building a filing index using simple logical subject headings will help you file what you need when you need it with limited maintenance overhead and distractions.
- ✓ Apply the same filing structure to your paper, electronic and e-mail files. You cannot afford to remember three separate filing systems.

28: DESIGNING A CLUTTER-FREE FILING SYSTEM

Just like designing a house designing your system is a thinking process. By asking simple questions you can design a simple system that defines your needs and requirements. In this design process we encourage you to think and describe your needs in response to the filters you use to focus your roles, the people you interact with, and the issues your must resolve. Using the table format, indicate your desire and add appropriate comments when needed.

Designing your work space

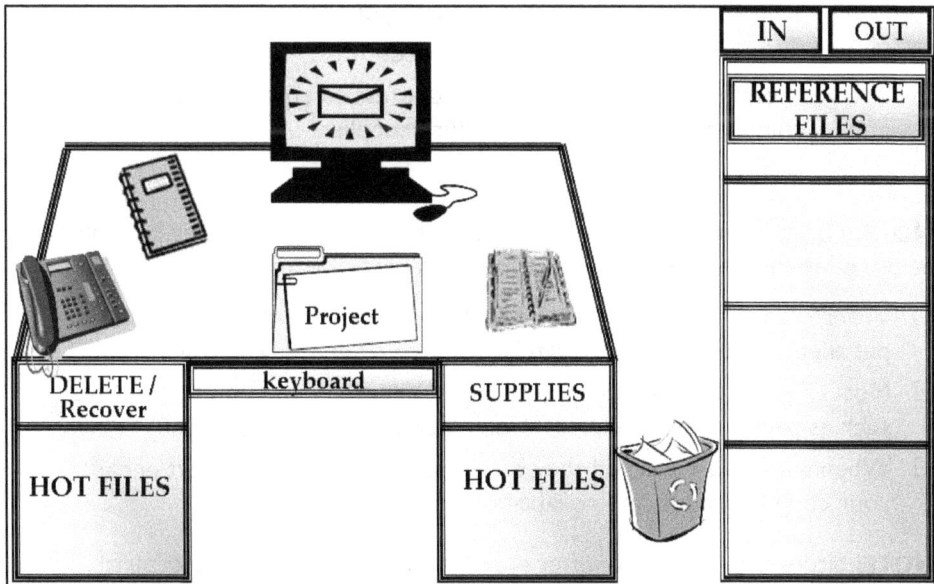

Before you jump into the filing system, it is important to look at your entire office environment, contents, and layout. Are you comfortable in the present layout or are there more suitable arrangements? What can you do to simplify and reduce clutter in order to enhance your concentration, and reduce distractions or interruptions? What seating arrangements are best for your communication with visitors?

Exercise: Arranging your office layout

The attached diagram, illustrates a simple layout. To help you think of your needs we have provided some simple questions for you to consider. Place a ✓ mark the ones that apply to you.

WORK SPACE

☐ Do you need to change your office layout to enhance your concentration and reduce distractions?

☐ What changes can you make to take advantage of daylight and brightness?

☐ Do you have adequate lighting to reduce eyestrain as you read and use your computer?

☐ When people walk by your door or workstation do they distract you and are you tempted to look up and socialize with them?

☐ Can you eliminate any clutter that reduces your effectiveness?

☐ Do you have adequate desk and filing space?

☐ Are you comfortable with your present access to equipment such as phone, computer, recycle bins, and office supplies?

☐ Where will you place your Hot File?

NOTE: For maximum ease of use we recommend that your paper Hot File be placed in the on your right or left side drawers of your desk.

☐ Where can you place your Reference and Archive files? Is it possible to put them out of your immediate work area or in a shared place?

☐ Most of us need easy access to supplies. Where would you store items such as paper, pens, staples…? (See office supplies shopping list.)

☐ When guests visit you will they be sitting in a manner that best enhances your communication and collaboration?

NOTE: Sitting opposite each other is often referred to as the adversarial seating position, while sitting beside each other is considered a more collaborative seating position.

Interruptions had a negative impact on my effectiveness. On the physical side, my office is located in the crossroads of two main corridors and facing the main entry to our work area. Our office building houses over four thousand people. My desk faced the door of my office so I was in full view of all traffic. Greeting socially conscious colleagues was a ritual that repeated itself several times a day. Such interruptions had a negative impact on my effectiveness. Minor adjustments to my seating arrangements and the blinds on my glass wall helped reduce the eye contact with every passerby. This reduced my interruptions and helped me focus on the tasks at hand as well as the guests in my office.

On the mental side, I found it helpful to compartmentalize my activities. This has helped me focus on one type of work at a time, for example, batch processing e-mail and voice mail has helped me a lot. Allowing a transition between my roles at work and home life helps me focus on my responsibilities as a father and husband. This has had a great impact on my life. Paul Kim

Designing paper files

While the file design principles are the same for your paper, e-mail, and electronic files, there are some differences brought by the use of related electronic technology. We encourage you to decide which files—paper, e-mail, or electronic—you consider your primary files and let that be the primary driver in your design. If you are graphically minded use a simple diagram similar to the network diagram illustrated earlier to build your structures.

Sometimes we find it helpful to start the design your information process using the paper files. Being tangible the paper file will help you experience this process in a more concrete way. For this reason we will start here with the paper file. Later we will relate the same experience to your e-mail and electronic files by indicating differences that take advantage of related technology.

Today there seems to be more paper in our "hoped for" paperless offices than ever before. Frankly, I find paper clutter not only confusing but also quite depressing. Some people, as part of their work plan, have the habit of shuffling bundles of paper from one side of their desks to the other. This is counter productive.

To reduce my paper clutter I have a "Pending" file, a "Probably Discard" file along with a well organized "Reference" file. This has helped me file what I need as soon as I get it and prevent paper from accumulating on my desk **MARIE DARLING**

HOT FILES

☐ Based on your roles, what are the major group headings you will use? (e.g., Leadership, Operation and Projects)

☐ What are the sub-headings associated with these?

 ☐ **Leadership:** Add the names of the people, groups, or sub groups you interact with for the benefit of your relationships with them. If possible, limit this list to your important and teachable people.

 ☐ **Operation:** Write the labels of functions, committees, or tasks you are involved in on a regular or periodic basis.

 ☐ **Projects:** List the titles of projects in which you presently and actively play a role.

NOTE:

- As you build your file headings refer to the tips on subject headings. As you build your tree (Grandfather, Father, Child) avoid complexity and try to stay within a limit of about three levels.

- As you are doing this you are building your filing index list that will be common to your e-mail and other electronic hot files. It may be helpful to examine your present files as a reference point but be careful and do not allow your old way of filing to direct your new way of filing.

☐ Do you need a waiting, pending, or follow-up, tickler folder (1 to 31 days and/or 1 to 12 months)?

☐ Do you need a reading folder? Should this be part of your Leadership or Operation folder?

NOTE:

- Reading is a critical professional development responsibility so designate a special place for easy access during your professional development or reading time.

- Some material is better filed in three ring binders that do not easily fit in filing drawers. Think of where you can place these.

REFERENCE FILES

☐ Where should you place these files to keep them within reasonable reach?

☐ Where will you place reference books, magazines, and periodicals?

☐ Should your reference material be placed in departmental or corporate files to reduce duplication and enhance efficiency?

NOTE: It is very likely that you may find some groups and subjects repeated from your Hot File. This is fine. These files will hold similar but older material.

ARCHIVE FILES

☐ How can you reduce the clutter created by these files and keep them out of sight?

☐ Should your archive material be placed in a departmental or corporate archive?

Note: It is very likely that the same groups and subjects will be repeated from your Reference File. This is fine. These files will hold similar but much older material.

INBOX

☐ Where can you place your inbox to ensure the least distraction and the temptation to frequently access it?

☐ What is the best structure for easy processing of your inbox? Do you need the material pre-sorted in multiple folders, for example, Important People, Reading, Signature Required?

OUTBOX

☐ Where can you place your Outbox to allow you to quickly place material in it and to provide others with easy access without distracting you?

☐ What is its best structure? Do you need special persons, department, or special function folders or subfolders?

DELETE BOX

☐ Where will you place your delete files or box?

BRIEFCASE

NOTE: The content of your briefcase is totally based on the functions and roles you play when you are away from your primary work place and it should be easily organized and maintained to reduce distraction and stress.

☐ Is your present briefcase adequate for your role and professional image?

☐ Can you keep it simple and clutter free so it communicates confidence and control to others?

Designing e-mail files

Your e-mail should follow the same structure as your paper files with some differences. For example:

- **Inbox:** Your e-mail system may enable you to develop simple rules tool to sort incoming mail into folders based on your roles and the important people with whom you interact. The rules tool is one of the most helpful—yet neglected—features of e-mail systems. This feature lets you direct and sort incoming mail into appropriate folders based on predefined conditions, priorities, people or key words in the subject or message text. Adopt the OHIO (Only Handle It Once) principle and simply drag the e-mail message from the Inbox to the appropriate Hot and Reference Folders.

- **Hot Folder:** As you follow the OHIO (Only Handle It Once) principle, your Hot folder should be relatively small. The pending and follow-up functions can be performed by the use of simple follow- up flags or simply dragging the e-mail in question to the "to do" list or to set up follow-up calendar appointments.

- **Reference and/or Archive Folder:** Because of the flexibility offered by e-mail technology and its search capability, material that does not need to be in the Hot file can be archived. This enables you to have one combined Reference/Archive folder. Most e-mail systems enable you to set automatic archiving rules. If your e-mail system does not offer such an archiving tool, set your own folder and periodically drag and drop older items to the Archive folders.

- **Outbox:** We recommend that you configure your e-mail system to hold your outgoing mail in the "outbox" until you click the Send/Receive button. This gives you more quality control if you need it.

- **Delete:** You can configure your delete folder to hold all deleted items and automatically destroy them based on predefined criteria. In a manner similar to that discussed with the paper system you can have your system destroy all documents that are older than three or four months.

Designing hard drive files

The following points provide an example of how, with some minor differences, your hard drive files can follow the same structure as your paper and e-mail file.

- **Hot Folder:** Think of the folder "Documents" as your main entry point into your document filing system. Establish the Hot folder below that. Using Microsoft Windows Explorer as an example, you can build a filing system that mimics the same structure as your paper file. Name this folder "1-HOT" so that it appears at the top of the filing tree.

- **Reference Folder:** Create and name another folder "2-REFERENCE" so that it appears second in the filing tree.
- **Archive Folder:** Create and name another folder "3-ARCHIVE" so that it appears third in the filing tree and can be populated with sub folders as needed (and as listed in the file index).
- **Delete Folder:** Windows will normally place deleted records and documents in a recycle bin. While in the recycle bin, items can be restored to their original location. Items in the recycle bin are erased based on user or system defined rules and frequency. Tip: Examine these rules and parameters to make sure they support your expectations.
- **Outbox:** Consider the "Sent Folder" in your e-mail system as your outbox of your hard disk data.
- **Briefcase:** Some may consider an electronic organizer, smart phone, or net-book to take material while traveling. If so, most operating systems provide ways to synchronize such files for compatibility and ease of use. However, sometimes these features are oversold, so be sure to understand how these systems interplay and support file sharing and updates; otherwise, you could be disappointed.

Note: Users of operating systems other than MS Windows may note that their computers follow similar file management, but use different names and labels.

Designing Web folders

The World Wide Web (WWW) has a wealth of electronic files that you can use. Most often you can consider this a Reference Folder. If you keep an extensive list of "Favorites" in your Web browser we recommend that you develop a structure similar to the one you established in the Reference Folder.

Search engines: While most of us are familiar with the power search engines like Google bring to the Web, few take advantage of such tools to search the content on their e-mail and electronic files. These tools are a key differentiator between the paper and other files. Learning the effective use of such tools can help greatly in overcoming the fear of filing, deleting, and reducing the burden of electronic filing.

Summary

✓ Ensure that your workspace is organized to reduce distractions and interruptions.

✓ Reduce clutter by designing your filing system based on a frequency of use filing methodology. This includes Hot, Reference, Archive, Delete, Briefcase, Inbox, and Outbox.

✓ Design your sub categories to support your roles (such as Leadership, Operation and Project).

✓ Keep your structure logical and easy to use; this will further reduce the maintenance overhead required.

✓ Follow the same structure for all your paper files, e-mail files, electronic files, and Web favorites.

29: BUILDING A CLUTTER-FREE FILING SYSTEM

The frequency of use filing methodology™ leads you to building a simple clutter free filing system. By now we hope you have thought of what you need and documented your design in a simple subject index list. If you have not done this yet, we encourage you to do so. In this chapter we will show you an example of a step-by-step **action plan** to help you build your simple, yet effective filing system.

Once again we recommend that you deal first with your **desk and paper files**. Being tangible, the paper file will help you experience the file building process in a concrete way. Later, we will relate the same experience to your e-mail and electronic files.

Building your work space

With your workspace design in hand, take time to make the necessary changes. Again, remember the operative phrase here is "keep it simple." Be courageous in making change. Change induces creativity in keeping a clutter-free office. Make sure you add items that bring you joy and refreshment. Strategically place items that help you focus on your higher values and priorities. While recently visiting a senior executive we were impressed by the number of art pieces made by the little hands of his small children. Another manager had pictures of his boat and the places he visited on many shores. Awards and mementos of high achievements are excellent to keep close so you can glance at them when tired or discouraged.

On the other hand, try to remove items that encourage collecting clutter such as bulletin boards that collect sticky notes and outdated notices. Remove old mugs and meaningless knickknacks. Tip: For the sake of good health, be aware of dust collectors, consider adding a living plant and clean regularly.

Building paper files

A common question we are often asked is, "What kinds of files should I have?" The key to rapid document retrieval is simple, proper labeling of folders and files. Here are some simple helpful tips:

- Use boxed, hanging files. This allows you to place smaller sub-files inside each hanging folder. For simplicity, use only one standard size of folders; do not mix legal and letter size files.

- Place labeled tabs in the front of the file. This gives quick fingertip access to the file as you add new material.

- Label files and drawers with big, **bold**, and easy to read lettering so you can see them quickly. Where possible use simple logical abbreviations.

- Avoid the use of elaborate filing color schemes. This may add complexity and may be a deterrent to quick filing.

- When holding paper together use a stapler instead of paper clips. Paper clips can catch other unrelated papers.

- As you add new files, update your subject list or index for ongoing reference.

In the past I considered myself a very organized person. I had all my "work in progress" files sorted in piles on my desk. I thought that having them in sight would keep them properly prioritized. Now I know that this was distractive and counter productive. Now my hot file is placed in the left hand drawer of my desk and on the top of my desk all I see is the one file or project I am currently working on. This has removed the distraction and has allowed me to be much more focused and productive. This has been the one thing I changed that has most improved my effectiveness. **CATHY WARD**

The following is a simple step by step task list to guide you. Plan adequate time for what could be a very enjoyable experience. Depending on the condition of your system, we recommend two to four hours for each session. Read the following task list and indicate your target completion date and any appropriate notes. Once completed cross give it a good check mark.

Exercise: organizing your files

The following exercise provides you with a step by step task list that we use in helping our clients organize their files.

TASK LIST

1. If you have not yet done so, go back to the design section and establish your best office layout for improved effectiveness. Make a sketch of this layout and make sure you have all the furniture and equipment you need. Rearrange your space, if necessary.

2. Mark or label where you will place essential supplies, inbox, Hot Files, Reference Files, Archive Files, outbox, delete box, garbage can, chairs, etc.

3. Examine your office supplies. Make sure you have an adequate supply of hanging files, plastic index tabs for the hanging files, manila folders, and a good medium felt marking pen.

4. Block an appropriate amount of time for this valuable effort. We recommend approximately two to four hours each time you work on your filing. You may need more than one session to organize your office.

5. Place a sign, **"PLEASE DO NOT DISTURB."** Do not accept any interruptions.

6. Place three boxes or garbage bags beside the exit door or nearby. Mark them respectively as **Donate, Garbage,** and **Recycle.**

7. **Remove the clutter.** Totally clear the top of all your office furniture. This includes your desk, filing cabinets, and chairs. Place unwanted clutter in Donate, Garbage or Recycle boxes or bags.

8. Empty the contents of the drawer labelled Hot Files placing it on the floor along with the material you removed from the top of your desk.

9. Examine your subject list, label appropriate hanging folders and sub-folders and place them in the space you marked Hot Files.

10. Populate your Hot Files by sorting all you had on top of your desk and all that you have piled on the floor. Mark additional folders and files as you need to and adjust your subject list. Your goal is to have a small number of files that will go in your Hot File space. Don't forget all other shelves and drawers that may hold Hot File material.

11. As you go along designate two piles for **Reference** and **Archive** material. Do not file these yet. Just pile them.

12. Delete, donate, and/or recycle any material that does not fit your new plan.

Note: As a general rule, anything that you have not touched, used or referred to in the past few months should not be placed in the Hot file.

13. Reorganize essential office supplies, inbox, outbox, delete files, garbage can, chairs, etc. according to your plan.

14. **Congratulations!** You have done the most challenging part. Be sure to take a well earned break before you start on your Reference and Archive files. Invite your friends and teachable people to see your office. This will encourage you to keep it tidy and you will help others in the process.

Note:

- Do not take time to process your inbox now. You can do this in your normal processing cycle, provided you plan extra time for it.

- Depending on the nature of your files you may find it worthwhile to simply put the piles you labelled Reference and Archive out of sight until needed.

Observations: It is rather interesting to note that many times our clients who have put aside filing the Reference and Archive material seldom had the need to go back and re-file it. However, the following steps are provided should you need to file your Reference and Archive material.

1. Empty all the contents of the space you allocated for the Reference Files and place it with the pile you have designated as Reference.

2. Label that space as Reference Files.

3. Examine your subject list and ensure that you have correct hanging folders and sub-folders for your Reference Files and place them where you marked Reference Files.

4. Populate your Reference Files by sorting the pile you designated as Reference. Make additional files as you need to and adjust your subject list as you go along.

5. As you work on your files designate any Archive material putting it in the pile you called Archive. Do not file this yet. Just pile them.

6. As you go along delete, donate and/or recycle any material that does not fit your new plan.

7. Continue until you have finished filing all your Reference files.

8. Empty all the contents of the space you allocated for the Archive Files.

9. Label that space as Archive Files.

CHALLENGES, CHANGES & CURES

10. Examine your subject list and ensure you have correct hanging folders as well as sub-folders for all your Archive Files and place them in the place you marked Archive Files.

11. Populate your Archive files by sorting the pile you marked Archive. Make additional files as you need to and adjust your subject list as you go along.

12. As you go along delete, donate and/or recycle any material that does not fit your new plan.

Office Supplies List

Essential Supplies List	Qty		Qty
Binder 3 Ring		Highlighters	
Binders 3 Ring - dividers		Light, Desk	
Box - business card holder		Notepad	
Box – Inbox		Paper for computer printer	
Box – Outbox		Paperclips and holder	
Boxes or garbage bags		Pens, blue or black	
Calculator		Pens, Marking (Medium Tip)	
Clock, Desk		Phone (optional headset)	
Computer system & peripherals (jump drive, speakers, etc.)		Planner or Diary	
Computer, Internet connection		Post It notes	
Computer, Office Software		Power cord/Surge protector	
Computer, printer and cartridges		Punch, paper (3 hole)	
Cutting blade		Rubber bands	
Date stamp and ink pad		Ruler	
Envelopes - 9X12		Scissors	
Envelopes for mailing #10		Scotch tape and dispenser	
Fax Machine		Staple remover	
Folders Hanging (box-bottom)		Stapler	
Folders Hanging - plastic tabs (Clear)		Staples	
Folders labels (1"X2.63)		Wastebasket and Recycle Box	
Folders, Manila			

Building e-mail files

In a manner similar to building your paper file you can build you e-mail files. The following steps provide a simple process to guide you.

TASK LIST

1. Set aside one hour of uninterrupted time to focus on this important process.

2. Examine your filing index or subjects list. Identify the ones you need for your e-mail file. Remember your e-mail filing should follow the same structure as your paper file, but it does not need to be identical.

3. **De-clutter:**

   A. Remove any unused or extra folders.

   B. Examine your toolbars and customize them for maximum efficiency.

   C. Assuming your inbox is your main directory, create a subfolder and label it (**Z-OLD MAIL** so that it is filed at the end of the filing tree**).** For this purpose we will consider any e-mail that is older than one day to be considered OLD MAIL.

   D. Highlight the OLD MAIL, drag it and drop it in the folder (**Z-OLD MAIL).**

   E. If you wish, do the same with the old folders.

NOTE:

- Do not worry! All your old mail is still alive and well. You can retrieve it if you need to from your (Z-OLD MAIL) folder.

- Starting that folder with the letter Z will place it at the end of the file folder tree and give you room to create new inbox sub folders above it.

4. Going back to your inbox route folder refer to your filing index list and create the following sub categories and their related folders;

   A. **LEADERSHIP (or PEOPLE)**: Make sub folders for each of the people you regularly communicate with for the benefit of the relationships. These may include your important and teachable people, as well as key family members or friends.

   B. **OPERATION:** Make sub folders for regularly managed issues, committees, or events.

   C. **PROJECTS:** Make sub folders for projects where you play an active role.

Note:

- By placing a (-) ahead of the folder name you instruct your system to place it first in the filing tree.

5. Consider using rules to prioritize your incoming e-mail. For example:

   A. Set up a rule to place all the e-mail you receive from your important people in the folder "-IP to Me". Be sure to create a folder (-IP to ME).

   B. Set up a rule to place all incoming e-mail copied to you from your important people in the folder "-IP copy to ME". Be sure to create a folder (-IP copy to ME).

6. Decide whether you need to use two separate folders or combine your material in a Reference/Archive folder.

7. Most e-mail systems provide Auto Archiving functions. Using the tools and options menu you can set global archiving rules. You can override these to set specific archiving terms for specific folders. If you decide not to use the auto archive features of your e-mail

   A. Create a new sub folder called "**3-ARCHIVE.**"

   B. Create appropriate subfolders.

8. Dealing with the –OLD FOLDER.

   A. As needed retrieve e-mail you need from the old folder and place it in your new file structure.

   B. Schedule regular time to move needed relevant e-mail from your old files into the new filing structure and delete or archive the rest.

9. As you go along delete material that you no longer need.

10. Congratulate yourself on a job well done. Share your pride with supportive friends and teachable people.

Building hard drives files

In a manner similar to building your e-mail files you can build your other electronic files. The following provides a step by step process to guide you.

TASK LIST

1. Open Windows Explorer. (Users of other operating systems will find similarities but please also consider the differences.)

2. Familiarize yourself with the search and find tools available in your system. Or download one of the very popular desktop search tools such as Google from the web. This will help you overcome some of your filing fears.

3. **De-clutter:**

   A. Delete any unused icons from your computer screen desktop.

B. Uninstall any programs that you do not use and remove them from your hard drive.

C. Perform a backup of all your critical files. Remove any unused or extra folders.

D. Assuming "**DOCUMENTS**" is your main directory, create a subfolder and label it **(Z-OLD FILES).**

E. Drag and drop your old files in the folder **(Z-OLD FILES).**

NOTE: Do not worry! All your old files are still alive and well. You can retrieve them if you need to from your (Z-OLD FILES) folder. Starting that folder name with the letter Z will place it at the end of the file folder tree and give you room to create new folders above it.

4. Assuming that "**MY DOCUMENTS**" is your main directory, build 3 new folders:

I - HOT

2- REFERENCE

3 - ARCHIVE

NOTE: Placing a number before the folder name gives it a priority above the alphabetical character that you use.

5. Examine you filing index and highlight the folders you need to create. For example you may find that in the 1-HOT folder you may create:

A. **LEADERSHIP (**or PEOPLE) folder with sub folders below it.

B. **OPERATION** folder with sub folders below it

C. **PROJECTS** folder with sub folders below it.

Remember your electronic filing should follow the same structure as your paper file **but it does not need to be identical.**

6. Follow the process and create folders and sub folders for **2- REFERENCE.**

7. Follow the process and create folders and sub folders for **3 – ARCHIVE.**

8. As you get new files place them in the appropriate folders.

9. **Dealing with the –OLD FILES**.

A. As needed retrieve files you need from the –**OLD FILES** and place them in your new file structure.

B. Schedule regular time to move, drag and drop needed relevant files from your old files into the new filing structure and delete or archive the rest.

10. As you go along delete material that you no longer need.

CHALLENGES, CHANGES & CURES

11. **Congratulate yourself on a job well done. Share your pride with supportive friends and teachable people.**

Building Web folders

In a manner similar to building your e-mail and hard disk files you can build your Web files and folders. Note one key difference: unlike other files, Web links are by nature only reference or research material.

TASK LIST

---

1. Open internet browser such as Internet Explorer. (Users of other systems will find similarities.)

2. Familiarize yourself with the search and find tools available in your system.

3. **De-clutter:**

    A. Using the Organize Favourites tool create a subfolder and label it **(Z-OLD LINKS).**

    B. Move all your links to that folder **(Z-OLD LINKS).**

NOTE: Do not worry all your old links are still alive and well. You can retrieve them if you need to from your (Z-OLD LINKS) folder. Starting that folder name with the letter Z will place it at the end of the file folder tree and give you room to create new folders above it.

4. Examine your filing index and highlight the folders you need to create. For example you may to create:

    A. **LEADERSHIP** folder with sub folders and links about your important and teachable people

    B. **OPERATION** folder with sub folders and links about issues you deal with regularly

    C. **PROJECTS** folder with sub folder and links about projects where you play an active role.

Remember your web links file should follow the same structure as your paper file **but it does not need to be identical.**

5. As you find new links place them in the appropriate folders.

6. **Dealing with the Z-OLD LINKS**

    D. As needed retrieve links you need from the **Z-OLD LINKS** and place them in your new file structure.

    E. Schedule regular time to move, needed relevant links from your **Z-OLD LINKS** into the new filing structure and delete the rest.

7. As you go along delete material that you no longer need.

8. **Congratulate yourself on a job well done. Share your pride with supportive friends and teachable people.**

A busy executive suite is a place where paper often flies in all directions. Filing important documents is often neglected in favor of more pressing matters. Due to more than five years of neglect our central executive archive library became a useless resource rather than a helpful asset. Distrust of this neglected system resulted in everyone from the CEO down keeping their own system of duplicated records.

As attempts to rely on external help failed I decided that "If it's to be, it's up to me." As a senior executive assistant I was convinced of the value brought by a well organized central reference and archive library. With management support and the help of other Executive Assistants we now have a system that is efficient and effective for all members of the executive suite. Based on this and my many years of experience I strongly recommend considering the benefits of a centralized reference and archive library for most busy executive offices. **MARIE DARLING**

Summary

✓ Your clear and simple design will help you use a simple step by step plan to build your clutter-free system.

✓ Your clutter-free workspace that enhances your focus and effectiveness is your first building block.

✓ Decide your primary information resource, paper, e-mail, or hard drive and which one should take priority.

✓ If possible starting with the paper files gives you a tangible, easy to visualize, first model to follow. Then move on to your e-mail, hard disks and web folders.

✓ Always start with the Hot Files. If you have time, go on to the Reference and Archive.

30: MAINTAINING A CLUTTER-FREE SYSTEM

The Second Law of Thermodynamics (Law of Energy Decay) indicates that that "every system left to its own devices always tends to move from order to disorder, its energy tending to be transformed into lower levels of availability, finally reaching the state of complete randomness and unavailability for further work"[64]

Stated differently, even the simplest, best system will rapidly deteriorate if not properly maintained. If you do not pay attention to the ongoing maintenance of your system it will disintegrate into practical confusion becoming a liability rather than an asset. Having invested time and energy to bring your system to a good state, you need to maintain it so it provides you with ongoing benefits.

Maintaining filters

Just like a well-run engine your filters need to be maintained. The maintenance frequency depends on the pace of change and the demands life put on you. You live in a changing world. Priorities, people and your needs change on a regular basis. Periodically, perhaps once every six to twelve months or as major changes occur, take time to examine and update your filters. Take time to review the chapter of filters to refresh your memory of its commonsense principles. Then, using your present filters take inventory.

A. Write down your achievements and the positive changes. Resist the temptation to undervalue your achievements. While being realistic you owe it to yourself to think success.

B. List the positive contributions your important and teachable people have made to your life. Commit to send appropriate acknowledgment.

C. Write lessons learned.

- Document your view of your changing world. What changes have happened personally and professionally that require a redefinition of your roles? What should be your response to these changes? Be sure to consider your personal health, spiritual, emotional, and mental development needs.

- Using a new set of filtering templates:

    - Redefine your roles using appropriate adjectives or attributes.

    - Update your people inventory focusing on the important and teachable people. Commit to communicate with the important people to ensure that they agree with you and support you in your redefined roles and goals.

    - Change and prioritize your issues filter to help you focus on the important.

    - Update your objectives and goals list. Make sure they are SMART.

    - Give your mission statement a good look and make appropriate changes, if needed.

    - As you do this, examine your communication protocols and update them. Mark a time in the future when you again plan to maintain your filtering system. Planning ahead will help you keep the discipline and the priority of this important exercise. The frequency of this filters maintenance exercise depends on your stage of life and the pace of change that surrounds you.

Maintaining your work space

Occasionally, say once every year examine your work space and see if there is any room for enhancement or change. This does not have to be major. We are all tempted to collect clutter and sometimes small change can be healthy. Consider an update of family pictures, a new lamp for improved lighting, a fresh new plant, or a relocation of a filing cabinet. Whatever the change make sure to keep your environment simple and clutter-free. In other words, if you are adding something consider removing something.

Maintaining Hot Files

Your Hot Files hold the information you need most frequently. It needs to be simple, crisp, and clean. We recommend that once a week you take time to review your past week and plan for what lies ahead. You do this examining and maintaining your Hot Files. In a way this is like a walk down memory lane. As you review your files:

- Record your weekly achievements and successes.

- Write notes of appreciation where appropriate.

- Record issues and challenges and diarize what needs to happen.
- Delete and discard unnecessary material.
- Move any files you no longer need to the Reference or Archive sections.

Maintaining Reference Files

Your Reference Files hold the information you may need in the future. This does not require as rigorous a maintenance plan as the Hot file. Depending on how active your Reference Files, we recommend that once a month or once a year you take time to review and maintain your Reference Files. Again, as you did with the Hot Files:

- Review and document your successes.
- Plan for possible enhancements and change based on lessons learned.
- De-clutter discarding old or not needed material.

Maintaining Archive Files

Maintaining the archive file is one of the areas often most neglected. This may be because most of us seldom access the Archive Files. To help you keep your Archive Files simple and clutter-free write a simple retention policy that is based on:

- **Regulatory and compliance requirements:** The nature of your business and the nature of the documents you are dealing with often dictate your required retention period.
- **Costs:** Storage and maintenance costs may influence your document retention policies. For example, maintaining paper records requires more space and cost than electronic files. The same applies to searching and retrieving information from such records. How often will you use it and what are the potential benefits?

Maintaining Sent Files

As a general rule we recommend that you be more diligent and retain documents that you have created for as long as you possibly can. The reason for this is that you are much more accountable for what you create or initiate versus what you receive from others. At the same time, if others follow the same rule, should you need a copy of something that was sent to you, the originator would likely be able to reproduce it. This does not mean that you keep your sent material all in your Hot Files. What we mean is that you may retain it in Archive for as long as you possibly and logically can.

Maintaining Your Delete File: Your Delete File holds the information you hope you will never need but are not ready to immediately discard. You may recall having to retrieve an item out of your recycle bin. That's the reason for the temporary delete function. Whether it is the computer recycle bin, your e-mail delete folder or your paper delete box, do not keep the files as Archive. They are designed to give you a short term retrieve option. With this in view, try to purge them every one to three months; otherwise they may overflow and cause more system clutter than you can afford.

Exercise: Maintaining files

Using the following table, write what you believe is a reasonable maintenance schedule. Using easy to remember frequency and dates, such as the same time, same day of the week or month, commit to a regular plan and mark it in your calendar.

FREQUENCY?

D=Daily, W=Weekly, M=Monthly Or A=Annually ↓

System To Be Maintained	↓	When?
• **Filtering System** (Roles, People, Issues, Objectives, and Goals)		
• **Inbox: Personal Communication Protocol** (For e-mail, phone, paper, and meetings)		
• **Hot Files** (e-mail, paper, and hard drive)		
• **Reference Files** (e-mail, paper, and hard drive)		
• **Archive Files** (paper and hard drive assuming e-mail archive will be controlled by auto-archiving function)		
• **Delete File** (paper and hard drive assuming e-mail will be controlled by its own system)		

By virtue of my role, I receive and collect a lot of material and media products. At one time my office furniture was hidden under the burden of paper and clutter I collected as a communications director. Organizing my office and reducing the clutter has had a most significant impact on my productivity. Now my daily commitment is to always have nothing that is not filed on any of my desks. It is rewarding to hear visitors' comments about the tidiness of my office. This is not only encouraging but also motivating to enhanced communication and productivity.

In our personal and business lives we each have more than we can handle. Unless you get organized you will always feel forgetful, overwhelmed, and frustrated. My advice to any overloaded person is to develop a simple system to categorize and file what you need, based on your various roles and the priorities you have established. Be committed to maintain your system and that will bring a feeling of control and you will not feel overwhelmed as you otherwise could. **SHELLEY FLETCHER**

Summary

✓ If not maintained, all systems deteriorate into decay and become more burdensome than useful.

✓ Maintaining your filtering system will help you identify changes to your roles and goals in response to your changing world.

✓ Maintaining your inbox based on your communication protocols will help ensure your communication commitments to your important people.

✓ Maintain your Hot Files on a weekly basis. As you do this, review and document achievement and plan for the week ahead. As you reduce the clutter you will keep this file crisp and clean helping you to find what you need quickly, reducing the time wasted in searching for information when you need it.

✓ Maintaining your Reference Files and Archive Files on a monthly or annual bases basis will keep them organized and accessible and maintained in accordance with regulatory or compliance requirements.

CHALLENGES, CHANGES & CURES

ACTION PLAN

- If it's to be, it's up to me

- If you want to be the master of an art, coach it

- Coaching tools, templates and discussion questions

31: YOUR PERSONAL ACTION PLAN

If it's to be, it's up to me

Eve is an operational business director in a large multinational corporation. Her staff of almost 200 managers and professionals looks up to her for direction and advice. Like most of her peers, her workday started early and went long and late. Back to back meetings, long e-mail lists and numerous interruptions kept the corporate culture spinning faster and faster. Eve's role had become that of a manager, firefighter, and troubleshooter. No doubt with her experience and skills she had become a very good firefighter. In response, her staff and others have developed a skill of searching out troubles and bringing them to her doorstep.

When we met Eve she confessed her guilt for a compromised personal life. Her gym membership was seldom used and her eating and sleep habits were often compromised. Following a recent medical check up, she knew that change was not optional. In her mid forties, with family health issues, she knew she had to make some changes. Following the Overcoming Overload workshop Eve made some changes and influenced her team to make changes that impacted the whole organization. As a result, Eve was given an award for excellence in leadership. Her team became known as the best place to work.

Eve's action plan started with filtering to prioritize and focus her roles and priorities. Eve decided that her top priority was to be a coach to her ten managers. With a coaching plan in hand, she blocked one day a week to give each of her managers uninterrupted, preplanned, one-on-one coaching time. Her objective was to help each of them grow their leadership and problem solving skills. She took specific countercultural actions and risks to make sure they had a chance to exercise their empowerment. Against her natural motherly instinct, she committed never to respond to a problem that could be dealt with by one of her managers or staff. The results were impressive. The most visible result Eve experienced was that her problem solving meeting participation dropped by more than fifty per cent.

While Eve had realized that the only person she could change was herself, she had a distinct sphere of influence that was broader than she could expect. Experiencing the joy of empowerment and self-confidence her managers followed her example in their relationship with their staff. Together with Eve, they gained the support of the Senior Vice President for some practical behavioral changes that significantly improved their meeting effectiveness. They

CHALLENGES, CHANGES & CURES

implemented new group e-mail handling protocols that controlled the urgency created by e-mail misuse and significantly reduced e-mail overload. By their example many other groups and divisions began to adhere to the same commonsense principles and practical tips they learned and applied. Eve and her managers became a model to many in the organization.

If they can do it so can you.

The Personal Effectiveness Framework™ is a toolbox that you can personalize and tailor in response to your changing needs. To a very great degree, change is a personal choice. Motivated by the promise of improved effectiveness or concerns for the negative impact of overload, many of our workshop participants have chosen to change. Our hope is that you will choose to exchange your overloaded world for one that is more effective and balanced.

Nothing will change unless you take the first step and have an action plan. Like Eve in the preceding story you can change only what you own and what you can control. Overcoming overload in an overloaded world is not easy. By nature, we easily surrender to bad habits. In addition, the corporate culture of most organizations is victimized by urgency and compromised priorities. We confess that some of the material presented in this book is counterculture. In an overloaded world, good behaviors are often counterculture. You will likely face opposition from draining people who have often contributed to your overloaded world. You will be tempted to avoid the efforts and discipline that lead to improved effectiveness and a balanced life.

You are not disarmed. While most dislike and oppose change they admire progress and leaders who seek it. As you acknowledge the challenges facing corporate leaders and as you endorse the emerging changes we outlined, you will be empowered to take personal action. The positive results you will experience will encourage you in your commitment to continual improvement. By your model others will be influenced and motivated to change. This will give you the opportunity to play one of the greatest roles you can ever have, **coaching others for common good.**

A reasonable action plan is a statement of faith and commitment. You must believe that you are embarking on a valuable endeavor that has positive consequences. You must be committed to reasonable discipline and changed behavior. Towards this goal, seek the support of your important people who will see change as needed progress that is for the good of all concerned.

Exercise: develop your action plan

The illustrated **Personal Effectiveness Framework** ™ is made of three major parts and each includes topics or sub-parts. Since it is not possible to do everything given to you we encourage prioritizing the topics you want to focus on and set objectives and **SMART** goals for each of your priority topics.

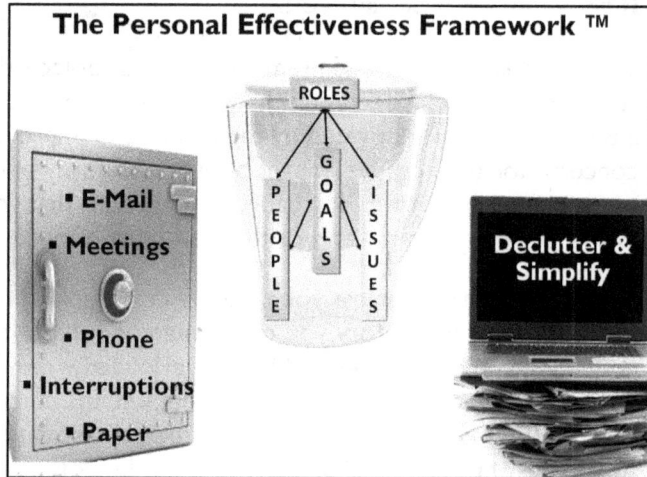

The Personal Effectiveness Framework ™

- E-Mail
- Meetings
- Phone
- Interruptions
- Paper

ROLES

PEOPLE / GOALS / ISSUES

Declutter & Simplify

Using the following table here is what we recommend:

1. Prioritize the three parts of this framework by placing an **A**, **B** or **C** in the space to the left of the title. A is the highest priority.

2. In a similar manner below each title, prioritize the sub-titles. Putting them in numerical order of priority - **1, 2, 3, 4**…

	Filter to Prioritize		Control to Improve		De-clutter to Simplify
	Roles		E-mail Overload		E-mail File
	People		Meeting Overload		Hard disk files
	Issues		Interruptions		Web folders
	Objectives		Phone Overload		
	Goals		Paper Overload		
	Mission Statement				
	Filter at a Glance				

3. Starting with your **A1** topic, use the following table to confirm your action plan and write your objectives and SMART goals.

Prioritized topic:		
The reason I am focusing on this topic is:		
Objective – What? What do I want to happen? (Accomplishment)	**How?** How will I know it happened? (Actions)	**By When?** Target date

4. Later, after you finish with your **A1**, move on to either **A2** or **B1** or **C1**.

5. Share you plan with others; this way you will not only encourage them by your model, but you will create a format that will hold you accountable and encourage you in your own commitments. When dealing with countercultural change support and accountability are key success factors.

Note: Sometimes we are asked how you prioritize the selected topic. **Keep it simple.** You can make your choice based on the topic:

- you find most interesting
- most likely to bring you the greatest benefits and/or
- easiest to implement

Information and work overload is a common and constant problem for many of us in the workplace.

This is a reality that I had to face. My first step in fighting my overload problem was to acknowledge that it was a personal problem that I had to solve myself. I also had to admit that if I did not conquer the problem that it could have a seriously detrimental impact on my life. Only then could I make the mental shift and take personal responsibility for fixing the overload problem.

The second step was to realize that it was a significant problem and this problem would not be solved with just a simple set of techniques and tools. Rather, this problem required an integrated solution. While techniques and tools were helpful, for me the real breakthrough came from changing my attitudes, and in clarifying my roles and goals. **DOUG STIRLING**

I lead a very large multi-facility health organization. At the same time, everybody around me knows that I am very active in my family life and very supportive of community involvement. This is not hard to do when you set the right priorities and communicate them. My advice to a young professional is take note. You will find yourself in your fifties a lot sooner than you think so pace yourself. There is more to life than money and work. The things you are giving up now to earn the big bucks cannot be recovered. **JOHN McGARRY**

I often find that I have to go away to where I cannot be reached by the normal tools that overtake our life. No e-mail, not cell phone, not even TV or newspapers. I find backcountry camping gives me a good place for this. I have done this many times and I feel I need to do more of this to sort of charge my batteries and restore my creative energies. Taking time to reflect and think is very important to me. I feel I owe it to myself and also I owe it to the organization I lead. If I do not, I am not going to be as effective as they deserve. **MATTHEW ANDERSON**

Summary

- ✓ Nothing will change unless you start with an action plan.
- ✓ Keep your action plan simple by prioritizing the topic of the Personal Effectiveness Framework™ and developing objectives and smart goals as you go along.

32: IF YOU WANT TO BE THE MASTER OF AN ART, COACH IT

The greatest way to help yourself improve and apply what you have learned is to become a coach to someone who struggles with the same issues. A coach is not a person who has all the answers. A coach is not one who is able to do something better than his or her protégé. **A good coach is one who is able to help his or her protégé do things better than they thought they could. You are a coach.** Being a coach is one of the most rewarding of life experiences. Intentionally or unintentionally, directly or indirectly, we all are coaches. By our example as well as our words, we each lead and influence others.

We are a sports family. Without good coaches my children would not have progressed as they did in their highly demanding sports. It is the same in life. Having a good coach is a most valuable asset.

In the absence of coaching we must learn through personal experience often repeating the same mistakes several times before we discover the solution. Coaching enforces the positive while at the same time bringing an honest, objective external set of eyes to help you see the negative and define what needs to change. The priority of a good coach centers on the development of the individual without necessarily having a vested interest in the expected action or outcome. **ANDREA SEYMOUR**

If you have found the material in this book helpful, you have an opportunity to master these skills by becoming a coach and helping someone else.

- Do you know any overloaded people?
- Do you care about the stress of your coworkers, friends and business associates?

If you answered yes to the above two questions, you have a unique opportunity to gain great rewards while helping someone else. You can enhance your effectiveness and overload management skills while at the same time making a positive impact on the world around you. Yes, you can be someone's coach. As people observe your changed behaviour, and hopefully the positive outcome that you have gained, they will be curious and receptive to your counsel and encouragement.

Ipsos Reid, the Canadian opinion survey company, reported last year that a majority of young employees have a hard time fitting in the workplace. As a member of the "millennial generation" I have clearly seen many of my colleagues experience discontent with their jobs as they search for the "perfect career."

Working in the field of higher education, I have come to appreciate the concept of coaching and mentoring that can take place on university and college campuses. When this mentorship is absent it leaves young professionals without direction attempting to find meaning. With guidance, they may come to learn to love their work environment, but without it they may find a critical gap in their professional careers.

My own personal experiences have developed this belief. I have been fortunate to receive the input and accountability of great coaches in my life. Whether providing counsel for future career choices, encouraging me to persevere through struggles, or challenging my previous thoughts and perceptions, these coaches and mentors have played an extremely influential role in the development of the person and professional that I am today. Because of their example, I have committed myself to be available to coach students; this role is a part of my career in education. The role of a coach is not to be taken lightly. The impact of the mentoring relationship can have transformational effects that last a lifetime. **NOEL HABASHY**

Over the years I have experienced and observed good leaders and poor leaders. Good leaders focus on inspiring, developing, and coaching people The highest responsibility of leaders is to create more leaders through coaching. Coaching people instills confidence and self esteem in people. A quote I read one time said, "We teach what we need to learn ourselves." Coaching has dual benefits. When I coach someone I learn greatly through the process. You cannot be a coach or mentor and not be a student at the same time. This multiplies the benefits of the coaching experience. Leadership is all about people. **KAREN MacDONALD**

While the ultimate beneficiary of coaching is the protégé, impacting lives for good energizes you as you see the positive impact you have on the lives of others. Effective coaching is based on:

CHALLENGES, CHANGES & CURES

1. **Convictions and shared values**: It is critical that your coaching be based on personal conviction in what you believe is best. Such values must be shared and accepted by your protégé in absolute honesty.

2. **Commitment to disciplined accountability:** Coaching has a cost. You must agree with your protégé that there is a price to be paid by each of you. You pay in time and commitment you make. Your protégé pays in terms of discipline and accountability and a sincere desire for **change and results**.

3. **Clear communication:** Clarity of communication is essential for good coaching. While verbal communication and body language are essential, sometimes it is helpful to have written communication. In dealing with challenging issues this may serve for ongoing reference and accountability.

4. **Honesty, integrity, and trust:** A coach is not perfect. An honest coach admits failures and expresses opinions with integrity. Sharing your experiences and struggles with integrity is critical to developing trust in your successful coaching efforts. At the same time your protégé must admit the need for help and commit to progress, not perfection.

Exercise: Commit to teachable people

1. Make a list of your teachable people and identify the ones you believe respect you and admire your behaviour. Engage them as individuals by:

   A. Asking them how they feel about the overloaded world in which we live.

   B. Sharing with them your experience and what you are doing to improve your effectiveness in overcoming overload.

   C. Offering to meet with them on a regular basis and work through some of these issues. If they agree:

      a. Define your next meeting time and place.

      b. Provide them with a copy of the template.

      c. Encourage them to take our **complimentary** Web-based **Effectiveness and Overload Gauge™** at http://www.nomoreoverload.com/OG/Survey1a.asp , **use Project code: BOOK,** or give them a copy of the Overload Gauge template. The survey/gauge results will give you a baseline and help you prioritize the discussion content.

d. Have them purchase their own copy of this book or lend them your own copy.

2. In your next meeting, using the **Overload Gauge results**, identify the areas that deserve the most attention and those on which your protégé wants to work. Help your protégé document an action plan. Agree on:

    A. Meeting regularly to review and discuss progress

    B. How often you will meet (weekly, bi-weekly, or monthly)

    C. How much time you will spend in each meeting (no more than 1 hour)

    D. How long the term of your coaching agreement will be (three to six months)

    E. How you will disengage from this agreement should life circumstances lead to changed priorities and/or if progress is not realized

3. Support your protégé with gentleness and accountability. If you need to, refer to the section on Discussion Questions for help.

At the end of one of my university graduate courses I was approached by three mature students who said to me, "We desperately need a mentor at work. Would you be our mentor?" These were people in their mid to late thirties. And I thought "WOW" and wondered what happened to all the leaders in their organizations. I get that a lot more often lately which proves to me that there is a dire need and that managers and leaders are not doing as good a job at mentoring at they might—albeit in healthcare, the management spans of control have reached unreasonable levels and this has to change.

My advice to young employees is that if your manager does not have the time or the skill to mentor you and coach you, take time to seek it out elsewhere. If you do not, you will likely feel lost and may not develop to your full potential. In the end, it is your career and you have to take responsibility for seeking out the supports you need to advance the scope of your experience and skills. **LYNN NAGLE**

Leaders cannot preach what they do not practice. Their examples influence others. Managers who deliver great results and demonstrate balanced and well-controlled personal priorities are more attractive to their employees. Regardless of how good a wellness programs you put in place, a toxic environment and management style will dilute all the benefits and potentially be seen very negatively, and create a lot of cynicism. It is necessary to address the culture and ensure it is congruent with your wellness goals.
VIOLETTE LAREAU

Summary

✓ We all coach and influence others by our example, words and habits.

✓ Overload is a prevailing problem in our society. This offers a unique opportunity for coaching and developing your skills while helping others as well.

✓ Successful coaching is based on convictions, shared values, commitment to disciplined accountability, clear communication, honesty, and integrity.

✓ Coach teachable people who respect you and are prepared to enter into a disciplined coaching agreement with you.

33: COACHING TOOLS: TEMPLATES AND DISCUSSION QUESTIONS

Templates

Templates are tools to help you write your thoughts so you can **see them and share them with others**. The objectives of these templates are to:

- Provide simple structures or a process to guide your thinking and/or your discussions as you coach your protégé

- Provide a reference point to help you keep discussions on track and avoid distractions or going off on tangents

- Provide a forum of clear accountability ensuring coaching commitments and disciplines are maintained

- Offer a yardstick to gauge progress and reward success

The templates we provide you are flexible, so use what we provide as an example and create your own templates to fit your needs and personal style. In the following sections we reference the Chapter number where you can see an example of the template as well as more detail about the applications. For twelve months after the publication of this book you can find sample templates on our website at: http://www.integrity-plus.com/templates.html.

Overload Gauge

- This gauge is intended to help you identify the most critical causes of overload that hinders your effectiveness. These are broken into three categories that relate to the solutions provided in the **Personal Effectiveness Framework**™. **Template examples and detail input descriptions are in Chapter 1.**

Meeting Effectiveness Gauge

- This template or tool will help you gauge your overall effectiveness in your meeting participation. In addition, you could translate this to actual cost and loss of value to your corporate and personal life. **Template example and detail input description are in Chapter 23.**

Roles Inventory

- This template serves to help you list, prioritize, and describe what you can best be and the high value roles you can play. Once written, these can be discussed and negotiated with others. **Template example and detail input description are in Chapter 14.**

People Inventory

- This template is to help you prioritize the people in your life as well as the reasons you need to prioritize them. This will help you examine your communication and the amount of time and activities you invest with them. **Template example and detail input description are in Chapter 15.**

Issues Inventory

- The objective is to prioritize the issues you deal with and develop a filing index of the information subjects that are important to the fulfillment of your roles. This should help reduce information clutter as well as de-cluttering and simplifying filing and information retrieval. **Template example and detail input description are in Chapter 16.**

Goals Inventory

- The objective is to write **SMART** goals that relate to what you wish to be and the roles you play. **SMART** goals are **S**pecific, **M**easurable, and **A**greed upon, **R**ealistic and **T**ime dependent. **Template example and detail input description are in Chapter 17.**

Filter at a Glance

- The objective is to provide a summary that can be easily referred to and updated. This is a tool by which you can make easy and quick filtering decisions. **Template example and detail input description are in Chapter 17.**

Self Directed Coaching and Progress Dashboard

- The objective is to provide a simple tool to help you gauge your progress and facilitate communication and accountability with your coach or protégé. **Template example and detail input description are in Chapter 19.**

Communication and Note Taking Sheet

- The objective is to provide **one place** to capture all notes, thoughts, interactions and related responses. This will also help you take meeting notes and indicate delegation and target completion dates. **Template example and detail input description are in Chapter 23.**

VIP: Thoughts and Tips

- The objectives are to reduce interruptions and distractions by sorting and batch processing thoughts related to **one person** and to provide an agenda or a list of points for future discussion. **Template example and detail input description are in Chapter 24.**

Office Supplies List

- The objective is to ensure that you have all the supplies needed for optimum operational efficiency. **Template example and detail input description are in Chapter 29.**

DISCUSSION QUESTIONS

Questions are more powerful than opinions in developing a coaching relationship. Your protégés are more likely to be committed to their own opinion as they articulate it as an answer to your questions. As you seek to interact with others you may find that asking the right question is essential for starting the dialogue and keeping your interaction on track. These questions can be used by:

1. Individuals seeking to coach others towards a more effective and balanced work and life
2. Leaders as they seek to interact with their teams in uncovering causes and symptoms, as well as solutions to increased effectiveness and overcoming overload
3. These questions are provided in a topical manner that relates to the sections and chapters provided in this book. You may find it helpful to refer to the related chapters. You may also find it helpful to use the templates provided in some chapters as a way of documenting your interactions and discussion.

ON CHALLENGES

- What do you think of the law of diminishing returns and how it applies to your personal and corporate culture?
- How does the supply and demand for talent impact you and/or professionals in your field?

- How does information technology positively or negatively impact your work environment?
- Can you recall an example of when you or your teams have been compromised by the culture of urgency?
- How do you gauge your level of overload?
- What are the key contributors to overload in your business environment?
- What are the key overload symptoms that bother you the most?

ON CHANGE

- How do you describe wellness?
- How do you describe not being well and how does it affect personal and corporate effectiveness?
- How is the quality of your work impacted if you are not totally well?
- What are the symptoms of adrenalin addiction in your workplace?
- How would you describe your top five strengths, qualities, or attributes?
- What activities give you the greatest sense of fulfillment and why?
- At work, to what extent are you able to do what you love the most? Explain.
- How do you describe effective collaboration and when was it most visible in your work environment?
- How would you describe an effective delegator? How do you rate your delegating skill?
- What does your boss need to do to improve his or her delegation?
- Would you consider your boss as your coach? Why?

ON CURES

On roles filters

- How would you describe the most important roles on which you like to focus? Why?
- What are the favorite roles you play and why?
- What percentage of your time is spent on the Leadership, Project, and Operation Stages? Would you like to see any change in this? Why?

On people filters

- How do you define your important people?

- As you examine your calendar what changes do you need to make to enhance your relationship with your important people?
- How do you identify your teachable people?
- How do you gauge your effectiveness as a coach to your teachable people?
- As you examine your calendar, what changes do you need to make to enhance the impact you make on your teachable people?

On issues filters

- How does urgency impact your life?
- How do you describe the sources of your urgent, emotionally draining issues?
- How do you describe the important issues you deal with and what are their primary sources?
- What are the important and *not* urgent issues you need to more carefully prioritize?
- How does your filing system support the roles on which you want to focus?

On goals filters

- What are the objectives or accomplishments you want to see happen over the next three or six months?
- Do you have written SMART goals that relate to your important roles? Are they documented?
- How engaged are your important people in your progress toward achieving your objectives? What makes you think so?

On a mission statement

- What would you say if asked, "What is your purpose for living?"
- How does your personal mission statement relate to your important and teachable people?
- To what extent does the mission statement of the corporation you work for or the associations to which you belong reflect your passion and commitments?
- If you were to develop a "modified corporate mission statement" that better reflects the role you play in the organization you work for, what would that mission statement say?

On overcoming e-mail overload

- When does e-mail become a cause for ineffectiveness and overload in your life?

CHALLENGES, CHANGES & CURES

- What are the reasonable e-mail responsiveness expectations for your important roles?
- How can you best communicate a reasonable e-mail protocol to your important people?
- What changes do you need to make to help you improve the effectiveness of e-mail as a tool in your work?

On overcoming phone overload

- What can you do to enhance the effectiveness of the phone as a workplace tool?
- What are the phone call return expectations for the important roles you play?
- How can you enhance the quality of your outgoing voice message?
- What can you do to enhance the quality of your phone communication?

On overcoming meeting overload

- In your organization to what extent do you waste time in meetings?
- What can you do to enhance the effectiveness of your meeting participation?
- When leading a meeting, what can be done to improve the meeting effectiveness and overall return on the time and effort invested?

On overcoming interruptions

- How do interruptions impact your productivity?
- To what extent do you contribute to the amount of interruptions and what can you do to help?
- How can the VIP sheet described in the personal interruptions chapter impact your productivity?

On overcoming paper overload

- To what extent has the electronic world had a positive or negative impact on the use of paper in your office?
- What can you do to reduce paper clutter in your office?

On developing a clutter-free filing system

- What do you think of the **"Frequency of Use Filing Methodology™?"**
- What is the primary filing tool you use (paper, e-mail files, or hard drive)?
- Would it be helpful to have common departmental Reference and/or Archive Files? How can they be best maintained?

- What document retention guidelines can best support your important roles? Can you establish common document retention guidelines for your team?
- How can you apply common filing structures to the paper, e-mail, and electronic files?

On building a clutter-free filing system

- Can you arrange a common teamwork effort to reduce office clutter?
- Can a common supply room be helpful? Who will maintain it?

On maintaining a clutter-free filing system

- What is a practical maintenance plan for your filtering system?
- What is a practical maintenance plan for your filing system?
- How can the maintenance plan you use help you review your roles and responsibilities and document your achievements as well as future plans?

On your personal action plan

- Examining the topics presented by the **Personal Effectiveness Framework**™, what should you focus on?
- What do you want to see accomplished in the next twelve weeks and what activities will you undertake to achieve this?
- How will you ensure that you will follow through with your plan?

On if you want to be the master of an art, coach it

- How would you describe the people who can benefit from improved effectiveness and work-life balance? What can you do to help them?
- What are the objectives you would like to accomplish from your coaching experience?

ENDNOTES

Chapter 1

[1] Edward M. Hallowell, "Overloaded Circuits: Why Smart People Underperform," *Harvard Business Review* 83, no. 1 (2005): 55–62, 116. Image illustration by Joel Lardner. www. joellardner.com.

[2] James C. Collins, *Good to Great: Why Some Companies Make the Leap ... and Others Don't.* (New York: HarperCollins Publishers, 2001).

[3] The survey will be available for only a limited time after publication.

Chapter 2

[4] The web templates will be available for only a limited time after publication.

Chapter 3

[5] Doris Janzen Longacre, *More-with-Less Cookbook* (Scottdale, Pennsylvania: Herald Press, 1976).

[6] Doris Janzen Longacre, *Living More with Less* (Scottdale, Pennsylvania: Herald Press, 1980).

[7] Paul Vieira, Productivity 'Abysmal'; Canadians stand to lose $30,000 each: Carney, [online], [cited 5 February 2010]; available from http://www.nationalpost.com/news/story.html?id=2523937.

Chapter 4

[8] McKinsey & Company, *The War for Talent: Organization and Leadership Practice,* [online], [cited 3 November 2009]; available from http://www.mckinseyquarterly.com/The_war_for_talent_part_two_1035.

[9] U.S. Census Bureau, [online], [cited 3 November 2009]; available from http://www.census.gov/. (Several tables are used for U.S. Census Bureau population figures.)

Chapter 5

[10] Richard A. Swenson, *The Overload Syndrome: Learning to Live within Your Limits* (Colorado Springs, Colorado: Navpress, 1998).

[11] Ibid., 138.

[12] Francis Narin, "Tech-Line Background Paper 3. Research Background."

Chapter 6

[13] Charles E. Hummel, *Tyranny of the Urgent* (Downers Grove, Illinois: InterVarsity Press, 1994), 4-5.

Chapter 7

[14] Edward M. Hallowell, "Overloaded Circuits: Why Smart People Underperform," *Harvard Business Review* 83, no.1 (2005): 55 – 56.

[15] Edward M. Hallowell, *CrazyBusy: Overstretched, Overbooked, and About to* Snap! *Strategies for Handling Your Fast-Paced Life* (New York: Ballantine Books, 2007), 4.

[16] Robert M. Yerkes and John D. Dodson, "The Relation of Strength of Stimulus to Rapidity of Habit-Formation," *Journal of Comparative Neurology and Psychology* 18, no. 5 (1908): 459-482.

[17] Archibald Hart, *Adrenalin and Stress* (Dallas: Word Publishing, 1995).

Chapter 9

[18] Sarah Cook, *The Essential Guide to Employee Engagement: Better Business Performance through Staff Satisfaction* (London: Kogan Page Limited, 2008).

[19] Paul Hemp, "Presenteeism: At Work—But Out of It," *Harvard Business Review* 82, no. 10 (2004): 51.

[20] *Health is cool! 2006 Survey (Volume 1),* [online] [cited 2 November2009]; available from http://www.dsf-dfs.com/en-CA/_Utilitaires/Prmtns/HlthCl.htm.

[21] Margo Vanover Porter, "Wellness at Work," *Association Management* 57, no. 4 (2005):52.

[22] Linda Duxbury and Chris Higgins, *The 2001 National Work-Life Conflict Study: Report One,* [online], [cited 4 November 2009]; available from http://www.phac-aspc.gc.ca/publicat/work-travail/report1/index-eng.php.

[23] Archibald Hart, *Adrenalin and Stress* (Dallas: Word Publishing, 1995), 71.

[24] Ibid., 76.

Chapter 10

[25] Max Lucado, *Discovering the Cure for the Common Life: Living in Your Sweet Spot* (Nashville: W Publishing Group, 2006), 1.

[26] Tom Rath, *Strengths Finder 2.0* (New York: Gallup Press, 2007), ii.

CHALLENGES, CHANGES & CURES

[27] Tom Rath and Barry Conchie, *Strengths Based Leadership* (New York: Gallup Press, 2008), 14.

Chapter 11

[28] John Donne, *Devotions Upon Emergent Occasions*, ed. Anthony Raspa (New York: Oxford University Press, 1987), 87.

29 Don Tapscott and Anthony D. Williams, Wikinomics (New York: Penguin Group, 2008).

Chapter 12

[30] Andrew Carnegie quote, [online], [cited 16 November 2009]; available from http://www.brainyquote.com/quotes/quotes/a/andrewcarn130735.html.

Chapter 14

[31] William Shakespeare, *As You Like It* (New York: Simon & Schuster, 1959), II, vii, 149-152.

[32] Thom S. Rainer, *Breakout Churches: Discover How to Make the Leap* (Grand Rapids, Michigan: Zondervan, 2005).

Chapter 15

[33] Gordon Macdonald, *Restoring Your Spiritual Passion* (Nashville: Thomas Nelson, 1986).

[34] Stephen R. Covey, *The Seven Habits of Highly Effective People: Restoring the Character Ethic* (New York: Simon and Schuster, 1989).

[35] David W. Augsburger, *Caring Enough to Confront* (Ventura, California: Regal Books, 2009).

Chapter 16

[36] Charles E. Hummel, *Tyranny of the Urgent* (Downers Grove, Illinois: InterVarsity Press, 1994), 6.

[37] Merrill E. and Donna N. Douglass, *Manage Your Time Your Work Yourself: The Updated Edition* (New York: AMACOM, 1993), 26.

[38] Edward R. Dayton and Ted W. Engstrom, *Strategy for Living* (Glendale, California: G/L Publications, 1976), 67.

Chapter 17

[39] Ibid., 31.

Chapter 20

[40] Jaroslav Pelikan, ed., *Luther's Works*. Volume 21 (Saint Louis: Concordia Publishing House, 1956), 88.

Chapter 21

[41] *The Latest on Workplace Monitoring and Surveillance*, [online], [cited 11 March 2010]; available from http://www.amanet.org/training/articles/The-Latest-on-Workplace-Monitoring-and-Surveillance.aspx.

[42] Kaitlin Duck Sherwood, *Tips for Overcoming Email Overload*, [online], [cited 16 November 2009]; available from
http://www.overcomeemailoverload.com/advice/TopTenTips.html.

[43] *Several Answers about Managing E-Mail*, [online], [cited 16 November 2009]; available from http://www.tmius.com/4tmcorn.HTML.

[44] Ellen Roseman, "Staying on Top of Your Virtual World," *Toronto Star*, 22 February, 2004, p. C1.

[45] Timothy Ferriss, *How to Stop Checking Email on the Evenings and Weekends*, [online], [cited 20 November 2009]; available from
http://www.lifehacker.com.au/2008/02/how_to_stop_checking_email_on_the_evenings_and_weekends-2/.

[46] Michael Linenberger, *Total Workday Control Using Microsoft Outlook: The Eight Best Practices of Task and E-Mail Management* (San Ramon, California: New Academy Publishers, 2006).

[47] Sally McGhee, *Take Back Your Life!: Using Microsoft Outlook to Get Organized and Stay Organized* (Redmond, Washington: Microsoft Press, 2005).

[48] Tim Speed, Dick McCarrick, Bennie Gibson, and Brad Schauf, *Lotus Notes Domino 8: Upgrader's Guide: What's New in the Latest Lotus Notes Domino Platform* (Birmingham, England: Packt Publishing, 2007).

Chapter 22

[49] Laura M. Stack, *Taming the Telephone*, [online], [cited 16 November 2009]; available from http://www.theproductivitypro.com/newsletters/newsletter10.htm.

[50] Laura M. Stack, *How to Leave Effective Voicemail Messages*, [online], [cited 16 November 2009]; available from
http://www.theproductivitypro.com/newsletters/num63August2004.htm.

Chapter 23

[51] Wayne J. Hunicke, *Improving the Quality of Your Meetings*, [online], [cited 16 November 2009]; available at http://www.advantagemgmt.com/resource/meetings.html.

[52] Ibid.

[53] *Getting the Most out of Meetings*, [online], [cited 16 November 2009]; available from http://www.mindtools.com/tmmeetng.html.

[54] Laura M. Stack, *Meetings! Where Minutes are Kept and Hours Wasted,* [online], [cited 16 November 2009]; available from http://www.theproductivitypro.com/newsletters/num61June2004.htm.

Chapter 24

[55] Patricia Pickett, "Interruptions Reduce Staff Productivity," *ComputerWorld Canada,* 5 September 2003: 25.

[56] Laura M. Stack, *Dealing with Interruptions from Visitors,* [online], [cited 16 November 2009]; available from http://www.theproductivitypro.com/newsletters/Number%204%20June%201999.htm.

Chapter 25

[57] *Paperless Office is Pure Fiction: Report,* [online], [cited 20 November 2009]; available from http://www.cbc.ca/technology/story/2006/11/10/tech-paperless.html.

[58] Christina Cavanagh, *Managing Your E-Mail: Thinking Outside the Inbox* (Hoboken, New Jersey: John Wiley & Sons, 2003), 34.

Chapter 26

[59] Tom Blackwell, *Pathologist's disorganization a "serious problem": inquiry,* [online], [cited 26 November 2007]; available from http://www.nationalpost.com/story.html?id=124945.

[60] Paul Waddington, *Dying for Information? A Report on the Effects of Information Overload in the UK and Worldwide,* [online], [cited 26 November 2009]; available from http://www.cni.org/regconfs/1997/ukoln-content/repor~13.html.

Chapter 27

[61] Susan Silver, *Organized to Be Your Best! Simplify and Improve How You Work* ([Los Angeles]: Adams-Hall Publishing, 2000), 105.

[62] Stephanie Winston, *The Organized Executive: The Classic Program for Productivity: New Ways to Manage Time, Paper, People, and the Digital Office* (New York: Warner Books, 2001), 103.

[63] Ibid., 92.

Chapter 30

[64] Frank Steiger, *The Second Law of Thermodynamics, Evolution and Probability,* [online], [cited 26 November 2009]; available from http://www.talkorigins.org/faqs/thermo/probability.html.

BIBLIOGRAPHY

BOOKS

Alesandrini, Kathryn. *Survive Information Overload: The 7 Best Ways to* Manage *Your Workload by Seeing the Big Picture.* Homewood, Illinois: Business One Irwin, 1992.

Augsberger, David W. *Caring Enough to Confront.* Ventura, California: Regal books, 2009.

Burleson, Clyde W. *Effective Meetings: The Complete Guide.* New York: John Wiley &Sons, 1990.

Butler, Ava S. *Team Think: 72 Ways to Make Good, Smart, Quick Decisions in Any Meeting.* New York: McGraw-Hill, 1996.

Caunt, John. *30 Minutes ... to Manage Information Overload.* London: Kogan Page, 1999.

Cavanagh, Christina. *Managing Your E-Mail: Thinking Outside the Inbox.* Hoboken, New Jersey: John Wiley & Sons, 2003.

Collins, James C. *Good to Great: Why Some Companies Make the Leap ... and Others Don't.* New York: HarperCollins Publishers, 2001.

Cook, Sarah. *The Essential Guide to Employee Engagement: Better Business Performance through Staff Satisfaction.* London: Kogan Page, 2008.

Covey, Stephen R. *The Seven Habits of Highly Effective People: Restoring the Character Ethic.* New York: Simon & Schuster, 1989.

Dayton, Edward R. and Ted W. Engstrom. *Strategy for Living.* Glendale, California: G/LPublications, 1976.

Douglass, Merrill E. and Donna N. Douglass. *Manage Your Time Your Work Yourself: The Updated Edition.* New York: AMACOM, 1993.

Ellwood, Mark. *Cut the Glut of E-Mail.* Toronto: Pace Productivity, 2002.

Flynn, Nancy. *The e-Policy Handbook: Rules and Best Practices to Safely Manage Your Company's E-Mail, Blogs, Social Networking, and Other Electronic Communication Tools*. New York: AMACOM, 2009.

Gleeson, Kerry. *The Personal Efficiency Program: How to Get Organized to Do More Work in Less Time*. New York: John Wiley & Sons, 2000.

Hallowell, Edward M. *CrazyBusy: Overstretched, Overbooked, and About to Snap! Strategies for Handling Your Fast-Paced Life*. New York: Ballantine Books, 2007.

Hart, Archibald. *Adrenalin and Stress*. Dallas: Word Publishing, 1995.

Izzo, John B. and Pam Withers. *Values Shift: The New Work Ethic and What It Means for Business*. Toronto: Prentice Hall Canada.

Jensen, Bill. *Simplicity: The New Competitive Advantage in a World of More, Better, Faster*. Cambridge, Massachusetts: Perseus Publishing, 2000.

Kieffer, George David. *The Strategy of Meetings*. New York: Simon & Schuster, 1988.

Lewis, David. *10-Minute Time and Stress Management: How to Gain an "Extra" 10 Hours a Week!* London: Judy Piatkus, 1995.

Linenberger, Michael. *Total Workday Control Using Microsoft Outlook: The Eight Best Practices of Task and E-Mail Management*. San Ramon, California: New Academy Publishers, 2006.

Longacre, Doris Janzen. *More-with-Less Cookbook*. Scottdale, Pennsylvania: Herald Press, 1976.

Longacre, Doris Janzen. *Living More with Less*. Scottdale, Pennsylvania: Herald Press, 1980.

Macdonald, Gordon. *Restoring Your Spiritual Passion*. Nashville: Thomas Nelson, 1986.

McGhee, Sally. *Take Back Your Life!: Using Microsoft Outlook to Get Organized and Stay Organized*. Redmond, Washington: Microsoft Press, 2005.

Morgenstern, Julie. *Time Management from the Inside Out: The Foolproof System for Taking Control of Your Schedule – and Your Life*. New York: Henry Holt and Company, 2000.

Moxham, Richard. *Taming Time: A Practical Guide to Time Management*. London: Spiro Press, 2001.

Pollar, Odette. *Organizing Your Workspace: A Guide to Personal Productivity*. Revised ed. Los Altos, California: Crisp Publications, 1999.

Rainer, Thom S. *Breakout Churches: Discover How to Make the Leap*. Grand Rapids, Michigan: Zondervan, 2005.

Rath, Tom. *Strengths Finder 2.0*. New York: Gallup Press, 2007.

Rath, Tom and Barry Conchie. *Strengths Based Leadership*. New York: Gallup Press, 2008.

Roberts-Phelps, Graham. *Telephone Tactics*. London: Hawksmere, 1999.

Shenk, David. *Data Smog: Surviving the Information Glut*. New York: HarperCollins, 1997.

Silver, Susan. *Organized to Be Your Best! Simplify and Improve How You Work*. [LosAngeles]: Adams-Hall Publishing, 2000.

Speed, Tim, Dick McCarrick, Bennie Gibson, and Brad Schauf. *Lotus Notes Domino 8: Upgrader's Guide: What's New in the Latest Lotus Notes Domino Platform*. Birmingham, England: Packt Publishing, 2007.

St. James, Elaine. *Simplify Your Work Life: Ways to Change the Way You Work So You Have More Time to Live*. New York: Hyperion, 2001.

Stack, Laura. *Leave the Office Earlier: The Productivity Pro Shows You How to Do More in Less time…and Feel Great about It*. New York: Broadway Books, 2004.

Streibel, Barbara J. *The Manager's Guide to Effective Meetings*. New York: McGraw Hill, 2003.

Swenson, Richard A. *Margin: How to Create the Emotional, Physical, Financial, and Time Reserves You Need*. Colorado Springs, Colorado: Navpress, 1992.

Swenson, Richard A. *The Overload Syndrome: Learning to Live within Your Limits*. Colorado Springs, Colorado: Navpress, 1998.

Tapscott, Don and Anthony D. Williams. *Wikinomics*. New York: Penguin Group, 2008.

Trout, Jack and Steve Rivkin. *The Power of Simplicity: A Management Guide to Cutting through the Nonsense and Doing Things Right*. New York: McGraw-Hill, 1999.

Winston, Stephanie. *Getting Out from Under: Redefining Your Priorities in an Overwhelming Word: A Powerful Program for Personal Change*. Reading, Massachusetts: Perseus Books, 1999.

Winston, Stephanie. *The Organized Executive: The Classic Program for Productivity: New Ways to Manage Time, Paper, People, and the Digital Office*. New York: Warner Books, 2001.

CHALLENGES, CHANGES & CURES

PERIODICALS

Hallowell, Edward M. "Overloaded Circuits: Why Smart People Underperform." *Harvard Business Review* 83, no. 1 (2005): 55–62, 116.

Hemp, Paul. "Presenteeism: At Work—But Out of It." *Harvard Business Review* 82, no. 10 (2004): 49-58.

Miller, Julie. "Why Wellness Works." *Managed Healthcare Executive* 13, no. 7 (2003): 24-25.

Porter, Margo Vanover. "Wellness at Work." *Association Management* 57, no. 4 (2005): 49-50, 52, 54.

Yerkes, Robert M. and John D. Dodson, "The Relation of Strength of Stimulus to Rapidity of Habit-Formation." *Journal of Comparative Neurology and Psychology* 18, no. 5 (1908): 459-482.

INDEX